D0982233

OTHER A TO Z GUIDES FROM
THE SCARECROW PRESS, INC.

The A to Z of Westerns in Cinema

Paul Varner

The A to Z Guide Series, No. 101

The Scarecrow Press, Inc.
Lanham • Toronto • Plymouth, UK
2009

Published by Scarecrow Press, Inc.
A wholly owned subsidiary of
The Rowman & Littlefield Publishing Group, Inc.
4501 Forbes Boulevard, Suite 200, Lanham, Maryland 20706
http://www.scarecrowpress.com

Estover Road, Plymouth PL6 7PY, United Kingdom

British Library Cataloguing in Publication Information Available

Library of Congress Cataloging-in-Publication Data
The hardback version of this book was cataloged by the Library of Congress as
follows:

Varner, Paul, 1948–
    Historical dictionary of westerns in cinema / Paul Varner.
        p. cm. — (Historical dictionaries of literature and the arts ; no. 26)
    Includes bibliographical references.
    1. Western films—Dictionaries. I. Title.
PN1995.9.W4V37 2008
791.43'627803—dc22   2007047509

ISBN 978-0-8108-6888-5 (pbk. : alk. paper)
ISBN 978-0-8108-7051-2 (ebook)

Printed in the United States of America

For Jeanine, Bart, and Tess—
Thanks.

Contents

Editor's Foreword

In the world of cinema, some things remain static and some things change. The Western was for a very long time a genre that remained static. In any given Western, it did not take long to identify the good guys and the bad guys; then after a bit of rousing action, the good guys beat the bad guys, righted various wrongs, and rode off into the sunset. At present, that sort of scenario is hardly imaginable and would not be very popular since it is no longer perceived as the real world. Nowadays the good guys have questionable characteristics, the bad guys often possess a streak of decency, and the cast of characters has broadened to include many who were previously nearly invisible. Women, gays, African Americans, and Native Americans finally appear as real people and not just convenient villains. These changes, which mirror changes in society, have given the Western a new lease on life, resulting in films that could not have been produced or conceived of in earlier decades.

With this, the Western—one of the oldest of film genres—has managed to retain its long-standing popularity and has actually expanded its audience. New films continue to appear, many attracting crowds and winning awards, making it a good time to publish *The A to Z of Westerns in Cinema*. The chronology charts the genre's long and impressive history, from the more obvious films of earlier years to the more varied and sometimes surprising ones of the present. This evolution, and what it means for the genre, is then explained in the introduction. The dictionary examines many of the more significant actors, producers and directors, sources and characteristics, locations and themes, and landmark films. Other entries analyze the vast array of types, from early and classic Westerns to a range of alternative Westerns and the hybrid "spaghetti Western." The volume concludes with a comprehensive bibliography.

The author of this volume is Paul Varner, who has taught at a number of schools over the years, recently as professor of language and literature at Oklahoma Christian University before moving to Abilene Christian University. He is a specialist in both Westerns in cinema and Westerns in literature, which is convenient because many of the films in this genre are based on novels. Dr. Varner has lectured on the Western and also written on some of the more significant authors and characters, his favorite being Hopalong Cassidy. He has also been the area chair of Westerns for several learned societies. Dr. Varner's accumulated and considerable experience with the genre gives him an impressive insight into what the Western once was and what it is in the process of becoming.

Jon Woronoff
Series Editor

Preface

The A to Z of Westerns in Cinema will hopefully be a useful tool for researchers, film critics, students, and other readers in understanding the different ways of viewing and appreciating cinema Westerns. The introduction and chronology will give an overview of how to approach Westerns as postmodern filmgoers and provide the history of Westerns at the beginning of the postmodern era.

This book is meant to be a comprehensive source for understanding Westerns, but it is a dictionary rather than an exhaustive encyclopedia. It suggests areas of importance and points to significant people, films, themes, and crucial issues. The body of material examining the history of Westerns as well as specific films, directors, actors, studios, and crucial issues is enormous, and the bibliography at the end should indicate what kind of research is possible in Western film studies. This volume should be the beginning point for anyone involved in serious study and enjoyment of Westerns.

Obviously, my criteria for selection of entries in the dictionary is subjective. Not all actors, directors, or films will be found here. Many issues that film critics deal with are missing. Again, the selection is intended to be suggestive rather than comprehensive. That being said, I have emphasized Westerns from recent decades rather than the early years of cinema simply because modern Westerns generally have more significance than those of the distant past and not as much has been written about Westerns from our own time. I have also attempted to recognize as many female actors, screenwriters, and directors who have contributed to cinema Westerns as possible because they deserve the recognition and because they are usually neglected in favor of the popular male cowboy stars. Among the entries included are people, places, and events from the actual history of the American West. For these entries, I am not concerned with actual historical facts. Instead, I give the basic information that any viewer of Westerns needs to know, often information filmmakers assume everyone knows.

Of course, I have attempted to maintain as thorough of a racial sensibility as possible. A problem arises, however, in dealing with cultural historical artifacts such as cinema Westerns, which obviously refer to Native Americans as Indians and often refer to all Hispanics, regardless of national origin, as Mexicans. Other racial epithets abound in the older films as well. I have attempted to use such terms only in the context of the historical culture of the films themselves.

The single most important research tool for the study of film and Westerns is the Internet Movie Database (IMDb). It contains a massive amount of facts, dates, cast lists, awards, trivia, and quotes on virtually every commercial film ever made. I am not trying to compete with the IMDb in my entries for actors, directors, or individual films. Instead of providing simple biographical data or plot summaries, which are easily obtainable online, I try to provide information on the individual's or film's significance.

In the introductory remarks to the bibliography, I indicate the sources I have relied on most heavily. An enormous body of material has accumulated through the years on such a popular film genre as Westerns, and I am indebted beyond words to the scholars and film historians who have gone before me. All errors in the following pages, however, are mine alone.

Chronology

1890 The year traditionally considered the official closing of the West according to the U.S. Census Bureau and also according to Frederick Jackson Turner, whose interpretation of the Western experience would dominate Western historical and cultural studies throughout the 20th century. By 1890, all remaining lands had been settled and, supposedly, all Native American tribes had been subdued and placed on reservations. **29 December:** The last significant "Indian battle," according to contemporary estimates, was the Battle of Wounded Knee in South Dakota.

1902 Owen Wister's *The Virginian: A Horseman of the Plains* became a national bestseller and established the Western as a fictional genre. Most of the basic plot characteristics of the Western as well as many of the clichés can be traced back to this popular novel.

1903 **1 December:** Edwin S. Porter's *The Great Train Robbery* appeared on-screen. Although only eight minutes in running time, it is the first narrative film and the first Western.

1907 George M. "Broncho Billy" Anderson and George K. Spoor established Essanay Film Manufacturing Company, the first major film studio, in Chicago.

1908 **3 November:** Butch Cassidy and the Sundance Kid reportedly died in a shootout near San Vicente, Bolivia. Thus, two of the last of the old-time outlaws of the West were still active when cinema Westerns were being made.

1914 William S. Hart appeared in his first Western, *The Bad Buck of Santa Ynez.* **28 March:** D. W. Griffith's *The Battle of Elderbrush Gulch* appeared, an early, significant Western starring Mae Marsh and Lillian Gish.

1917   26 March: John Ford began a long career directing with some Harry Carey Sr. one-reelers.

1923   16 March: *The Covered Wagon*, directed by James Cruze, was one of the first Western epics ever released. A true high-budget blockbuster for its time, the film stock would be raided for years for cheap inserts into other films.

1924   21 June: *Wanderer of the Wasteland*, based on a Zane Grey novel, was released, the first Western filmed in Technicolor.

1925   15 October: *The Vanishing American*, the first Western to use Monument Valley for its setting, premiered in Los Angeles. **27 December:** William S. Hart released his last film, the silent *Tumbleweeds*.

1928   25 December: *In Old Arizona*, a Cisco Kid Western starring Warner Baxter, was released. It was the first Western talkie as well as the first talkie filmed outdoors. The era of sound had begun.

1930   19 April: *The Light of Western Stars*, the last silent Western, was released. As with many films of this time, including Westerns, both a silent version and a sound version were made. The silent era officially closed.

1931   1 December: *Range Feud*, a Buck Jones Western, appeared, with John Wayne in his first Western.

1935 William S. Hart said goodbye to his fans. Well into the sound era, Hart re-released his last film, the silent *Tumbleweeds* (1925), and added an introduction to the film in which, walking beside Fritz, he laments the passing of the old ways, thanks him for being faithful through the years, says goodbye to his viewers, and walks his horse up and over the hill into the sunset. **23 February:** Gene Autry's first starring film, *The Phantom Empire*, began playing. The science-fiction Western would be the beginning of a long career for the singing cowboy. **23 August:** William Boyd's first Hopalong Cassidy film was released.

1936   16 November: Cecil B. DeMille's *The Plainsman* was released. This big-budget epic, starring Gary Cooper and Jean Arthur, was DeMille's one effort to make one of his trademark epic spectacles in the Western style.

1938   20 April: Roy Rogers starred in his first Western, *Under Western Stars*. His popularity was established, and thereafter he would be billed as "King of the Cowboys."

1939   2 March: John Ford's *Stagecoach* was released. Although John Wayne received secondary billing, this was the film in which he became an A-list Western star. **1 April:** Hollywood descended on Dodge City, Kansas, for the week-long world-premier celebration of *Dodge City*, starring Errol Flynn and Olivia de Havilland. Flynn and other stars of the film, such as Ann Sheridan, as well as celebrities such as Humphrey Bogart, arrived by train to begin the festivities. The high-budget spectacular was another attempt to change Westerns from B movies into respectable cinema.

1940   12 October: Tom Mix, speeding across the Arizona desert in a 1937 Cord Sportsman, failed to negotiate a turn and crashed, dying in a blaze of glory worthy of his Western film exploits.

1942   28 November: Buck Jones was guest of honor at the prestigious Cocoanut Grove nightclub in Boston when a fire broke out, killing more than 500 people, including Jones.

1944   John Wayne helped organize the Motion Picture Alliance for the Preservation of American Ideals, a reactionary anticommunist organization. Wayne and Ward Bond would be later presidents of the organization, which in the 1950s would collude with the House Un-American Activities Committee in its search for communists and communist sympathizers in Hollywood. The actors made many enemies in Hollywood and their efforts divided the film community along political lines. **13 May:** Roy Rogers's and Dale Evans's first film together, *Cowboy and the Senorita*, appeared.

1946   23 April: Howard Hughes's *The Outlaw*, starring Jane Russell, opened in San Francisco. The theater owner was immediately arrested for film obscenity. Nevertheless, the movie was soon showing across the country to shocked yet curious audiences. Westerns were suddenly glamorous and sexy. **30 December:** Following soon after *The Outlaw*, David O. Selznick's and King Vidor's *Duel in the Sun* premiered at the Egyptian Theatre in Los Angeles, just in time to qualify for the Oscars.

Jennifer Jones's sensuous portrayal of the "half-breed" Pearl, who destroys two men's lives, provided considerable controversy and publicity. Coming at a time when wholesome B Westerns were marked to a youth market, *Duel in the Sun* and *The Outlaw* marked a decided shift to erotic Westerns, which would become more pronounced in the 1950s.

1947   31 December: Roy Rogers, "King of the Cowboys," and Dale Evans, "Queen of the Cowgirls," were married in Oklahoma City, Oklahoma.

1949   24 June: *The Hopalong Cassidy Show* aired on NBC. The era of television Westerns had begun.

1950   1 June: Audie Murphy's first Western, *Sierra*, was released. Murphy, the United States' most decorated soldier in World War II, came home a hero and by the late 1940s had become one of the most popular Western stars. From 1950 to 1969, 25 of the 28 films he starred in were Westerns, such as *Destry* (1954) and *Hell Bent for Leather* (1960). **12 July:** Anthony Mann, film noir director, aired *Winchester '73*, starring Jimmy Stewart, an attempt to bring noir to Westerns. **15 November:** *Rio Grande* premiered, bringing to a close John Ford's Cavalry Trilogy, which also included *My Darling Clementine* (1946) and *Fort Apache* (1948). The three films, starring John Wayne, developed Ford's post–World War II vision of U.S. foreign policy.

1952   January: The first of Budd Boetticher's Western noirs, *The Cimarron Kid* (1952), starring Audie Murphy, appeared. Boetticher's great Westerns would all appear in the 1950s, culminating with a series of Randolph Scott films, including *Seven Men from Now* (1956) and *The Tall T* (1957). **24 July:** *High Noon* premiered. The film had already stirred controversy when its screenwriter, Carl Foreman, was summoned before the House Un-American Activities Committee for questioning into his communist sympathies. Foreman was later blacklisted from Hollywood as a communist sympathizer. So *High Noon* is often considered to be an allegory of what happens to good people hunted by anticommunist zealots, such as senator Joseph McCarthy.

1953   27 November: *Hondo*, filmed in 3D and starring John Wayne, was released. The audience had to wear special glasses to get the full effect. The gimmick never really caught on.

1954   10 February: *Phantom Stallion*, starring Rex Allen, last of the singing cowboys, was released. It is often considered the last truly B Western, and thus it signaled the end of the B Western era.

1955   Jacques Bazin, highly influential French film critic and co-founder of *Cahiers du Cinéma*, wrote approvingly of Western films, legitimizing Westerns as worthy of serious film study. **21 September:** The last of Ronald Reagan's gunfighter Westerns, *Tennessee's Partners*, appeared. The trilogy also included *Law and Order* (1953) and *Cattle Queen of Montana* (1954).

1957   30 May: John Sturges's *Gunfight at the O.K. Corral*, nominated for two Academy Awards, premiered.

1959   4 April: Howard Hawks's answer to *High Noon* (1952), *Rio Bravo*, appeared, starring John Wayne. The film showed what a truly American lawman would do when facing a similar situation to the left-leaning sheriff played by Gary Cooper in *High Noon*.

1960   23 October: *The Magnificent Seven* opened, and a brief period of the new Western epic commenced.

1962   22 April: *The Man Who Shot Liberty Valance* appeared.

1964   John Ford directed his last Western, *Cheyenne Autumn*.

1967   1 February: *A Fistful of Dollars* was released in New York. The spaghetti Western had arrived. Early criticism and fan reaction was derisive and harsh, while box office receipts piled up.

1968   4 July: John Wayne's *The Green Berets*, a Vietnam combat movie, premiered in Atlanta, Georgia, on Independence Day. Although not a Western, the film inadvertently helped change the direction Westerns would take in the future. Released at the height of antiwar sentiment, *The Green Berets* revealed John Wayne's jingoistic patriotism and also showed the venerable cowboy fighter as simply old. Wayne's reputation would never be the same. His day had long passed, and America said goodbye to one of its last heroes.

1969   18 June: *The Wild Bunch* premiered in Los Angeles, the most violent Western and one of the most violent films of any genre to date. **24 October:** *Butch Cassidy and the Sundance Kid* appeared and modernized the Western.

1970   7 April: John Wayne received his only Oscar, for best actor in *True Grit* (1969). **23 December:** *Little Big Man* appeared, one of the first truly revisionist Westerns. The way cowboys and Indians were played out on film would never be the same again.

1974   7 February: Mel Brooks's Western spoof *Blazing Saddles* began its run in theaters across the United States. The putdown of the Western genre was so hilarious and yet so severe that many felt sure the Western as a significant film genre was dead.

1979   11 June: John Wayne died. With his death, there could no longer be any question that the era of classic Westerns was over.

1980 Michael Cimino's *Heaven's Gate*, a highly publicized, big-budget film, became a major box-office failure. Critics said it was so great a failure that it killed the Western forever. For much of the early 1980s, production companies refused to gamble again on Westerns.

1981   20 January: Ronald Reagan became president of the United States, the only Western film actor ever to be so elected. In his campaigns and later presidential speech rhetoric, he exploited his image in Westerns as a tough, all-American cowboy for political purposes.

1991   25 March: Kevin Costner's *Dances with Wolves* won 7 Academy Awards while being nominated for 12. The success proved that Westerns could still be made successfully. But the film also ushered in a new era of alternative Westerns, with its fundamentally different perspective on the history of the frontier West.

1993 Maggie Greenwald's *The Ballad of Little Jo*, a Western with a cross-dressing female hero, began an era of numerous postmodern feminist Westerns in which gender roles are reversed. Feminist Westerns that followed include *The Quick and the Dead* (1995), *The Missing* (2003), and *Gang of Roses* (2003). **29 March:** *Unforgiven*, directed by and starring Clint Eastwood, won four Academy Awards while being nominated for nine. Eastwood won his first of many Oscars and was established without question as one of the dominant actors and directors of the late 20th and early 21st centuries.

1995   10 May: Jim Jarmusch's postmodern *Dead Man*, starring Johnny Depp, was released in the United States a year after its European release. The film proved the Western genre capable of adapting to the postmodern era.

2001   17 August: *American Outlaws*, a Western aimed at a teenage audience, was released.

2003   15 August: Kevin Costner's *Open Range* appeared.

2005   16 December: *Brokeback Mountain*, a modern Western, was released after a publicity campaign lasting several months and with accompanying controversy over the story line of a long-standing homosexual relationship between two traditional working cowboys. The film won four Academy Awards after being nominated for nine.

2007   7 September: *3:10 to Yuma*, starring Russell Crowe, a remake of the 1957 classic, was released. **5 October:** *The Assassination of Jesse James by the Coward Robert Ford*, starring Brad Pitt, was released. Together, these films signaled the health of the Western genre in the early 21st century.

Introduction

When early filmgoers watched *The Great Train Robbery* in 1903, many of them shrieked in terror at the end of the last scene, when one of the outlaws turns toward the camera and fires a gun, seemingly directly at the audience. The puff of smoke was sudden, and it was hand-colored so it looked real. We look back today at that primitive movie in wonderment and see all the elements that would become part of the Western genre. Because *The Great Train Robbery* was the first narrative, commercial movie, the Western genre is the only film genre whose history exactly parallels the history of popular film itself. The story takes place in the West in the late 19th century, and it contains the basics of what would become the Western myth. These basics would develop, as the century progressed, into the three essential elements of a Western movie: the Western moment, myth, and place.

The Western moment refers to that barely existent time in U.S. history after the Civil War ended in 1865 when the country turned its attention westward and began the final process of settling the rest of the country. The U.S. Census Bureau determined that by 1890 the West had been settled, so most Westerns take place sometime between 1865 and 1890. But these dates have little relevance to Westerns. Most never indicate a historical date. Many indicate dates well before 1865 or well after 1890, some after the turn of the 20th century. As *The Great Train Robbery* was being filmed in New Jersey, much of the western United States remained as primitive as it had in the true Western moment. Thus, early Western filmmakers were telling stories set within the memory of many of their viewers. Al Jennings's *A Bank Robbery* (1908) was filmed in an Oklahoma town that was as much a part of the old West at the time of the filming as it had been 20 years earlier. Jennings himself had been a genuine Western outlaw years before. So the earliest Westerns told stories that their audiences truly understood.

Through the years, memory of the historic old West faded and movies began portraying not a recent West but a West that was no more. Silent-era Westerns such as those of William S. Hart tended to look back nostalgically and romanticize the West. Popular Western novelists such as Zane Grey, Max Brand, and Clarence Mulford described a West that never was, and movies followed the trend. B Westerns of the 1930s and 1940s tended to compare the historic Western moment to the contemporary moment, identifying the former as a time when goodness and purity were possible and the latter as a time corrupted by modern influences. Thus we see Gene Autry and Roy Rogers Westerns taking place in the 1930s and 1940s but with everyone still riding horses and traveling by stagecoach. In many B Westerns, stagecoaches travel alongside automobiles. High-budget Westerns before World War II like *Stagecoach* (1939) and *The Plainsman* (1936), while not as simplistic as B Westerns, nevertheless maintained the trend of portraying the historic old West as a period in which America grew up, a period in which a man could make his way in the world unlike any other time in history.

By the 1940s and 1950s, the true historical Western moment had become almost irrelevant in Westerns except as a mythical period when humanity was forced to live at the most elemental level, to confront raw nature and human evil in the form of outlaws or Native American tribes unaided by modern technology. The Western moment, then, for John Ford in his Cavalry Trilogy as well as the later John Wayne films, became a time period useful for working through the nation's social and cultural problems with war, civil rights, and ultimately its past and treatment of indigenous peoples. Anthony Mann and Budd Boetticher used the Western moment to portray intense character trials and character development in their noir Westerns.

While no one remarked on it at the time, the history of Westerns through the 1950s was based on certain assumptions that we now collectively refer to as the classic Western period. These movies interpreted the historic Western moment primarily in terms of white, male, Anglo-Saxon history. Westerns of the 1960s began questioning this narrow view of history. Spaghetti Westerns and other antimyth Westerns blurred the Western moment to such a degree as to be unidentifiable. All that mattered was that it was not a period to look back on nostalgically. It was not a time when a man could discover what his real character was. It was not a time to be proud of in U.S. history. Thus in Sergio

Leone's Dollars Trilogy or in Sergio Corbucci and other Italian directors' Django movies, there are no good characters, no noble cowboy heroes. The Western moment has become a time of human corruption.

Alternative Westerns since the 1980s have attempted to respond to antimyth films and the attack on classic Westerns by looking at elements of the West ignored by such directors as John Ford. Kevin Costner's *Dances with Wolves* (1990) is the first major film to look at the United States' treatment of Native Americans through the perspective of Native cultures. Other alternative Westerns treat racial and gender themes. The way we look back at the historic old West in our movies today has fundamentally changed since the genre's beginnings in 1903.

Westerns, though, are not solely concerned with the time period of the old West. They also base their narratives on the Western myth, which refers to the accumulated stories, customs, codes of behavior, and traditions developed in movies and fiction from the beginning of the genre to the present. Westerns do not reflect actual history. They reflect the myths that have accumulated through the years.

What Billy the Kid was like as a real human being at a real moment in history is relevant to a Western only as one element out of many. The myth in movies such as *The Outlaw* (1943) or *The Left Handed Gun* (1958) gives us a handsome and devilish but likeable left-handed gunfighter, still just a kid, still with a measure of puckish innocence. The Western myth was fully developed in the classic Western period when the role of whites in relation to Native Americans, the role of women in relation to cowboy heroes, and the role of violence and gunplay in establishing justice were all codified. When viewers saw Tom Mix, Roy Rogers, Gary Cooper, and John Wayne on-screen, there was no question what character qualities they possessed. Antimyth Westerns and later alternative Westerns have been reimagining the Western myth since the 1960s to include women, Native Americans, and all ethnic groups that were a part of the historic West.

But a Western would not be a Western if it was not located in a specific locale. The place that unifies all Westerns is usually considered the trans-Mississippi western United States. Classic Westerns focused on the high plains regions of the West or such majestic areas as Monument Valley. Rarely were they set in coastal California or the Northwest. The idea has always been that in vast stretches of unpopulated frontier, humanity functions at its most elemental level. The landscape of a Western has become a formative factor in character development. It often serves as an antagonist that must be conquered, as in *A Far Country* (1954) or *The Covered Wagon* (1923). Antimyth Westerns such as *The Wild Bunch* (1969) or *A Fistful of Dollars* (1967) stretched the Western place to below the border into Mexico, where that landscape served as a foil to the more recognizable landscape of classic Westerns. Early fans and critics of spaghetti Westerns were often outraged that these movies were filmed in Spain and Italy in locations that only suggested a true Western setting. Place was becoming much less important. Several later postmodern Westerns use place to simply indicate the genre. *The Quick and the Dead* (1995) takes place in a Western town but with no historical context whatever. The mere suggestion of the movie set, along with its interpretation of the myth, makes it a Western.

Today, the three elements that traditionally define a Western often seem blurred or altogether absent. Nevertheless, in order to watch a Western you must still be aware of the historical context of the genre. In Westerns, perhaps more than in any other movie genre, the traditions and myths developed by the genre are assumed to be understood by all viewers. Even such bizarre postmodern Westerns as *The Dead Man* (1995) and *Gang of Roses* (2003) depend on a certain knowledge of previous Westerns.

Unfortunately, a generation of moviegoers has grown up without knowing the assumptions on which Westerns are based. Many viewers today have never seen a Western in their lives. Their entire knowledge often consists of occasionally surfing television channels or encountering references in popular culture, such as John Wayne or Clint Eastwood imitations. For postmodern viewers of Westerns, then, the old stories of the West are in the background but no longer hold the imagination. After all, postmodernism by definition repudiates the myths of the past, including Western myths. Since those myths were all told from a white masculine perspective, because they were stories of white men beating up on Native Americans and women and "winning" the West, many have lost interest in cinema Westerns. Few postmodern movie watchers can accept the values on which classic Westerns were based and often have little acquaintance with new postmodern Westerns. The "question of questions" about cinema Westerns is whether they will continue to thrive in the 21st century.

The Dictionary

– A –

ABILENE, KANSAS. Certain historically significant **towns** appear often in Westerns. Abilene was one of the first great cow towns. Early in the Western period it became a rail junction and thus a destination for the great early cattle drives from Texas. Like **Dodge City**, Abilene symbolizes the conjunction of civilization in the east and the Western frontier. The town is usually depicted as crowded with cowboys, saloons, and saloon girls. Gunshots punctuate the night. Only the toughest of lawmen, such as **Wild Bill Hickok**, can tame such a town. *Abilene Town* (1946) and *Gunfight in Abilene* (1967) celebrate this great cow town of the **Great Plains**.

ACCORD, ART (1890–1931). Art Accord was featured in numerous **silent** Westerns as a ruggedly handsome, clean-cut **cowboy hero** known for his fist-fighting ability in such films as *The White Outlaw* (1929). But Accord's real claim to fame was his inability to make the transition from silents to talkies. Early sound technology simply could not pick up the nuances of his peculiar voice. Several silent stars experienced similar difficulties, but most persevered and overcame initial resistance. Accord could not overcome his difficulties. As a result of a career-ending disappointment, he entered a life of crime, ending up dead in a Mexican jail, perhaps by suicide.

AFRICAN AMERICANS IN WESTERNS. While African Americans populated much of the historical West, they were largely neglected or relegated to submissive roles in Western cinema for most of the 20th century. The early silents of **D. W. Griffith** portrayed African Americans as brutes incapable of containing their lust for white women. *The Birth of a Nation* (1915), while not specifically a Western, represents Griffith's racist attitudes. Later Westerns develop the role of the **comic Negro**, a racist caricature that remained in Westerns through the 1950s. Some films were produced, however, with predominantly African American casts and marketed to African American audiences. **Herb Jeffries**, the Bronze Buckaroo, made a career as an early African American cowboy star.

African Americans were demeaned in early Westerns mainly through racist stereotyping. A typical stereotype was the loyal servant who wanted to be cared for by white people and who performed only menial tasks. This character was naturally funny, childlike, self-deprecating, and always cowardly. Other African American stereotypes were singers, dancers, entertainers, and loyal, dependent servants ill-equipped to care for themselves. In films set following the Civil War, these characters were often former slaves who voluntarily stayed on the plantation to serve just as they had before the war. Any African Americans who were sympathetic to reconstruction were depraved, savage, and uncivilized. Of course, these characters also had heavy dialects and were highly superstitious.

One example of how unexamined racism drives the plot of a Western is in *The Lonely Trail* (1936), starring **John Wayne** and Ann Rutherford, where an elaborate network of plantation servants (former slaves happy to remain around) is in place to warn the white Texas landowners of the approach of the reconstruction police. When the vicious police arrive, the servants jump up and begin dancing and playing the harmonica and banjo. It was no doubt very funny to original audiences.

As with other cultural issues, race issues have often been treated indirectly in Westerns. Cavalry Westerns of the 1940s and 1950s, such as **John Ford**'s **Cavalry Trilogy**, often made oblique comments about black and white racial tensions by addressing issues between various white ethnic groups. Unfortunately, these Westerns usually displaced the racism with the different ethnic groupings banding together in their oppression of, for example, the savage **Apache**.

As the **civil rights** movement got underway in the United States in the 1960s, Westerns began to revise the role of African Americans, and notable African American actors began successful careers. Woody Strode in *The Man Who Shot Liberty Valance* (1962) played a transitional role as faithful yet still respected companion to Tom Doniphon (John Wayne). Later he played strong characters in *Sergeant Rutledge* (1960) and *The Professionals* (1966). Ossie Davis in *The Scalphunters* (1968) played a conventional role as a runaway slave paired with a white mountain man, but instead of a black-white friendship, the racial antagonism is pronounced and racial tension is emphasized.

Revisionist Westerns have repeatedly attempted to recognize the legitimate historical role of African Americans during the **Western moment**, just as the role of Native Americans has been reconsidered in Westerns of the period. During the 1970s, a series of "black" Westerns appeared, such as *Duel at Diablo* (1966); *The Red, White, and Black* (1970); *The Legend of Nigger Charlie* (1972); and *The Soul of Nigger Charlie* (1973). Sidney Poitier, a prominent civil rights activist as well as actor, directed *Buck and the Preacher* (1972), starring in it along with Harry Belafonte and a nearly all–African American cast.

Perhaps the most important transitional moment in the history of African Americans in Westerns occurred in Mel Brooks's ***Blazing Saddles*** (1974) through Cleavon Little, who as sheriff subverts, comically, most previous stereotypes of his race. The popularity of the film and the memorable comic scenes did more to change the public's attitude toward race than any other Western.

The last decades of the century saw, with mixed success, attempts to integrate African Americans into the historical Western moment as naturally as they had been perceived in contemporary U.S. society. At times, color-blind casting has simply ignored racial differences. Nevertheless, the dominant role of African Americans in Westerns has always been as "**racial others**." *See also* CIVIL RIGHTS WESTERNS; COMIC NEGRO; FETCHIT, STEPIN; TOONES, FRED.

ALLEGORIES, WESTERNS AS. If Westerns are primarily about the time in which they are produced, not the time in which they are set, then Westerns of the cold war period are often interpreted as allegories of the tensions between the Soviet Union and its allies and the United States, Great Britain, and their allies. Westerns such as ***High Noon*** (1952) and ***The Ox-Bow Incident*** (1943) are usually seen as allegories of contemporary issues: individual rights versus rights of the state, mass hysteria in the face of common threats from outside. *High Noon*, for example, was produced during the national hysteria over communists brought on by the McCarthy hearings.

ALLEN, BOB "TEX" (1906–1998). Born Irvine E. Theodore Baehr, Tex Allen—as he was known in his Westerns—had a long career in a wide variety of Hollywood films and Broadway plays. In 1936, Columbia, having just lost its top cowboy star, Ken Maynard, cast the journeyman actor in the Bob Allen, Ranger series, six films made between 1936 and 1937. The best is probably *The Reckless Ranger* (1937), unique in its sympathy for sheep men in their conflict with cattlemen. Allen's **sidekick** was Wally Wales and his horse was Pal. After **singing cowboys** began dominating **B Westerns**, Allen's Western career ended. He went on to a long career in theater and in the 1950s was known more for his Broadway roles than his old Westerns. *See also* CATTLEMEN VERSUS SHEEP MEN.

ALLEN, REX (1920–1999). "The last of the **singing cowboys**," so Allen was billed in his later acting years, along with Monte Hale. After World War II, **Republic** developed these two singing cowboys. Allen made only 19 Westerns, beginning with *The Arizona Cowboy* (1950). To be billed as a clean-cut role model for young fans, Allen, as part of his contract with Republic, pledged to not smoke or drink in public and to always wear cowboy dress. As a veterinarian in *Border Saddlemates* (1952), Allen's character, who is treating a boy's pet fox that is about to die, assures the boy that God loves animals the same as humans. Then he sings about God saving the animals in Noah's ark. Allen's production unit folded in 1953. Known for his deeply mellow voice, Allen turned to recording and to being a longtime narrator for Disney films.

ALTERNATIVE WESTERNS. The Vietnam War, the civil rights movement, the women's rights movement, the American Indian movement, and other historical events of the 1960s and 1970s brought paradigmatic changes in American culture that affected every form of art and certainly every facet of the U.S. film industry. Westerns changed as well, first with the appearance of **antimyth Westerns** such as those of **Sergio Leone** and then with the development of alternative Westerns, sometimes called **postmodern Westerns** or revisionist Westerns, which reflect end-of-century cultural changes. Three types of alternative Westerns, according to Richard Slotkin, have appeared since the 1970s: **formalist Westerns, neorealist Westerns**, and **cult-of-the-Indian Westerns** (also called counterculture Westerns).

Alternative Westerns, reflecting the postmodern consciousness, are substantial departures both stylistically and ideologically from Westerns earlier in the century. They tend to reflect end-of-century gender and race concerns and usually mix dark, grimy reality with elements of fantasy. *The Quick and the Dead* (1995) tells the story of a quick-draw contest, with the fastest gunfighter being a **woman** (Sharon Stone). *The Ballad of Little Jo* (1993), with close attention to **historical authenticity**, tells the story of a frontier woman forced to conceal her gender for decades merely to survive. *Dead Man* (1995), filmed in black and white, uses techniques of surrealism to tell its story. Recent Westerns are still considered "alternative" rather than mainstream because they are countering a tremendous body of cinema and a powerful cultural force of the previous century. *See also* AFRICAN AMERICANS IN WESTERNS; CIVIL RIGHTS WESTERNS; CROWE, RUSSELL; FEMINIST WESTERNS; HACKMAN, GENE; INDIANS; MYTHOLOGICAL HISTORICISM AND ALTERNATIVE WESTERNS; WOMEN, STEREOTYPES.

ALTMAN, ROBERT (1925–2006). After graduating from the University of Missouri with a degree in engineering and flying fighter planes in World War II, Robert Altman entered the film industry by making industrial films. During the 1960s he mostly worked in television. After making his first hit film, *MASH*, in 1970, he began a long career of successful hits, including two significant Westerns: *McCabe and Mrs. Miller* (1971) and *Buffalo Bill and the Indians, or Sitting Bull's History Lesson* (1976). Both films celebrate the end of **classic Westerns** and work squarely in the **antimyth** tradition. *McCabe and Mrs. Miller*, starring **Warren Beatty** and Julie Christie, is a charming story of entrepreneurship in the old West involving a brothel. *Buffalo Bill and the Indians, or Sitting Bull's History Lesson*, starring Paul Newman, concerns Buffalo Bill Cody and his Wild West show. Characters like Annie Oakley, Sitting Bull, and even president Grover Cleveland work their way through the story. Both Westerns exemplify Altman's style, seen in his non-Westerns as well, of questioning and debunking every possible **cliché** of American myth. Altman's is a West demythologized.

***AMERICAN OUTLAWS* (2001).** Colin Farrell, Scott Caan, Ali Larter, Gabriel Macht, Les Mayfield (director). Postmodern America is calling all myths to account, and when it comes to Westerns, the **outlaw** myths are all open for reinterpretation. Thus, *American Outlaws* reinterprets the **Jesse James** stories for a new generation, a generation brought up on MTV. Executive producer Jonathan A. Zimbert explains some of the film's rationale on the film's website: "Throughout history, outlaws have always been popular, particularly among young people who consider themselves outlaws, rebelling against the older establishment. . . . The James Gang is kind of like a rock and roll band out on the road on their first tour together. This is something today's audience can relate to" (www.americanoutlaws.com).

The film begins during the Civil War and portrays the ambivalence of most Missourians toward both sides of the war. When the James and Younger families return to Missouri after the war, they find trouble waiting. First, both families are targeted by Federal authorities because they fought on the "wrong" side. Then Cole Younger (Caan) is arrested and subject to be hanged. Thus, the friends become an outlaw gang and set out to free Cole. Jesse's fiancée, Zee (Larter), proves an effective gang member, masterminding their first outlaw act. But the James brothers and the Youngers become sympathetic outlaws in American myth because they save the common people from greedy barons. The evil railroad owner, Thaddeus Rains (Harris Yulin), comes through Missouri, forcing farmers to sell their land to him and resorting to **violence** if they refuse. The only hope against U.S.-government backed greed and corruption is the new American outlaws. From Missouri the gang moves West, saving the weak and innocent and attacking the inhuman machine of American capitalism. But as time goes on, Jesse (Farrell) realizes he just wants to settle down with Zee and lead a normal domestic life. He is arrested in Florida on his honeymoon.

This is the Jesse James for a new generation. Other versions of the legend have celebrated railroad moguls as the heroes fighting against ruthless outlaws. But postmodern audiences question older ideas of economic progress. The new Jesse James upholds the moral values of the 21st century while acknowledging older domestic values. Jesse, for example, refuses to kill except as a last resort. Zee refuses Jesse sex until after they are married. Jesse and Frank find satisfaction in murder or robbery merely for the thrill. The moral center of the film is the question of whether powerful, government-sanctioned greed and corruption justifies the response of the American outlaws.

The film's cult following was short lived, but its appeal to a young generation not brought up watching **classic Westerns** was significant. No doubt the superb performance by its cast of fashionably dressed young stars contributed to its success as well. *See also* ANTIMYTH WESTERNS; OUTLAWS.

AMIS, SUZY (1962–). Suzy Amis is most remembered for her role as Little Jo Monaghan in **Maggie Greenwald**'s *The Ballad of Little Jo* (1993)—a character who passes for a male rancher, undetected except by an Asian ranch hand who becomes her lover. Only at little Jo's death does the community discover that she was really a woman. In *The Ballad of Little Jo*, the fashion model Amis proved to be a superior actress. Her one other Western is *The Last Stand at Saber River* (1997) opposite Tom Selleck. *See also* FEMINIST WESTERNS.

ANDERSON, BRONCHO BILLY (1880–1971). Between 1908 and 1915, Anderson, the first cowboy star of the movies, created over 375 silent shorts, including "Broncho Billy," and developed standard production procedures often used in later years for making low-budget, quickly produced films. Anderson's standard production formula called for one Western a week on a budget of around $800 (occasionally grossing as much as $50,000), working from a skeleton script with little time for costume changes, actors' makeup, or, naturally, rehearsal. The emphasis was on speed. Anderson could make a 19-scene film on location in one day, shooting one scene after another without significant pause.

Although he had the cowboy look—he posed for a *Saturday Evening Post* cover as a cowboy before his film career—Broncho Billy was not a natural cowboy actor. Anderson convinced Edwin S. Porter to give him a role in **The Great Train Robbery** (1903) on the basis of his horsemanship, but he could not even ride a horse. During the first take, Broncho Billy attempted to mount the horse on the wrong side and fell off. Wisely, Porter used him in walking roles instead. In all, Anderson played three characters: the brakeman, a passenger who is shot in the back, and one of the robbers.

Most of his early movie jobs, however, were off camera, working first for Vitagraph and then Selig Polyscope. In 1907 he took a crew to Colorado for a series of Westerns that received lukewarm response. But Broncho Billy's break came in 1908 when he helped establish the **Essanay Company** with a studio in Niles, California. Anderson set out to film Westerns in California, but he could not find anyone to act lead in his films—partly because actors were scarce in California and partly because film acting still had a poor reputation. As a last resort, Anderson took the lead role in the first short he filmed—*Broncho Billy and the Baby* (1915). By acting in the lead role as well as directing and producing, Anderson kept a low overhead in production, often taking only two cameramen and a regular cast of three to four actors on location to sites in Colorado, California, Las Vegas, and Catalina Island.

Typical Broncho Billy films were praised in their time for realism created by location filming. Inevitably, the films used sentimental themes with sharp distinctions between right and wrong, bad guys and good guys. Because the films were shot with such rapidity, there was little continuity in Brocho Billy's character. In some films he played villains while in others he played heroes of sterling virtue out to right the wrongs afflicting the oppressed.

Broncho Billy's outfit was simple; realistic without looking like a costume. "He wore a simple and modestly colored shirt, often a waistcoat [apart from Hart and, occasionally, Mix, few other Western stars did this] and leather cuffs, adorned with a single star, around the lower arms" (Everson 1978, 183). Working cowboys wore these cuffs to avoid rope burns, but cinema cowboys rarely put them on. Anderson also trademarked garish sheepskin chaps, a feature seldom seen in later Western costumes.

The Broncho Billy films, distributed mainly in nickelodeons, made Anderson one of the first recognizable movie stars. Appearances in New York occasioned small riots. By 1912 he was earning $125,000 a year, a substantial increase from the 50¢ an hour he earned working with Edwin S. Porter.

While George M. Anderson became famous as Broncho Billy, he saw himself as a producer as much as an actor. In this producer role, Anderson signed comedian Charlie Chaplin to an Essanay contract in 1915 and is often considered responsible for Chaplin's rapid rise to fame. Anderson subsequently appeared in Chaplin comedies, as well as numerous other comedies, and Chaplin appeared in a Broncho Billy Western.

After silent films began showing in large theaters as features instead of in nickelodeons as one- or two-reel shorts, Anderson's career began to decline, partly by choice. His last Westerns, made after an absence of several years while making comedies, are some of the only surviving Broncho Billy films and are not generally considered his best.

Anderson went into a long retirement in 1923, disappearing from the movie industry entirely. In the 1940s an effort was made to find the old cowboy actor, and he was rediscovered after a nationwide search. Thereafter he reconnected with Hollywood, even appearing in a television special with **John Ford** to reminisce about the old days. In 1957 the Academy of Motion Pictures Arts and Sciences honored Anderson "for his contributions to the development of motion pictures as entertainment." Broncho Billy Anderson's last Western was *The Bounty Killer* (1965). *See also* COSTUMES; FORMULAS, CLASSIC WESTERN.

ANDREWS, ARKANSAS "SLIM" (1906–1992). Born Lloyd Andrews, Arkansas Slim was one of the famous comic **sidekicks** from the 1930s. He was tall and lanky, had a handlebar mustache, and seemed more of a hillbilly than a cowboy. He is best known as **Tex Ritter**'s companion, who faithfully trod along behind on a mule named Josephine. The two worked well as a team, though a *Variety* review of *The Golden Trail* (1940) suggested that Andrews should have been left unrestrained: "Evidently the guy is being held in check, for no apparent reason" (Kramer 1998, 63).

ANDREWS, DANA (1909–1992). Dana Andrews began his career primarily in Westerns, landing solid secondary roles in such well-regarded films as *The Westerner* (1940) and *Belle Starr* (1941). An actor with great promise never fulfilled, Andrews fought alcoholism most of his life, which affected his career considerably. During the

1950s, he played lead in several low-budget Westerns such as *Comanche* (1956); *Strange Lady in Town* (1955), opposite Greer Carson; and *Town Tamer* (1965). Andrews mastered the art of conveying the psychological intensity of troubled characters.

In *The Ox-Bow Incident* (1943), Andrews delivered a skilled performance as an innocent man accused of rustling and murder. Andrews's character (Donald Martin) purchases some cattle and neglects to get a bill of sale. Then, while moving into the territory, he picks up a Hispanic companion and an old man suffering from dementia. On a drearily cold night at the Ox-Bow, an angry mob finds these three men with the cattle and believes it is the herd taken from a man who has been murdered. In this noir Western, Andrews masterfully portrays a desperate man trying to reason with those beyond reasoning and maintain some semblance of personal human dignity as the rope is placed around his neck. Moments after the hanging, the mob finds out he was indeed innocent.

ANGEL AND THE BADMAN **(1947). John Wayne, Gail Russell, Harry Carey Jr.**, and James Edward Grant (director). The wounded and unconscious "badman," Quirt Evans (Wayne), is taken in by a Quaker family who espouse strict nonviolence. Delirious for days, he finally wakes up and continues his recuperation in the Quakers' home. During Evans's recovery, a strange thing happens to both the hardened **outlaw** and the naïve, innocent girl (Russell): the young girl, who has been tending to the badman's injuries, falls in love with an outlaw, and the outlaw turns out to be not so bad after all. Evans is torn between his obvious love for the Quaker girl and his realization of the life that awaits him. The family adopts Evans, and he becomes devoted to the father and mother and the younger brother. Yet their life of gentleness and nonviolence seems alien to him. What he knows is the practical ways of life necessary for survival.

At one point Evans confronts a heavy-handed landowner who has cut off water to the Quaker families in the valley below. Evans forces the landowner to open the dam, but more importantly, he forces the landowner to go down to the Quakers and apologize. They treat the astonished man royally, overwhelm him with goodness, and send him home with two baskets of pies, doughnuts, and goodies.

The old life, however, haunts the **gunfighter** and complications arise. At one point he is given a Bible. A fellow outlaw reads it and is changed. Eventually Evans changes. At the end, instead of riding off into the sunset, Evans rides off with his fiancée, the young Quaker girl, vowing to be a farmer.

On one hand, this is a powerful story, though the film borders on B quality. It mirrors the true story of many settlers who turned in their guns for the plow as they settled the West—the story often untold in Westerns. On the other hand, the film seems at odds with other Wayne pictures. Wayne presumably felt strongly about the story, since he produced it, but his character is incompatible with the values Wayne usually expressed, especially in the later films.

Gail Russell and her family in the film give superb performances. Russell's character, Penelope Worth, seems naïve and simple, but she is a very complex character, driven like her father and mother by sincere beliefs. Penelope watches Evans while he is unconscious and delirious. During this time, she sees through to his deep subconscious, to the hidden goodness within him, and while shocked, she is not deterred; this insight becomes the key to her devotion to him.

ANTIMYTH WESTERNS. Concurrent with the 1960s' revolution of cultural values, cinema Westerns began to challenge assumptions upon which **classic Westerns** were based. Perhaps the most obvious result was the **deterritorialization** of the classic Western by Italian directors such as **Sergio Leone,** who shot their films in Europe, usually Spain but sometimes Italy. These **spaghetti Westerns** removed geographic space as a regenerative force and developed antiheroes who no longer claimed moral rightness as an absolute. Good and bad mix freely, most notably in Leone's *The Good, the Bad and the Ugly* (1967). The moral center is based on self-preservation and self-gratification. **Post-Westerns** were clearly influenced by the popular ideas of mid-century existentialism as advocated by Jean-Paul Sartre and Albert Camus. Because they did not adequately deal with social issues such as sexism, homophobia, and racism (against **Native Americans**, **African Americans**, Hispanic Americans, and even Asian Americans), antimyth Westerns made a transitional philosophical statement and then were superseded by **alternative Westerns**.

APACHES. The **Native American** Apache tribes nearly always appear in Westerns as the most brutal of all **Indian** tribes. Their territory covered the southwest U.S. border with Mexico, and their most famous chief was Geronimo. Numerous Westerns portray Apaches as engaging in "**savage war**" simply because it is their evil nature to do so. In **John Ford**'s *Stagecoach* (1939), the helpless stage is attacked for no reason by warring Apaches. Early in the film, when rumors of an Indian uprising are mentioned, the mere fact that it is Apaches who are on the war path is enough to put terror into all hearts. In Robert Aldrich's *Apache* (1954), Burt Lancaster played Massai, an ambivalent Apache warrior who escapes from transportation to Florida in order to return to the homelands and live out his life in peace. One of the few sympathetic portrayals of the tribe is Walter Hill's *Geronimo: An American Legend* (1993). Ron Howard's *The Missing* (2003) involves a young girl's captivity at the hands of Apaches.

ARNESS, JAMES (1923–). Born James Aurness in Minnesota, James Arness is best known for his 20-year role as Marshal Matt Dillon on television's *Gunsmoke* series. Prior to his years in **television Westerns**, Arness played a variety of supporting roles in Westerns and non-Westerns, several with **John Wayne** (who became a close friend), most notably *Hondo* (1953). Trivia buffs may remember the broad-shouldered, six-feet-seven Arness as the Thing in *The Thing from Another World* (1951), his first starring role in a film. The actor's first starring role in a Western was opposite **Angie Dickinson** in Andrew McLaglen's *Gun the Man Down* (1956), a film produced by Wayne. His only other Western starring role was in *Comanche Stallion* (2006). Arness is the brother of actor Peter Graves.

ARTHUR, JEAN (1900–1991). Jean Arthur's most famous Western role is Marian Starrett, the winsome farm wife in *Shane* (1953). She loves her husband (Van Heflen) and son (**Brandon De Wilde**) but is drawn perilously close to Shane (**Alan Ladd**), the ex-gunfighter and idol of her son. However, 17 years earlier Jean Arthur played quite a different role in Cecil B. DeMille's *The Plainsman* (1936). As **Calamity Jane**, Arthur played a rough-talking, masculine muleskinner who falls in love with **Wild Bill Hickok** (**Gary Cooper**) and follows him to **Deadwood**. Some critics wondered how a glamorous star like Arthur could be credible as a Calamity Jane, but Arthur had a long career in Hollywood, playing many kinds of roles. Her Western career spanned back to numerous silent shorts of the 1920s such as *Ridin' Rivals* (1926), where she played opposite Buddy Roosevelt and Wally Wales.

ATES, ROSCOE (1895–1962). Roscoe Ates played comic supporting roles in film and television from the 1930s to the early 1960s. From 1946–1948, he held down the regular role of Eddie Dean's **sidekick**, Soapy Jones, known for his comic stutter. *Tumbleweed Trail* (1946), a **Producers Releasing Corporation (PRC)** production starring Dean and Shirley Patterson, represents a typical **B Western** film in which Ates appeared. **Television Westerns** gave Ates regular work throughout the 1950s.

AUTRY, GENE (1907–1998). Gene Autry was a well-established entertainer before coming to Hollywood, a star on the nationally popular radio program National Barn Dance on WLS radio station in Chicago. He was born a cowboy on a Texas ranch and was working as a railroad telegraph operator when Will Rogers, the famous Oklahoma comic actor, heard Autry sing during a layover in Oklahoma and encouraged him to enter show business. Autry began entertaining as a blackface minstrel in itinerant medicine shows. He acknowledged a significant influence from early country-folk singer Jimmie Rodgers; few of his pre-Hollywood songs had anything to do with Western themes. Early in his film career, Autry was dubbed "the Lavender Cowboy" because he did not fit the usual type of **B Western** cowboy: He was not tall, big-framed, or obviously rugged. Instead, he was clean, well-groomed, and splendidly outfitted in lavish **costumes** consisting of a tall white hat and flashy shirts, usually jet-black affairs ornamented with gold braids. His horse, **Champion**, typically had a role in each film.

Autry's first film was a 13-chapter **serial**, *The Phantom Empire* (1935), a very early science-fiction Western. As would become the usual style in his films, Autry played himself as a radio performer who, along with youngsters Frankie Darro and Betsy King Ross, stumbles into a plot involving, first, evil professors trying to steal the ranch to mine radium and, second, the underground lost kingdom of

Murania, ruled by Queen Tika. The film displays great **stunt** riding by Betsy, a nationally renowned horse champion; robots; ray guns; and cliff-hanger escapes. Through it all, Gene and **sidekick Smiley Burnette** find ingenious ways to get to a microphone and perform songs on their national radio show. The film has become a cult favorite because in many ways it is preposterous to the point of being camp; for example, the robots are clearly actors dressed in aluminum foil–like costumes. At the same time, the film typifies an element of B Westerns that rejects the **classic Western** myths and seeks, in an almost postmodern manner, to question norms of reality.

Autry went on to make numerous streamlined musical Westerns for **Republic**. Burnette, as Frog, sidekicked and sang duets through most of the films. During World War II, the popular singer left films for service in the Air Transport Command. While Autry was gone, Republic signed **Roy Rogers** to be its lead **singing cowboy**, so Autry signed with Columbia for the rest of his film career.

Gene Autry epitomized the singing cowboy; his films revolved around music. In *The Old Corral* (1936), a film in which Rogers played a bit part as one of the Sons of the Pioneers, the group robs a bus simply to attract attention so they can get a radio contract. At one point Sheriff Autry arrests Rogers and forces him to sing with the group as his punishment. As in nearly all Autry films, the setting of *The Old Corral* is contemporary. Champion is given feature billing as well.

Autry's films also illustrate the difficulty of classifying Westerns as A Westerns or B Westerns. Stars such as Gene Autry were as big at the box office as most A-list stars, and Autry's films, though distributed as B Westerns, were often budgeted similar to A Westerns. His movies uniformly departed from the classic tradition of cinema Westerns, but so did many A Westerns. The only reason to classify Autry's pictures as B Westerns is because of how studios produced and distributed them.

One specific way that Autry's films departed from the classic tradition was in their treatment of **women**. According to Philip Loy, Autry's female characters were "far more independent and aggressive than were most Western heroines of the 1930s" (2001, 242). In fact, Autry said in his autobiography that his heroines were 1930s women waiting for the advent of Gloria Steinem.

Especially after 1939, "Autry's role was not to romance his leading ladies, but to educate them in the ways of the West and to prepare them for responsibility, not to remove them from it. In that sense, Autry's Westerns are a transition into the changed image of women which permeated Westerns during World War II" (Loy 2001, 246). Rarely after 1939 was there much romance in his films. Instead, Autry's male character served as a father figure to the female lead, often teaching a prideful young thing a bit of humility.

Just as **William Boyd** and Roy Rogers had their lists of rules for clean living for boys and girls, so Autry had his "Cowboy Code":

1. A cowboy never takes unfair advantage—even of an enemy.
2. A cowboy never betrays a trust.
3. A cowboy always tells the truth.
4. A cowboy is kind to small children, old folks, and animals.
5. A cowboy is free from racial and religious prejudices.
6. A cowboy is helpful, and when anyone is in trouble he lends a hand.
7. A cowboy is a good worker.
8. A cowboy is clean about his person and in his thought, word, and deed.
9. A cowboy respects womanhood, his parents, and the laws of his country.
10. A cowboy is a patriot.

After the days of B Westerns ended, Autry moved his operation to **television Westerns** and prospered throughout the 1950s and 1960s. In 1961 he became the first owner of the California Angels baseball team.

– B –

BACALL, LAUREN (1924–). Although Lauren Bacall played on Broadway at a very early age, it was not until she appeared on the March 1943 cover of *Harper's Bazaar* that she got her break. **Howard Hawks**'s wife, Nancy, pointed Bacall out to her husband and the director assigned her to play opposite her future husband, Humphrey Bogart, in *To Have and Have Not* (1944). While she made her reputation early in non-Western films, Bacall has one memorable Western to her credit. She played opposite **John Wayne** in his last picture, *The Shootist* (1976). As Bond Rogers, the strong-willed rooming house proprietor, Bacall is a match for rough-but-aging John Bernard Books (Wayne), the notorious gunfighter.

BANDOLERO! **(1968). Jimmy Stewart**, Dean Martin, Raquel Welch, **Roy Barcroft**, Andrew V. McLaglen (director). *Bandolero!* is probably Dean Martin's best film. Here he played the **outlaw** leader Dee Bishop, who botches a bank robbery and gets caught. He is saved at the gallows by his brother Mace (Stewart), who impersonates a traveling professional hangman. On the way out of town they accidentally kidnap the beautiful señorita Maria (Welch), whose husband they had killed in the robbery and whom widowhood had made the richest person in the county. Off they go across the border. The señorita has not been to Mexico since her marriage, but she knows the countryside and the bandolero leader.

Much of the film is devoted to displaying Welch's charms. Just before Dee and Mace are killed in the final gunfight, Dee and Maria fall in love, though we never really know why. The sheriff (George Kennedy) is also madly in love with Maria (though she is not in love with him) and pursues the outlaws, foolishly hoping to impress her. Kennedy plays a good-hearted, honest but inept bumpkin, certainly not worthy of the wealthy and refined senorita.

Andrew V. McLaglen's film has great scenery and wonderful music by Jerry Goldsmith. It is a beautiful story, a 1960s pre-Vietnam-era Western showing that cultural changes are on the way. One way that *Bandolero!* bridges this major cultural transition period is through Stewart's character. Here is a Western that is moving past the **classic-Western** era, yet Stewart's character has not changed. Stewart is oddly teamed with Martin and Welch, who are playing characters from a different kind of Western.

BARCROFT, ROY (1902–1969). Born Howard Harold Ravenscroft, Roy Barcroft appeared in over 300 films for **Republic** between 1937 and 1957. In each film, the hefty actor usually sported a dark mustache and wore the typical dark hat of the bad guy. Virtually all his films were low-budget Westerns and **serials**. After his **B Western**

days, Barcroft found work in **television Westerns** and feature films. His best work was some of his last—***Bandolero!*** (1968) and *Monte Walsh* (1970).

BARDOT, BRIGITTE (1934–). The famous French beauty was 34 and near the end of her acting career when she made her only Western, *Shalako* (1968), opposite **Sean Connery**. She played a gorgeous European gentlewoman in a Western filmed in Great Britain and in Germany.

BARRY, DON "RED" (1912–1980). Born Donald Barry De Acosta, Red Barry was an exceptionally short actor for leading roles. A typically prolific contract player for **Republic Studios**, he was the first star of the popular Red Ryder series, which started in 1940. After the Red Ryder series, he appeared regularly in character parts, notably in **Roy Rogers** films. Barry's character was usually wound tight, ready to fight at any moment. Evidently his off-screen personality fit his screen persona. After his **B Western** days, Barry continued playing supporting roles in feature Westerns as well as **television Westerns**. *Plainsman and the Lady* (1946) is sometimes considered his best Western film although he also played a prominent role in *Seven Men from Now* (1956), opposite Lee Marvin. In 1980 he committed suicide by shooting himself.

BASIC PLOT FORMULAS. Frank Gruber, a writer of popular Western novels, has codified seven basic plot formulas of which all **classic Westerns** partake in one way or another:

1. *The Union Pacific story.* The plot concerns construction of a railroad, a telegraph line, or some other type of modern technology or transportation. Wagon train stories probably fall into this category.
2. *The ranch story.* The plot concerns threats to the ranch from rustlers or large landowners attempting to force out the proper owners.
3. *The empire story.* The plot might involve building up a ranch empire or an oil empire from scratch, a classic rags-to-riches plot.

4. *The revenge story.* The plot often involves an elaborate chase and pursuit, but it may also include elements of the classic mystery story.
5. *The cavalry and Indian story.* The plot revolves around taming the wilderness for white settlers.
6. *The outlaw story.* The outlaw gangs dominate the action.
7. *The marshal story.* The lawman and his challenges drive the plot.

Of course, other plot types, such as the gunfighter plot, could be developed, but most would probably still be a variation of these seven basic plot formulas. *See also* FORMULAS, CLASSIC WESTERN.

THE BATTLE OF ELDERBRUSH GULCH (1913). With much of the acting company he would use two years later in his epic *The Birth of a Nation* (1915), **D. W. Griffith** produced a primitive, two-reel **silent** Western that is foundational to the development of later Westerns. *The Battle of Edlerbrush Gulch*, from **Biograph**, is almost exclusively an action film with lots of gunplay and plenty of **Indians**. Two waifs and a young mother with child in arms come into a hardened Western town. Lillian Gish played the unnamed young mother, and Mae Marsh played a waif (Hattie) many years younger than her real age. Crazed Indians attack Elderbrush Gulch after they tried to steal Hattie's two puppies for food. Hattie was rescued just as she was about to be scalped. One of the Indians was killed. Griffith creates elementary panoramic shots for these battle scenes, foreshadowing his later work with epic films. In the melee, the unnamed mother loses track of her baby, thus creating the "child-in-danger" theme. Children cower in the cabin awaiting their certain death. Through the battle, the young mother wanders around looking for the baby. Eventually Hattie heroically rescues the baby. The cavalry arrives and all are saved.

Several scenes between the mother and Hattie border on inappropriately comic. Very little dialogue—in other words, very few storyboards—detracts from the continual action. Notably absent from the primitive filmmaking is the **running insert**, a staple in virtually every Western since the **silent era**. Despite innovative film techniques, Griffith's extreme racism, as is well-known from *The Birth of Nation*, makes the 24-minute Western nearly unwatchable today.

BEATTY, WARREN (1937–). One of Hollywood's most enigmatic actors, Warren Beatty has worked in critically acclaimed films such as *Bonnie and Clyde* (1967) and notable box office disasters such as *Ishtar* (1987). Opposite Julie Christie, Beatty played John McCabe, an entrepreneurial town builder, in **Robert Altman**'s *McCabe and Mrs. Miller* (1971)—a role often considered one of the most poignant performances among early **antimyth Westerns**. The final scene of the guerrilla-warlike shootout in the snow overturns the traditional formulaic showdown.

BEERY, NOAH (1882–1946). The brother of **Wallace Beery** and father of **Noah Beery Jr.**, Noah Beery appeared in numerous **silent** Westerns, nearly always as the classic heavy. Perhaps his most memorable role was that of the cruel sergeant in *The Mark of Zorro* (1920). After the advent of talkies, Beery's strong, domineering voice carried him through a long career of character acting.

BEERY, NOAH, JR. (1913–1994). The son of **Noah Beery** and nephew of **Wallace Beery**, Noah Berry Jr. married Buck Jones's daughter, Maxine Jones. His long career began as a child in *The Mark of Zorro* (1920), which starred Douglas Fairbanks and his father. His career as a Western actor consisted mainly of character roles and **sidekick** roles to such stars as **Buck Jones**, **Tom Mix**, and **Johnny Mack Brown**. Beery's most notable role was that of Buster McGee in **Howard Hawks**'s *Red River* (1948) who, when asked by Matt what Tess looked like, replied bashfully, "Oh Matt, do you remember that little filly I used to own?" "That is what I thought," Matt replied.

BEERY, WALLACE (1885–1949). The brother of **Noah Beery** and uncle of **Noah Beery Jr.**, Wallace Beery had a huge frame, a bulbous face, and a twinkle in his eye when he smiled, all of which suited him to a large variety of roles in a very successful film career. Early in the **silent era** he was primarily typecast as the heavy and as such appeared in several silent Westerns. In **James Cruze**'s epic *The Pony Express* (1925), Beery played a comic role as Rhode Island Red. But Beery's most substantial role was that of Pancho Villa in *Viva Villa!* (1934), a film nominated for a best picture Academy Award. The role demonstrated Beery's versatility as an actor as he alternated between a brutal **outlaw** leader bent on revenge and an idealistic revolutionary beloved of his men and country. Westerns have always been fascinated with the exoticism of Mexico just across the border, with all of its revolutions, and Beery helped establish the classic image of Pancho Villa in Western myth.

BEST, WILLIE (1913–1962). Born in Mississippi, Willie Best was an **African American** actor in Westerns of the pre–civil rights era. As with **Fred Toones** and **Stepin Fetchit**, Best was cast exclusively as the **comic Negro** in several films. He was often billed as "Sleep 'n' Eat." A typical Best film is *The Kansan* (1943) in which he played Bones, a hotel handyman and porter who, stereotypically, is slow moving, lazy, and cowardly. At one point the villains force his carriage to stop, and Best is pulled out moaning and shaking. His last film, a Western, was *South of Caliente* (1951).

BILLY THE KID (1859?–1881). Possibly no fact of Billy the Kid's true life is without dispute. What his real name was, where he was really born, how old he was, even facts surrounding his actual death are questions historians have never settled. Only one known photograph survives of the real Billy the Kid. However, the facts concerning the legend of Billy the Kid are well-known, and they are the only facts that matter for understanding cinema Westerns. Evidently Billy the Kid was born William H. Bonney in Brooklyn, New York, around 1859. When he came to New Mexico Territory as a teenager, he carried himself with youthful swagger, dressed colorfully, and had an extraordinarily fast gun. Somewhere along the way he developed a friendship with lawman Pat Garrett, who eventually killed the Kid in 1881. Before his death, Billy had killed 21 men.

Most Westerns have included, in one way or another, most of these basic details. Garrett later published the biography that established most elements of the myth for posterity. Legend nearly always pictures the Kid as a left-handed **gunfighter**, which in Western **code** has usually hinted at **homoeroticism**; his relationship with Garrett has certainly been seen as a homosexual affair. Numerous film versions about Billy the Kid have been made, the most prominent starring Jack Buetel in *The Outlaw* (1943), Paul Newman in *The Left Handed*

Gun (1958), and Emilio Estevez in *Young Guns* (1988). Virtually all films portray Billy the Kid as a misunderstood **outlaw**.

BINARY OPPOSITIONS, DUALISM, AND OPPOSITES IN CONFRONTATION. Typical Western plots are built from such traditional binary oppositions as freedom versus responsibility, the town versus the wilderness, East versus West, civilization versus savagery, and strong masculinity versus weak femininity. The **cowboy hero** often is a loner, yet he restores community at the end of the film, community of which he cannot be a part. Thus, **Shane** rides back into the distant landscape at the end. Occasionally opposites merge, as when **Wyatt Earp** marries Clementine, but more often one opposite will dominate the other.

BIOGRAPH. The name Biograph is short for the American Mutoscope and Biography Company, one of the earliest film production companies, established in 1896. Because it held patents on certain types of camera technology, Biograph became, for a time, one of Thomas Edison's chief rivals. Eventually they teamed up to establish the Motion Picture Patents Company to protect cinema-related patent rights. Biograph's studios were in New York, and the company produced over a thousand silent films from 1908 to 1916, including numerous early Westerns.

BLAKE, ROBERT (1933–). Although better known for his non-Western roles, Robert Blake has appeared regularly in Westerns throughout his career. Billed as Bobby Blake, he began his career in the *Our Gang* television series and then gained an early reputation for his role as Little Beaver in over 20 films in the Red Ryder series from 1944 to 1947. His most significant Western role, however, was in Abraham Polonsky's **antimyth** *Tell Them Willie Boy Is Here* (1969) in which Blake played Willie, an innocent **Native American** accused of murder and pursued in a massive hunt.

BLANCHETT, CATE (1969–). As Maggie Gilkeson in Ron Howard's *The Missing* (2003), Australian Cate Blanchett played one of the finest roles in post–September 11 American cinema Westerns. After Gilkeson's daughters are abducted by **Indians**, the single mother sets out in pursuit. Like **John Wayne** in *The Searchers* (1956), she becomes obsessed with finding her children, as one obstacle after another falls her way. Blanchett, who has been nominated for an Oscar three times and has won once, provides a brilliant performance, among the best by a female actor in cinema Westerns. *See also* WOMEN.

BLAZING SADDLES **(1974).** Cleavon Little, Slim Pickens, Gene Wilder, Madeline Kahn, Mel Brooks (director). By 1974, many were seeing Westerns as a fading cinema genre. The **classic** era of **John Ford** had passed by. **John Wayne**'s career appeared virtually over, and he had lost credibility with the American public due to his conservative political views. The time was ripe for making fun of the staid old out-of-fashion Western, and Mel Brooks took advantage of it. *Blazing Saddles* became one of the most influential Westerns of the 20th century.

In the film, the governor sends a new sheriff (Little) to police a small southwest town, hoping that the townspeople will reject their new black sheriff. Fortunately, Sheriff Bart teams up with the former Waco Kid (Wilder), now an alcoholic, to tame the town and overcome its prejudices, all with laughs aplenty. Little, especially, brings out the inherent racism in Westerns by spoofing first the classic **comic Negro** character and then the **B Western cowboy hero**, decked out in gaudy costumes and riding colorful show horses. Never again would black actors in Westerns be relegated to submissive roles based solely on their race. With its German saloon singer, the film also spoofs Westerns like *Destry Rides Again* (1939) (this time the singer is Madeline Kahn, not **Marlene Dietrich**). *See also* AFRICAN AMERICANS.

BOETTICHER, BUDD (1916–2001). Born Oscar Boetticher Jr. in Chicago, Illinois, Budd Boetticher directed films that are only recently gaining a reputation comparable to the movies of **John Ford** and **Anthony Mann**. Like Ford and Mann, Boetticher is now considered one of the great directors of the **classic** era. While in college at Ohio State University, Boetticher visited Mexico, where he developed a lifelong passion for bullfighting and became a matador himself. His personal life, Hemingway-like, was often reflected in his films. His entry to

Hollywood came in 1941 as a technical advisor on a bullfighting film. By 1943, after some general studio work, he became an assistant director. Boetticher began directing his own films in 1944, but it was not until 1951 that he began directing Westerns, starting with *The Cimarron Kid*, a Universal picture starring **Audie Murphy**.

Boetticher is often characterized as a maverick filmmaker who was frequently at odds with the Hollywood establishment. Only in recent years has he been recognized for artistically significant work on a series of Westerns from the 1950s starring **Randolph Scott**, produced by Harry Joe Brown, and most written by Burt Kennedy. These films, sometimes viewed as a series, are *Seven Men from Now* (1956), *The Tall T* (1957), *Decision at Sundown* (1957), *Buchanan Rides Alone* (1958), *Ride Lonesome* (1959), and *Comanche Station* (1960). These films were commercial successes and early on were critically acclaimed by French critics such as Alfred Bazin, who called *Seven Men from Now* an "exemplary Western."

Unlike the often dark, tragic vision of Anthony Mann, Boetticher's comedy reflected the complexity of all his characters—villains, heroes, and **women**. Yet his comedy also reflected the similar absurdist comic vision of his contemporaries in French intellectual life. For Boetticher, nothing was simple—no villain is all bad, no hero is all good, no woman is all virtuous. Randolph Scott exemplified the Boetticher vision of masculinity while Karen Steele, especially, and **Maureen O'Hara** were two of the most complex female characters in 1950s Westerns.

In 1960, at the height of his career, Boetticher left Hollywood for seven years to research and develop the film he hoped would secure his reputation, a film based on the life of matador Carlos Aruza. This move was interpreted as turning his back on Hollywood, and he suffered greatly for this personal quest. *Aruza* was released in 1971.

Together with Audie Murphy, he attempted one last Western, *A Time For Dying* (1969), and had other mutual projects planned before Murphy's death in 1971. Thereafter, Boetticher maintained steady work in television production, away from Westerns, until his death in 2001. *See also* FRENCH CRITICISM.

BOONE, RICHARD (1917–1981). A student of the famed Actors Studio, Richard Boone always seemed destined for greatness as a classically trained actor. Yet, partially due to a bad temper frequently displayed on the set, he never fulfilled what he thought his destiny might be and, as a result, led a troubled life. Best known as the suave **hired gun** in his long running **television Western** series *Have Gun, Will Travel* (1957–1963), Boone also played secondary parts in a number of 1950s Westerns such as **Delmer Davies'** *Return of the Texan* (1952); *Siege at Red River* (1954); *Ten Wanted Men* (1955), starring Randolph Scott; and *Man Without a Star* (1955), starring **Kirk Douglas**. His most notable film Western, though, was *Rio Conchos* (1964) in which he starred as an ex-Confederate officer intent on preventing a gunrunner from selling guns to the **Apaches**.

BOND, WARD (1903–1960). Born Warell E. Bond in Nebraska, Ward Bond became one of the standard members of the **John Ford** "Stock Company," appearing regularly in the John Ford and **John Wayne** Westerns of the 1940s and 1950s. No doubt his best role was that of Rev. Captain Samuel Johnson Clayton in *The Searchers* (1956). Unfortunately, Bond is probably most remembered not for his character parts but for his relentless pursuit, along with Wayne, of communists in the Hollywood film community during the 1950s, as president of the super-conservative Motion Picture Alliance for the Preservation of American Ideals.

BORGNINE, ERNEST (1917–). Born Ermes Effron Borgnino in Connecticut, the Oscar winner played in numerous Westerns, including *Vera Cruz* (1954), throughout the 1950s and 1960s. His most famous role was in **Sam Peckinpah**'s *The Wild Bunch* (1969) as the ruthless killer Dutch Engstrom. As with numerous secondary American actors of Westerns, Borgnine went to Europe to film Westerns in the 1970s, playing the lead in *Those Desperate Men Who Smell of Dirt and Death* (1969). In one of his last Westerns, the Mexican film *The Revengers* (1972), Borgnine again teamed up with **William Holden** in a film reminiscent of *The Wild Bunch*. Ernest Borgnine has proven himself a remarkably versatile actor over a very long film career.

BOUNTY HUNTERS. A common character in cinema Westerns is the independent gunman making his living by hunting wanted outlaws and other desperados. The posters picturing criminals commonly said, "Wanted, Dead or Alive," giving bounty hunters the right to kill without fear of legal consequences. The character rarely appears before the 1950s when **Anthony Mann** uses one in *The Naked Spur* (1953). It was the Italian **spaghetti Westerns** of the 1960s and 1970s, however, that developed the character more fully. *"For a Few Dollars More* begins with the words 'Where life had no value, death, sometimes had its price. That is why the bounty hunters appeared'" (Frayling 1981, 127).

BOYD, WILLIAM (1895–1972). Born in Hendrysburg, Ohio, William Boyd worked as a wildcatter in the Oklahoma oil fields before making his way to the California fruit orchards, evidently planning all along to try for the movies. He landed his first part in 1919 in a Cecil B. DeMille silent and continued working regularly for DeMille. From 1919 to 1934, Boyd appeared in nearly 70 films. Among his major roles for DeMille was the lead in *The Volga Boatman* (1926) and the part of Simon of Cyrene in *The King of Kings* (1927). His career nearly ended when another actor named William Boyd was involved in a sordid Hollywood scandal and the two Boyds were confused for one another.

In 1935 Harry Sherman cast Boyd, now "Bill" Boyd, as the lead in *Hop-Along Cassidy*. The original character, from a series of novels by Clarence Mulford, had a permanent limp from a gunshot wound. Boyd, who had rarely mounted a horse before, sprained his ankle doing so and, conveniently for the film, developed a limp. In the film he is introduced as Bill Cassidy, but he gets shot and thereafter everybody on the ranch calls him old Hopalong. This is the only movie in which Hopalong limped. Sherman ran the **Hopalong Cassidy series** through 54 episodes after which Boyd took over production for 12 episodes. The series was so successful that Boyd became completely identified with his character.

A smart businessman, Boyd bought all rights to the character of Hopalong Cassidy after Sherman relinquished interest. He was one of the first to purchase rights to a property for television. When the film series started winding down, Boyd began franchising the Hopalong Cassidy character on everything he could market—lunch pails, bicycles, milk bottles, costumes. He also launched a radio series, a magazine, and a long-running comic book series. Then in 1950, *The*

Hopalong Cassidy Show became the first network dramatic television series. By this time Boyd was showing his age pretty well and so ended the Hopalong Cassidy era with a few parades and rodeo appearances. By the early 1950s, Hopalong Cassidy had run its course and Boyd retired to Palm Desert, California. In 1968 after surgery on a lymph gland, he ceased all public appearances or photographs because of his perceived disfigurement.

William Boyd was a much better actor than he is usually given credit for. Even in the 1950s after the "Hoppy Craze" ended, Cecil DeMille asked him to play Moses in *The Ten Commandments* (1956). Boyd wisely declined, knowing that Hopalong Cassidy playing Moses would probably not help the picture. Even if his acting was not recognized, many believe that William Boyd revolutionized American popular culture by being one of the first to market his film character far beyond the limits of a movie theater. *See also* TELEVISION WESTERNS.

BRADY, PAT (1914–1972). Born Robert Patrick, Brady entered show business at age four and Western films in 1937 as the bass player for the Sons of the Pioneers. Although Brady played Charles Starrett's **sidekick**, he is best remembered as one of **Roy Rogers**'s sidekicks, often as Sparrow Biffle, because of his tall, lean frame.

BRAND, MAX (1893–1944). Born Frederick Faust, Max Brand is perhaps the most prolific Western author of all time, writing over 400 novels, nearly all Westerns. He died on the battlefield in World War II, but his estate had such a backlog of unpublished novels that even today a new, unpublished Max Brand Western comes out about every two months. In his last years before the war, Brand worked in Hollywood as a screenwriter, particularly on the popular Dr. Kildare movies based on his medical novels. Over 40 Max Brand novels have been adapted to film, including three films based on his novel *Destry Rides Again*: one starring **Tom Mix** (1932) and two directed by George Marshall—one starring **Jimmy Stewart** (1939) and another titled *Destry*, starring **Audie Murphy** (1954). Only the Tom Mix version remains relatively faithful to Brand's original novel.

BRANDO, MARLON (1924–2004). Sometimes considered the greatest actor in U.S. cinema history, the Nebraska-born Brando dominated the film industry throughout his career. He won two Oscars and was nominated for a best actor Oscar for one of his Westerns, *Viva Zapata!* (1952). He directed and starred in the 1961 *One-Eyed Jacks*, which costarred **Katy Jurado**, and starred in *The Apaloosa* (1966) and *The Missouri Breaks* (1976). While Brando's professional reputation rested on non-Westerns, like most great actors of his era, Brando proved adept in the Western genre.

BRANDON, HENRY (1912–1990). Brandon's most famous role came in *The Searchers* (1956), where he portrayed the dastardly Indian chief, Scar, a truly savage **Indian** with no redeeming qualities. By the end of the film, however, Ethan Edwards (**John Wayne**) nearly becomes Scar's equal in pure barbaric savagery. In his other Westerns, including Robert Aldrich's *Vera Cruz* (1954), Brandon was inevitably cast as an Indian despite being of German heritage.

BRENNAN, WALTER (1894–1974). Although he has three Academy Awards for best supporting actor, Walter Brennan is frequently remembered for the kindly, eccentric, backwards, and usually comic characters he played in over 100 films, many Westerns, from the 1930s to the 1960s. His first credited role was in *Tearin' into Trouble* (1927) with Wally Wales.

Two events early in life helped determine that Brennan's acting roles would often be comic, character roles. In World War I he experienced a gas attack that permanently affected his vocal chords. Thus, even at a relatively early age Brennan had the voice of an old man. Additionally, in 1932, Brennan lost his front teeth in a stuntman accident. Thereafter he often played roles in which he could remove his false teeth. One of his best scenes occurs in **Howard Hawks's** *Red River* (1948) when old Groot (Brennan) loses his teeth in a card game. Thereafter he can only have his teeth back at mealtimes.

Brennan was the first actor to accumulate three Academy Awards (and one more nomination). His Oscar for a Western was for his role as Judge Roy Bean in William Wyler's *The Westerner* (1940), opposite **Gary Cooper**. Neither in this film nor in *My Darling Clementine* (1946) did Brennan play his usual character role of an elderly country bumpkin. In fact, few **John Ford** villains are as ferocious as Brennan's role as Old Man Clanton in *My Darling Clementine*.

For **Anthony Mann**, Brennan played **Jimmy Stewart**'s partner in a cattle drive and a gold mining enterprise in *A Far Country* (1954). His character's death midway through the picture is a formative moment for change in Stewart's character. Brennan worked in six films for Howard Hawks, including *Rio Bravo* (1959), where he played Stumpy, the cranky old jail keeper. After *Rio Bravo*, Brennan devoted most of his time to **television Westerns**, starring in such popular shows as *The Real McCoys* and *The Guns of Will Sonnett*. *See also* STUNTS.

BRIDGES, LLOYD (1913–1998). Although Bridges had been acting in films for 18 years and had played in numerous Westerns, director Fred Zinnemann chose Bridges to play the youthful deputy Harvey Pell in **High Noon** (1952), his most famous Western role. The young deputy, seeking to bolster his reputation, eagerly anticipates sheriff Will Kane's (**Gary Cooper**) departure from town in the face of the coming showdown. Kane sees through Pell's weak character and knows that no help will be forthcoming. Besides, Pell has taken Kane's place in the exotic Helen Ramirez's (**Katy Jurado**) affections. A memorable scene is a brutal fight inside the livery barn, which nearly wears down the sheriff just before he must face Frank Miller (Ian MacDonald) and his gang at noon.

BRONSON, CHARLES (1921–2003). Born Charles Dennis Buchinsky, Bronson was one of the toughest guys on the screen from the 1950s to the 1970s. His deep, craggy face; flat, gravelly voice; squinty eyes that made him seem to be perpetually gazing into the sun; and, especially, light, muscular frame held Bronson in good stead as a solid action hero. His four best Westerns are often considered to be Robert Aldrich's **Vera Cruz** (1954), John Sturges's **The Magnificent Seven** (1960), **Sergio Leone**'s *Once Upon a Time in the West* (1968), and Buzz Kulik's *Villa Rides* (1968). Harmonica, the eerily mysterious harmonica player-gunfighter in *Once Upon a Time in the West*, is generally deemed Bronson's best role.

BROOKS, RICHARD (1912–1992). Born Ruben Sax, Richard Brooks earned numerous Academy Awards for writing and directing. He was nominated best director for his only Western as a director,

The Professionals (1966). This film is frequently seen as the front-runner to the enormous numbers of Italian **spaghetti Westerns**, mostly set in Mexican deserts and full of bizarre action sequences much like Brooks's *Blazing Saddles* (1974), although Brooks's style emphasized understatement and subtlety of psychological emotion, matters unknown in most Italian westerns.

BROTHERS IN ARMS (2005). Jean-Claude La Marre (director). Billed as a hip-hop Western, *Brothers in Arms* is a typical **postmodern Western**. The story involves a gang of **African American** cowboys planning to hold up a bank and thus extract revenge upon the white owner and his cruel son. The film is not a spoof of **classic Western clichés** but an effort to reenvision the West for postmodern sensibilities. The contemporary hip-hop music is reminiscent of the streamlined Western swing music in Westerns of the 1930s and 1940s. This film is usually compared with *Gang of Roses* (2003), also directed by Jean-Claude La Marre. *See also* PUNK WESTERNS.

BROWN, JOHNNY MACK (1904–1974). With his smooth manner and dashing looks, Johnny Mack Brown was destined to a Hollywood career, and his earliest films placed him in the heady company of ladies such as Mary Pickford, Greta Garbo, **Joan Crawford**, and Marion Davies. When talkies arrived, the studios felt his voice was unsuited to romantic roles. Beginning in the 1930s, Brown regularly appeared in Western **serials** such as *Wild West Days* (1937), with its 13 cliffhanger episodes in which his character saves a ranch and its platinum mine from a scheming gang that bribes **Indians** to do their dirty work. Brown was the best-dressed cowboy in his pictures. He loved plenty of fringe and sharp contrasts for black and white pictures.

BROWNE, RENO (1921–1991). Born Josephine Ruth Clarke, Reno Browne (sometimes credited as Reno Blair) appeared in 13 budget Westerns for Monogram. She was usually associated with **Whip Wilson**, but she also appeared with **Johnny Mack Brown** and Jimmy Wakeley. She was an expert rider and claimed to have done all her own stunts. Her horse was Major. Usually she played **pants roles**, carried a gun, and maintained her independence as a **woman**. A typical Browne film is *Fence Riders* (1950) in which she played an independent woman, who is at home in the West, owns a ranch, and does not need a man to save the ranch for her. During her film career, Browne also starred in her own radio series and comic book series; she was a cowgirl personality who also performed in a few films. She was married to Lash LaRue for a while and also toured with her own music group, Reno Browne and her Buckaroos, which evolved into Bill Haley and the Saddlemen (later the Comets).

BRYNNER, YUL (1920–1985). Yul Brynner traded in mystery and exoticism throughout his career, whether as the lead in *The King and I* (1956) through countless productions; Pharaoh Rameses in *The Ten Commandments* (1956); the Mongolian emperor in *Taras Bulba* (1962); or a robotic **gunfighter** in *Westworld* (1973). Consequently, his age and date of birth were always up to question. Usually his birthdate is listed as 1915, but in a biography about Brynner, his son states his father was born in 1920. Brynner himself provided variable information about his origins. "Ordinary mortals need but one birthday," he was fond of saying. Russian-born Brynner came of age in Paris, where he developed his skills in music and acting and also worked as a trapeze artist for a while. After coming to the United States in 1941, he began a career on stage in classical theater and musical theater. He was selected for *The King and I* in 1951 and came back to this musical throughout his professional life, touring and playing on Broadway into the 1980s. He won the best actor Academy Award for his role in the 1956 film version.

But while Broadway audiences remember Brynner, with his trademark shaved head, for his singing and dancing, he also played in some excellent Westerns, beginning with John Sturges's ***The Magnificent Seven*** (1960), in which he played a gunfighter who rounds up six other hired guns in order to pursue the Mexican bandit Calvera (Eli Wallach). The role became Brynner's trademark, reprised in *Return of the Seven* (1966), and, essentially, in *Invitation to a Gunfighter* (1964) and *Catlow* (1971). In this role, Brynner spoke with his cultivated accent and stared down his victims with steely eyes and an aristocratic smirk that could intimidate anyone. His futuristic Westerns of the 1970s, *Westworld* (1973) and *Futureworld* (1976), brought his gunslinger character to science fiction, and he actually donned hair for his role as the revolutionary Pancho Villa in *Villa Rides* (1968). Yul Brynner died of lung cancer in 1985, but before his death he filmed a public service announcement denouncing cigarette smoking to air on television after his passing. *See also* GUN-FIGHTER, SOCIAL ROLE OF.

BUDDY MOVIES. This term was first used by Molly Haskell to describe a particular kind of sexist Western coming to prominence since the 1960s. In buddy movies the friendships between a particular set of male friends transcends any male-female relationships that might present themselves. Examples from the **post-Western** era include *The Professionals* (1966), ***The Wild Bunch*** (1969), ***The Magnificent Seven*** (1960), and ***Butch Cassidy and the Sundance Kid*** (1969).

BUFFINGTON, ADELE (1900–1973). Born Adele Burgdorfer, Buffington is often considered, along with fellow screenwriter Betty Burbridge, as a writer whose talents, because she was a **woman**, were wasted on low-budget Westerns. Whether wasted or not, her talent was responsible for the script or story of over 100 Westerns throughout the **B Western** era. She began her career in Hollywood as a teenager working on set for **Thomas Ince**. She often used the masculine pseudonyms Colt Remington and Jess Bowers. *See also* GIBSON, HOOT.

BURBRIDGE, BETTY (1895–1987). A prolific screenwriter for low-budget Westerns, Burbridge has traditionally exemplified the plight of **women** writers in Hollywood from the early sound era who could only get low-grade work. This is unfortunate since reassessment of her work has revealed a talent for providing female roles counter to usual **B Western** typecasting. *Colorado Sunset* (1939) brings women's concerns to the front of the plot through a group of wives seemingly right out of a Greek comedy who demand that their husbands rebuff a protection association's threats and vote **Gene Autry** as sheriff. In one scene, a mob of women resort to fisticuffs to get their way. The three female co-leads strong-arm their male counterparts while being influential businesswomen in town. A trademark of a Burbridge script is the female owner of a radio station. Burbridge herself appeared in over 60 silent shorts before turning her hand to writing over 100 Westerns from 1924 to 1949, including many Gene Autry Westerns and **Three Mesquiteers** Westerns.

BURNETTE, SMILEY (1911–1967). Born Lester Allen Burnette, Smiley Burnette earned the nickname "Frog" due to his unusual voice. A singer and a songwriter in his own right, Burnette frequently burbled comic frog-like sounds in his songs. Besides his trademark voice, he always wore a black hat with a pointed crown and the front brim pinned back hillbilly style. Frog rode with **Sunset Carson**, **Roy Rogers**, and other cowboy stars, but he is usually associated with **Gene Autry** since they starred together in over 60 films. As a Western singer/songwriter, Burnette is best remembered for his duet with Autry, "Ridin' Down the Canyon" sung in *Tumbling Tumbleweeds* (1935). Burnette was the only **sidekick** to star in his own Westerns. He was top-billed in four **Republic** films, all in 1944: *Call of the Rockies*, *Bordertown Trail*, *Code of the Prairie*, and *Firebrands of Arizona*. In all four he was top-billed over Sunset Carson.

***BUTCH CASSIDY AND THE SUNDANCE KID* (1969).** Robert Redford, Paul Newman, Katharine Ross, George Roy Hill (director). One of the most famous **buddy movies** of all time, *Butch Cassidy and the Sundance Kid* is a good-hearted comedy based on the historical exploits of these famous members of the Hole in the Wall Gang. The film takes place at the turn of the 20th century as the two outlaws, Butch (Newman) and the Sundance Kid (Redford), realize their days of easy robbing are coming to an end. **Etta Place** (Ross), a schoolteacher turned outlaw and the Kid's love interest, makes the group a trio. The film follows them to New York City and eventually to Bolivia, where they plan on renewing their occupation. A classic hit song by B. J. Thomas, "Raindrops Keep Falling on My Head," came out of the movie. It was played during a scene with Etta, the Kid, and Butch riding a bicycle around in circles in the rain during their happier days.

One of the things that made the film so popular and so different in its time was that it took the new kind of **cowboy heroes** of **antimyth Westerns** and made them likeable. **Clint Eastwood**'s Man with No Name was a tough antihero, but he was not particularly likeable.

Newman and Redford, on the other hand, played **outlaws**, who were historically ruthless and despicable by any standard, and made them fun-loving buddies always able to make everything into a good time. The outlaws are chased through the Bolivian countryside, and eventually they run up on a sheer cliff with no hope of escape. Their backs are to the edge of the precipice, which drops down to the deep gorge and raging river below. "Jump!" yells Butch. "I can't swim," the Kid frantically replies. Butch chuckles, "Hell, the fall will probably kill ya." They jump.

As with other Westerns of the late 1960s and early 1970s, such as *The Wild Bunch* (1969) and *The Shootist* (1976), this film sought to move the chronological time of the old West into the 20th century. Interestingly, the historical period in which the early action takes place is 1903, the year the first film Western, *The Great Train Robbery*, was made. *See also* END-OF-THE-WEST FILMS.

B WESTERNS. *B Western*, a term now losing currency, technically refers to low-budget films shown as the second part of double features, becoming popular in the 1930s and the 1940s. But the term has also been used to refer to any low-budget film, including many **silent-era** Westerns, as well as **serial** films that were shown on Saturday mornings to young audiences. Although most movie genres were represented by B movies, science fiction, comedies, and Westerns dominated. Beginning in the 1950s, low-budget Westerns moved from matinee houses to television.

Most B Westerns in the 1930s had budgets well under $30,000 per picture. However, some stars' pictures could be budgeted higher. When **Buck Jones** left Columbia for Universal Pictures in 1934, for instance, not only was his salary increased but Universal also gave him responsibility for producing his own films. Universal underwrote the films with a budget of $65,000 per picture. By the 1930s, **Republic Studios** was investing even more in **Gene Autry** films. Paramount even budgeted **Hopalong Cassidy** movies at over $125,000 per picture. Autry and Cassidy films were, however, unusual.

Although there are numerous B films that had budgets and production values nearly that of lower-budget A films and vice versa, production and distribution of the two kinds of films varied greatly. A films, the major top-billed productions of a double feature, depended on a percentage of the box office profits for revenue whereas B films were rented to theaters at a flat rate. There was a tremendous consumer market for B films, which could nearly always make a profit if made cheaply enough. And generally, studios that made A films did not make B films.

B Westerns, then, were produced by a host of minor studios in Hollywood, collectively known as "**poverty row**." Republic and Monogram led the group, but other studios included **Producers Releasing Corporation** and **Mascot**. These studios produced numerous films rapidly, often working on multiple projects at a given studio at the same time using the same casts and crews. Most actors worked under **standard picture-commitment contracts**, which meant they worked every day and were paid the same regardless of how many pictures they made. More fortunate actors worked under **term player contracts**, which gave them a regular yearly salary.

B Westerns basically developed out of a long tradition of low-budget moviemaking held over from the silent era. Hundreds of silent Westerns were made cheap, in assembly-line fashion, similar to the later Westerns of the 1930s. After the phenomenal success of **William S. Hart**'s darkly realistic Westerns, numerous imitators began mass-producing Westerns. Since Hart's austere style was easy and inexpensive to imitate and since an easy profit could be made, large numbers of silents were made quickly in the Hart style. William K. Everson notes that Aywon studios' *Another Man's Boots* (1922) was a virtual copy of Hart's *Square Deal Sanderson* (1919).

For most of the 20th century, B Westerns were dismissed contemptuously by film critics, being compared to A Westerns in much the same way that pulp novels were compared to serious literary novels. B Westerns were often condemned because they were deliberately designed as commercial products valued for their consistency rather than their originality. Certainly, for those working in the B Western studios, there was very little prestige compared to mainstream Hollywood culture. However, as film critics and cultural critics have begun studying Westerns more seriously, they have discovered that the classification of these particular films based on how they were originally distributed and displayed is outdated and not very useful. Literary critics take no notice of a novel's original publication methods or of bookstore sales. William Faulkner's *Absalom, Absa-*

lom! sold less than 1,000 copies when it was produced in 1926 whereas *Gone With the Wind*, published the same year, sold millions—yet nobody would judge either novel on the basis of its sales. When critics, then, look at the 1930s and 1940s low-budget Westerns based on their own merits, several facts tend to emerge. Many low-budget Westerns took artistic risks that A Westerns could not afford to take and in some ways, by their nature, were more innovative than their counterparts. Many A Westerns, despite higher budgets, have little artistic integrity. From a postmodern perspective, it might be argued that these B films, because they undercut the classic Western myths, may actually deserve more serious analysis than higher-budget **classic Westerns**. The trend today is no longer to separate out B Westerns from A Westerns, but to refer to the B films, if one must make a distinction, as low-budget Westerns.

Since B Westerns were made on the assumption that consumers would buy tickets for even the cheapest product, they often sported cardboard-looking sets, utterly common props, and plenty of stock footage show stunt riding, large crowd scenes, Indian battles, and other features not practical to film on limited budgets.

Nevertheless, B Westerns introduced many elements into the Western genre. The cowboy star with a specific persona and a trademark costume became an essential ingredient. Thus, a whole series of cowboy stars spent entire careers in B westerns: **Tom Mix**, **Buck Jones**, **Johnny Mack Brown**, Tim Holt, and many others. But B Westerns also introduced the **singing cowboy**, led above all by **Roy Rogers** and **Gene Autry**. The resultant vision of the old West became a sanitized frontier in which serious violence was rare and cowboy heroes were clean-living models for young boys and girls to emulate. Only in the world of B Westerns could **Hopalong Cassidy**'s sidekick, Andy Clyde, walk into a saloon and order milk. Cassidy himself spent hours in saloons playing cards, without any evidence of ordering a drink.

– C –

CALAMITY JANE. One of the most colorful traditional female characters in Westerns, Calamity Jane was, historically, Martha (Calamity)

Jane Canary (1848–1903), author of a famous autobiography and entertainer in Wild West shows near the end of her life. How much of the Calamity Jane legend squares with historical fact will probably always remain conjecture. The essentials of the legend that play out in numerous Western films and **television Westerns** is that Calamity Jane was a cross-dressing female scout for General Crook, a buffalo skinner, a sharpshooter, and the beloved of **Wild Bill Hickok**. Her character has been played as glamorous, by **Jean Arthur** in *The Plainsman* (1936) and Frances Farmer in *Badlands of Dakota* (1941); as comic, by Doris Day in *Calamity Jane* (1953; directed by David Butler), a film musical; and as dirty, unglamorous, and crude, by Ellen Barkin in *Wild Bill* (1995).

As with most historical characters, film versions of Calamity Jane isolate a few features of her character and gloss over anything inconvenient to the story. Evidently, the real Calamity Jane was unlikable, even repulsive. Nothing about her could be termed glamorous. Yet Calamity Jane the legend serves her purpose, playing the **pants roles** either for the irony of the part or for a comic effect.

CALHOUN, RORY (1922–1999). Born Francis Timothy McCown in Burbank, California, Rory Calhoun used his chiseled good looks and sturdy build to keep him in steady work in movies and television from the 1950s through the 1980s. **Alan Ladd** discovered him in 1943 when he saw Calhoun riding a horse. Impressed with his natural horse-handling ability, Ladd urged him to get a screen test. Early uncredited bit parts in a few war movies followed, and then his break occurred when he played James Corbet in the vintage boxing movie *The Great John L.* (1945). With this film, along with a name change, Calhoun began a steady career. As a professional gambler, he played opposite Marilyn Monroe and **Robert Mitchum** in the high-profile Western *River of No Return* (1954). Later Westerns included *Way of a Gaucho* (1952), *Four Guns to the Border* (1954), *The Silver Whip* (1953), and *The Yellow Tomahawk* (1954). After 1958 Calhoun moved to television for most of his remaining career. *The Texan* (1958–1960) was his most well-known **television Western** series.

Massacre River (1949), a romantic Western, was perhaps Calhoun's finest cinema Western. He played an Army officer (Lieutenant Phil Acton) in love with Kitty Reid (Cathy Downs), the sister of a fellow officer, Randy Reid (Johnny Sands). Unfortunately, his love is unrequited as Kitty pledges love to Lieutenant Larry Knight (Guy Madison), who proves unworthy of her and falls for the wiles of a **dance hall girl** named Laura (Carole Mathews). Larry resigns his commission and leaves town with Laura. While Kitty descends into despair, Phil pursues Larry and Laura into **Indian territory**, vowing justice. He finds the two, but a pending fight to the death is interrupted when all three must turn their attention to surviving an **Apache** attack.

CAMERA, MOVING. While in modern films the camera moves as needed to make a scene effective, early cinema Westerns employed only stationary cameras. Hollywood culture considered a mobile camera as artsy and European. Thus, even the battle scenes in an epic feature like **James Cruze**'s *The Covered Wagon* (1923) appear more like still photography than dynamic action scenes. **John Ford** was one of the first directors to take the camera off its stand. In *The Iron Horse* (1924), Ford mounted the camera on the front of the locomotive, allowing it to film varying sets of riders simultaneously as the train moved forward rapidly. The effect was to produce real action as it happens rather than as it might have happened.

CANUTT, YAKIMA (1895–1986). Born Enos Edward Canutt in Washington, Canutt earned his nickname from his rodeo-days billing—the Man from Yakima. In many ways, Yakima Canutt developed the role of stuntman into an integral part of the early motion picture business. In film after film, sometimes credited, often not, Canutt performs some incredible work with runaway horses, stagecoaches missing the turn high on a cliff, and other such **stunts**, all original feats at the time. Perhaps his most famous stunt is from *The Devil Horse* (1926) when Canutt, in a lengthy scene, hangs underneath a furiously bucking horse, desperately holding on to its neck. Canutt especially thrived from a long association with **John Wayne** and appears in many of Wayne's early films.

CAPTIVITY NARRATIVES. Inevitably associated with **Indian** captivity of young girls rather than young boys, early frontier narratives—such as that by Mary Rowlandson, *The Narrative of the Captivity and the Restoration of Mrs. Mary Rowlandson* (1682)—began a trend in popular literature of portraying the frontier as exotic yet savage and chaotic. The problem with captivity narratives in U.S. culture is that they exhibit the basest forms of racism both in the narrative and in the readership of film audiences. The dilemma is fundamentally racist: a savage race kidnaps young white girls in order to contaminate their race and their virtue. **John Ford**'s *The Searchers* (1956) is perhaps the most famous **classic Western** based on captivity fears. When Ethan Edwards (**John Wayne**) finally finds Debbie (Natalie Wood), captured as a child and now a woman, he tries to kill her for her own good because she has become Indian and no longer deserves to live. The film shows the extent to which such racism can destroy character. *The Missing* (2003) is also based upon a captivity narrative plot, but it avoids the same racism by making the protagonist a mother (**Cate Blanchett**) seeking to recover her daughter (Evan Rachel Wood) from the **Apaches**. *See also* ORIGINS OF THE WESTERN.

CARDINALE, CLAUDIA (1938–). The former beauty queen has been a legend in Italian cinema for decades. Her roles in cinema Westerns began as the kidnapped Mexican of an American landowner in *The Professionals* (1966). The professionals hired to recapture her, played by Lee Marvin, Burt Lancaster, Robert Ryan, and Woody Strode, discover a very different young wife than what they expected. The beautiful young woman wins the men over and gains her freedom from a tyrannical husband. Her most famous role, however, was in **Sergio Leone**'s *Once Upon a Time in the West* (1968) in which she played Jill McBain, a prostitute turned wife and mother, whose family is brutally murdered by the deadly gunfighter Frank (**Henry Fonda**). Cardinale provides much of the focus in the film as her character goes about recovering from her loss and finding the right men (**Charles Bronson** and Jason Robards) to destroy Frank. **Ennio Morricone**'s haunting "Jill's Theme" plays as Jill searches through the ruined homestead for reasons why her family was murdered, and it then becomes the theme of the film. Cardinale is still a force in Italian cinema.

CARD PLAY AND THE COWBOY HERO. The stereotypical **cowboy hero** plays cards and plays them well. Inevitably he can spot a crooked dealer and handles cheaters quickly and efficiently. Yet the cowboy hero is an amateur, and he naturally suspects the honesty of all professional **gamblers**. The game of choice in Westerns is poker, not just because it was historically the game of choice in the West but because, unlike other games of chance, successful poker play depends less on the intellectual skill of the cowboy hero than on his individual character. Inevitably, card play scenes in Westerns are placed early so that they will develop the hero's, or the villain's, character. How a man, or occasionally a **dance hall girl**, plays cards often determines how he will respond in other situations in the film. The man who can play honestly and skillfully but without emotion, who can win as well as lose with equanimity, is a man deserving our respect. The cowboy hero must know all the tricks used by cardsharps but never use them himself—and he must know how to deal with those who deal crookedly. Thus in *My Darling Clementine* (1946), we see **Wyatt Earp** (**Henry Fonda**) casually call out the professional gambler (Earle Foxe) for cheating. In the same film, **Doc Holliday** (Victor Mature) proves his superior poker skills to all players throughout his part of the West.

CAREY, HARRY (1878–1947). Born in the Bronx, Harry Carey developed a film career that started in the earliest days of nickelodeon silent pictures and stretched through World War II. By 1916 he was starring in such Westerns as *A Knight of the Range* with Olive Golden and **Hoot Gibson**. He married Golden that same year, and their son, **Harry Carey Jr.**, became a significant Western actor in his own right. Golden left acting for many years after *A Knight of the Range* but resumed her career in the 1950s and 1960s with appearances in such cult favorites as *Billy the Kid versus Dracula* (1966), starring **John Carradine**. Carey himself became a major **silent** Western star. *Satan Town* (1926) is probably his best film in the lead role. It is based on a traditional revenge plot, but as with *Hell's Hinges* (1916), the town becomes as much the antagonist as any character. During the Alaskan Gold Rush, Bill Scott (Carey) arrives in Satan Town seeking revenge on a crooked lawyer who had betrayed him long ago. Contemporary reviews point to a complex film with significant character development as well as action. Unfortunately, as with many silents, this Western is evidently lost forever.

Harry Carey did not make the transition to talkies well and never regained his status as a major Western star. His rough, hard-lined face caused him to be cast as characters older than his actual age. He did, however, continue a successful career of secondary roles in both **B Westerns** and major productions, particularly those by **John Ford**. In fact, Ford dedicated *3 Godfathers* (1948) to Carey, and in *The Searchers* (1956), he provided a visual tip of the hat to Carey when **John Wayne** takes a Carey-like pose in the doorway in the last scene. As a character actor, Carey appeared in several of the great Westerns of the 1940s such as *Angel and the Badman* (1947) and *Duel in the Sun* (1946). His last Western, *Red River* (1948), in which he appeared with his son Harry Carey Jr., was released after his death. *See also* SILENT ERA CINEMA.

CAREY, HARRY, JR. (1921–). Harry Carey Jr. grew up in a movie family, his father, **Harry Carey**, having played in Westerns since the silent era. The title of Carey Jr.'s autobiography sums up a long career: *Company of Heroes: My Life as an Actor in the John Ford Stock Company*. Few character actors have been seen in as many Westerns from 1948 to the present as Carey Jr. His first significant film was *Red River* (1948), followed by most of the **John Ford** Westerns of the time, such as *She Wore A Yellow Ribbon* (1949), *The Searchers* (1956), and *Cheyenne Autumn* (1964). Still active, Carey Jr.'s most recent Western is *Comanche Stallion* (2006).

CARRADINE, JOHN (1906–1988). Born Richmond Reed Carradine, this actor was called upon anytime, it seemed, that a casting director needed a tall, sophisticated gentleman with a voice befitting the dignity of an education. Probably his most famous role was that of the Southern **gambler** Hatfield in *Stagecoach* (1939). In *Cheyenne Autumn* (1964) he played a gambler named Jeff Blair in a comic set scene in a saloon. While the **Indians** are attacking and the town is lapsing into chaos, Blair and **Wyatt Earp** (**Jimmy Stewart**) nonchalantly continue their game. Carradine often appeared with **John Wayne,** and as a tribute, Wayne had Carradine play the gambler role in Wayne's last film *The Shootist* (1976). Tall, angular, and thin, with a gorgeous, deep baritone voice, exuding sophistication and class, John Carradine was typecast as the consummate professional gambler or representative Southern gentleman from back East. Strangely, many remember Carradine for his role as Count Dracula in perhaps the worst Western ever filmed, *Billy the Kid versus Dracula* (1966). He was the father of David Carradine.

CARSON, SUNSET (1920?–1990). Virtually every detail of Sunset Carson's early biography is in dispute because Carson deliberately falsified the details through the years. He was probably born Winifred Maurice Harrison in Gracemont, Oklahoma, somewhere between 1920 and 1924. Carson claimed to have been discovered by **Tom Mix** while performing in rodeos. After an audition with **Republic Studios** in 1944, Carson appeared in *Call of the Rockies*, second billed to **Smiley Burnette**. The two made four films together, with Burnette in the lead. Carson's first leading role was in Republic's *Sheriff of Cimarron* (1945). For two years Carson was a regular star for Republic, but in 1946 Republic's Herbert J. Yates fired him when he appeared at a studio party drunk, with an underage girl in tow. After a two-year absence from pictures, Carson made a series of obscure films with Astor Pictures and then gave up acting in 1952 to become a circus performer. His last film was a low-budget science-fiction Western, *Alien Outlaw* (1985), costarring Lash La Rue. Carson's costume in the film consisted of a regular white neckerchief and a set of pistols butts facing forward. His horse was Cactus.

CATTLE INDUSTRY VERSUS FARMING. Westerns celebrate the cattle industry; only rarely do they celebrate **farming**. The cowboy is a glamorous character while the farmer is typically a strong laborer (often ethnic) trying to sustain a family on a homestead. Historically, farmers and cowboys in the late 19th century were merely itinerant agrarian laborers. But on-screen, vast stretches of grazing pasture and clumps of herding cows needing little attention from the ranchers appears more appealing than stretches of farms with workers struggling over their plows.

CATTLEMEN VERSUS SHEEP MEN. One Western convention is that cattlemen and sheepherders do not mix. Cowboys look with contempt on sheep men, and range wars break out when sheep come into cattle country. Sheep just seem unnatural intruders on the cattle range. They devour all the range grass, making the range worthless for future cattle raising. One of **John Ford**'s earliest films, *The Gun Packer* (1919), is based on this rivalry. By 1967 the convention was so established that Andrew V. McLagen could direct a comic Western starring Doris Day, *The Ballad of Josie*, in which a female sheep-herder brings her sheep onto the range and organizes women in the town to make sheep acceptable.

CATTLE QUEEN OF MONTANA **(1954). Ronald Reagan, Barbara Stanwyck, Jack Elam**, Allan Dwan (director). When Ronald Reagan was elected president of the United States in 1981, he deliberately cultivated an image of the all-American cowboy, riding his horse around his ranch, often dressed in blue jeans and a cowboy hat. He used imagery based on the **myth of the West** in his speeches. *Cattle Queen of Montana* is a fairly neglected Western. In fact, it has often been considered a **B Western** though it was a full-budget film. Barbara Stanwyck gives a skilled performance and a young Jack Elam shows why he became one of the favorite bad guys of all time. But the *Cattle Queen of Montana*'s real significance is that it is perhaps Ronald Reagan's best Western.

Sierra Nevada Jones (Barbara Stanwyck) and her father drive cattle from Texas to Montana to establish their legal claim to a small ranch. But a band of **Indians** attack, kill Pops, drive off the cattle, and leave Jones with nothing. What really happened was that the bad Indian Natchakoa (Anthony Caruso) is in the pay of a wealthy land grabber, McCord (Gene Evans). But Natchakoa's rival is Colorados (Lance Fuller), a college-educated Indian who is trying to civilize his people in the white people's ways. Colorados aids Jones, and the two come perilously close to a relationship. In the background is one of McCord's newest hands, a professional gunfighter named Farrell (Ronald Reagan). Farrell is a left-handed gunfighter, so his motivations are suspect. However, affection develops between Farrell and Sierra as well as between Sierra and Colorados. Farrell turns out to be an undercover federal agent investigating McCord, so he is a good guy after all. Together, Colorados and Farrell work to get Sierra's cattle and land back and to put McCord away. Sierra even works for the government to help trap McCord. The film affirms all the values President Reagan would affirm as true American values: self-reliance, hard work, good ultimately triumphs over evil, and the government in its limited role always serves the good of private landowners.

CAVALRY TRILOGY. For three consecutive years after World War II, **John Ford** issued a cavalry movie with **John Wayne**: *Fort Apache* (1948), *She Wore a Yellow Ribbon* (1949), and *Rio Grande* (1950). During this period in the United States, American culture was beginning to undergo the major social upheavals that would characterize the 1950s and 1960s. Whether Ford intended it or not, these three films explore the major cultural issues of the day by placing them in a different time period; by associating them with the ultimate American myth, that of the West; and by creating the enclosed world of an army outpost on the frontier. The film army's **savage war** against the **Indians** seemed to parallel the intense war America had just completed victoriously. But the movie's Indians, who threaten to destroy the great American experiment based on its **Manifest Destiny**, probably represent the immediate threat of communism, which had spread so quickly across Europe. The internal social tensions between various ethnic (particularly Irish) noncommissioned officers and solidly Anglo-American officers surely reflected the contemporary black-white racial tension in the United States that could not yet be treated seriously by Hollywood. By changing the conflict from blacks versus whites to Irish versus Anglo, Ford made serious commentary acceptable to filmgoers. *See also* AFRICAN AMERICANS IN WESTERNS.

CHAMPION. Champion, **Gene Autry**'s sorrel-colored horse, was the only cowboy star's horse to have his own television series after his movie days were over: *The Adventures of Champion* (CBS: 1955–1956). *Melody Trail* (1935) was Champion's first film, but Autry actually used seven different Champions during his film and television career. According to the official Gene Autry.com website, the seven Champions were the original Champion, the Lindy Champion, Champion Jr., Little Champ, Touring Champ, Television Champ, and Champion Three. Only the original Champion had white stockings on his legs and a distinctive blaze down his face. He died while Autry was away for service during World War II.

CHASE AND PURSUIT. Virtually all adventure films have a chase-and-pursuit scene as an integral part of the plot, and Westerns are no different. Films such as **Anthony Mann**'s *Winchester '73* (1950) base the entire plot around chase and pursuit—in this film, pursuit after the elusive super Winchester that men die to possess. More often, however, the term *chase and pursuit* refers to the classic chase on horses as a **cowboy hero** such as **Roy Rogers** on **Trigger** races across the plains with a **moving camera** tagging along. This kind of chase, with wild, scattershot shooting, is usually confined to the low-budget Westerns of the 1940s.

CHEYENNE AUTUMN **(1960). Richard Widmark, John Ford** (director). *Cheyenne Autumn* was John Ford's last Western, released just as **spaghetti Westerns** were poised to make significant changes in cinema Westerns. Critics have often noticed a contrast between Ford's sympathetic portrayal of **Native Americans** here compared to his stereotypical treatment in earlier Westerns. *Cheyenne Autumn*, based on a story by Mari Sandoz, depicts a small Cheyenne band's desperate attempt to escape reservation life in **Indian territory** and return to their ancestral home 1,500 miles to the north. They flee their barren existence on the reservation, which has been compromised by corrupt government mismanagement, and then find themselves pursued by the U.S. cavalry.

Despite Ford's sympathy for the United States' historical treatment of Native Americans, he has often been criticized for casting white or Hispanic actors in the leading Native American roles, leaving genuine Native Americans in the background as extras. **Victor Jory**, ubiquitous bad man in dozens of old Westerns, played the old Cheyenne chief who dies early on. Two other chiefs are played by Ricardo Montalban and Gilbert Roland. The leading squaw is played by Dolores del Rio. Also, Sal Mineo played the hot-headed young warrior.

Richard Widmark played Captain Thomas Archer, who is in charge of the pursuit and shows sympathy for his foe and reluctance to accomplish his task. **Jimmy Stewart** and Arthur Kennedy played **Wyatt Earp** and **Doc Holliday**, respectively, involved in a poker game in **Dodge City** in an isolated scene inserted purely for comic effect. *See also* CARD PLAY AND THE COWBOY HERO.

throughout the first half of the 20th century. Although the film and television roles are most commonly associated with **Duncan Renaldo**, the character was played by numerous actors. The first film version, a silent titled *The Caballero's Way* (1914), was based on a 1907 O. Henry story of the same name. Besides Renaldo, actors who played the role through the years included Warner Baxter, Cesar Romero, and Gilbert Roland. Renaldo played the role from 1945 to 1950 when the series was moved to television for 156 episodes. The 1929 film, *In Old Arizona*, with Baxter in the lead, was the first Western talkie as well as the first talkie filmed outdoors. The original Cisco Kid was not Mexican and was quite disreputable. Gilbert Roland's Cisco was a debonair charmer of women, while Renaldo's version assumed a significant adolescent audience. Cisco rode through the countryside seeking adventure with his comic **sidekick** Pancho. Much unfortunate Hispanic stereotyping typifies all versions of the character. *See also* MEXICANS.

CIVILIZATION VERSUS WILDERNESS. Underlying every Western is the subtext of encroaching civilization. When John Bernard Books (**John Wayne**) walks down the street in an opening scene in *The Shootist* (1976), we know that the **Western moment** is coming to an end as telephone wires are clearly evident in the background. This is the inevitable moment in the future of every Western. First the wilderness must be tamed, then civilization will be welcomed. But this inevitability produces much of the tension in Western plots. We are led to admire the Western frontier and the men and women hardy enough to populate it. The civilized characters—the schoolteachers, the Southern gentlemen, the eastern dudes—are generally portrayed as weak, not hardy enough to survive the rigors of frontier life. *Hell's Hinges* (1916) develops this theme through a pair of easterners, a brother and a sister, who come to civilize the town through mission work. The brother becomes corrupted, but the **cowboy hero** (**William S. Hart**) becomes civilized as he tames the town and falls in love with the sister.

CIVIL RIGHTS WESTERNS. As in all historical cinema, Westerns concern themselves more with cultural issues contemporary with their audiences than with issues relating to the historical setting itself.

CHRIST-FOOL THEME. This term, evidently coined by Richard Slotkin, refers to hero figures who, though superior to others in prowess, humble themselves to save others. In *A Fistful of Dollars* (1967), the Man with No Name (**Clint Eastwood**) enters town on a donkey, wearing a serape. He is a Christ figure who temporarily plays the fool yet redeems the town and takes the sins upon himself. In *Shane* (1953), the hero rides into the valley out of nowhere, puts away his guns, dresses humbly, and plays the fool in order to appease the family he stays with and be an example to their young son who looks to Shane for his values. Shane deflects a saloon fight, but in the end he brings his guns to town and redeems the settlers. Then he rides back into the unknown from whence he came.

CINECITTÀ STUDIOS, ROME. Cinecittà Studios was primarily sponsible for the large numbers of Italian Westerns produced in 1960s and 1970s. The studio had been specializing in epic ac films (such as the 1950s Steve Reeves Hercules movies) before entered the Western market and issued a lengthy series of **spagl Westerns** (such as the **Django**, Sartana, and Stranger series) playing upon the popularity of **Sergio Leone**'s **Dollars Tri** Cinecittà's productions were invariably low-budget affairs "flimsy sets, variable colour matching, and the inadequacies **Techniscope** process" (Frayling 1981, 121). Since the da spaghetti Westerns, Cinecittà Studios has become the domina duction company in Italy.

CINEMASCOPE. 20th Century Fox pioneered this wid process in the 1950s and used it effectively for Westerns. It v replaced by Panavision. The trade name is frequently used t any widescreen process—the process of squeezing a wide fr a standard frame. By using the CinemaScope process, fil were able to provide stunning color and glossy images for p scenes as well as **chases** and gun battles. *From Hell to Tex* has sometimes been considered the standard for early v Westerns.

THE CISCO KID. The Cisco Kid was a recurrent characte comic books, radio shows, Western films, and **televisior**

Thus throughout their history, cinema Westerns have struggled with racism. As the American culture itself began serious examination of civil rights for **African Americans**, so did Westerns of the 1960s. In the 1950s African American racial issues were treated by recasting them as a **Native American** versus white struggles. Such films as **John Ford**'s *Sergeant Rutledge* (1960) and Ralph Nelson's *Duel at Diablo* (1966) began serious treatment of American racial tensions using actors Woody Strode and Sidney Poitier as sympathetic African American characters, but the most significant civil rights Westerns of the 1960s and 1970s were comedies. John Sturges's *Sergeants 3* (1962) stars Frank Sinatra, Dean Martin, Peter Lawford, and Joey Bishop—the Rat Pack. The fifth member of the Rat Pack was Sammy Davis Jr., an African American whose mere presence in the film as a comic equal to the white characters made a powerful cultural statement. However, the most significant advance toward integrating African Americans into Westerns as equals resulted from Cleavon Little's brilliant comic performance of an African American sheriff in Mel Brooks's *Blazing Saddles* (1974). From that point on, the civil rights issue of full integration into the casts of cinema Westerns was settled.

CLASSIC WESTERNS. After the **silent era** ended, Westerns had trouble making the transition to sound because they depended on action, not talk. It did not seem that sound could add anything to Westerns, and people wanted to watch the talkies. **B Westerns** filled the void and began their own traditions, especially with **singing cowboy** movies. Cecil B. DeMille's *The Plainsman* (1936) and **John Ford**'s *Stagecoach* (1939), however, resurrected large-budget Westerns not seen since the days of **James Cruze**'s *The Covered Wagon* (1923). The classic Western tradition that began in the 1930s continued until the early 1960s. The height of the classic era was probably the 1950s with such films as *High Noon* (1952) and *Shane* (1953). The films of this era, while of immense variety, shared basic assumptions about the **myth of the West** and about American culture and values. As with all Westerns, they commented on contemporary concerns through mythical narratives.

According to John G. Cawelti (1999), "The classic Western projected contemporary tensions and conflicts of values into a mythical past where they could be balanced against one another and resolved in an increasingly ambiguous moment of violent action" (97). For American culture during this period, "the Western served as an unofficial myth of America's situation in the world" (Cawelti 1999, 98). These movies particularly emphasized the role of the **gunfighter**, whether an individual or an official lawman, who purified through **regenerative violence** a town or community corrupted by the domination of **outlaws**. This archetypal conflict reflected the United States' new role as the major superpower in conflict with the Soviet menace during the cold war. As the later problems posed by the Vietnam War and the **civil rights** movement came to preoccupy Americans' worries, the classic Western began its long decline. However, because classic Westerns dominated the movies for so long, **antimyth Westerns** inevitably came along after the 1960s and called into question the values of these older films.

CLICHÉS. Because Westerns are mythical, they depend heavily on familiar conventions, symbols, and characters. At times these features of Westerns become clichés. Among the most common clichés are the opening scenes: Two lonely riders saunter into town against a bleak **landscape**. A dog runs across the road ahead without giving the men the slightest glance—the opening of William Wellman's *The Ox-Bow Incident* (1943). A group of men dressed in pre–World War I U.S. Army uniforms saunter into town against a bleak landscape. Children play beside the road ahead without giving the men the slightest glance—the opening of **Sam Peckinpah**'s *The Wild Bunch* (1969). A solitary man awaits something, standing high in the desolate rocks above the rutted road below. Two companions appear. He joins them, and they saunter into town—the opening of *High Noon* (1952). A lone rider and horse move slowly across the stark and barren landscape. Upon closer inspection, we realize he is the hero of the film—the opening of both Fritz Lang's *Western Union* (1941) and Robert Aldrich's *The Last Sunset* (1961). Somber music invariably plays and in films after the 1960s, the credits often roll. Dramatic action to come is strongly implied, and the suspense holds our interest. The cliché may be used often, but it is often used effectively.

Other clichés abound in Westerns. Often the hero is himself a reformed **outlaw**. (But, of course, his crimes must have been rather minor.) The villain is frequently the actual culprit in a situation in which the hero himself is accused. The villain typically knows in advance that the railroad is coming through; therefore he must eliminate undesirables from property he hopes to purchase and then sell to the railroads. When the **cowboy hero** makes a dramatic entrance through the batwing saloon doors, the man playing the piano abruptly stops. And, of course, when the movie ends the hero rides off into the sunset. *See also* COMIC NEGRO; FORMULAS, CLASSIC WESTERN; HIRED GUNS; BASIC PLOT FORMULAS.

CLIFT, MONTGOMERY (1920–1966). Clift was one of many Hollywood actors who showed incredible promise yet had a short career. His first major role was his only major Western role, that of Matt Garth in **Howard Hawks**'s *Red River* (1948). As Garth, Clift played the adopted son of Thomas Dunson (**John Wayne**), a greedy cattleman and Texas landowner. On a cattle drive, Garth splits with Dunson and takes over the drive. This takeover leads to the famous scene in which Garth and Dunson square off in a fisticuffs showdown. The fight turns into a **homoerotic** embrace as Garth proves he is a man and Dunson accepts him into the brotherhood of men. Clift's handsome physique and strong masculine-romantic features inevitably led to roles opposite top female leads such as Joanne Dru in *Red River* and Marilyn Monroe in one of his last films, *The Misfits* (1961).

COBURN, JAMES (1928–2002). After a short career in television, the University of California at Los Angeles–trained actor played significant supporting roles in Westerns throughout the 1960s, getting his first big break as the knife-throwing member of 1960's *The Magnificent Seven*. His career moved beyond that of supporting actor when the urbanely suave actor began playing a spy of international intrigue in the Flint series, beginning with *Our Man Flint* (1966), which were spoofs of the popular James Bond movies. If Coburn could pull off a spy-movie spoof, why not a Western one? So, in 1967 he starred in *Waterhole #3*, a comic send-up of the Western genre in which he played a card shark. In a famous scene, Lewton Cole (Coburn) is called out on the street for a classic quick-draw showdown. The challenger stands in the street, ready to draw fair and square. Cole looks outside, steps out of the saloon, sizes up the situation, shrugs, walks over to his horse, pulls out a high-powered rifle, and blasts away. The man falls, aghast at this violation of the **code of the West**. Of course, we all laugh.

After *Waterhole #3*, Coburn, like other American Western actors, headed to Europe to play in **spaghetti Westerns**. His best was another Western comedy, this one by **Sergio Leone**: *A Fistful of Dynamite (aka Duck, You Sucker!)* (1971). Here he played a happy-go-lucky political revolutionary in Mexico, whose specialty is pyrotechnics. The film celebrates explosions—lots of explosions, everywhere. Coburn's entrance on-screen is probably his most memorable scene. Carefully placed, carefully timed explosions are going off up and down the road, and through the smoke comes Coburn, riding a super-modern, super-cool, turn-of-the-century motorcycle. **Ennio Morricone**'s sound track, with its usual unidentifiable sound effects set to music, highlights a classic Coburn moment—the Western hero doing nothing if not with style. The film is typical Leone but lighter.

In 1973 Coburn played Sheriff Pat Garrett in **Sam Peckinpah**'s *Pat Garrett and Billy the Kid*, his last major Western. Coburn, however, continued film acting for many years, and his deep gravelly voice made him ideal for voiceovers. Even in aging roles toward the end of his career, Coburn maintained his smoothly sophisticated persona. *See also* GENRE FILMS AND WESTERNS.

CODE OF THE WEST. "A man's gotta do what a man's gotta do." **Cowboy heroes** of **silent-** and **classic-era Westerns** base their actions and beliefs squarely on a code of masculine behavior that stretches back to the days of chivalry. In *High Noon* (1952), Will Kane (**Gary Cooper**) knows he must return to town and face Frank Miller even though his new bride begs him to drive away for her sake. The code clearly states that a man can never turn away from a challenge. He must defend his honor and manhood. When he fights, a man must fight fair, with guns, face to face. There are simply some things that men must do, and there is never a need for explanation.

The code was strictly a male ethic, and its ideals of behavior related strictly to men's relationships with each other. The closer a man's ties to other men, the stronger his sense of honor and duty to the code. The weaker his ties to other men, the more feminine he was and, thus, less concerned about honor. In Westerns, shopkeepers do not need to adhere to the code of the West. Essentially, the determining consideration in any given action was the esteem with which other men would view it. Honor could only be conferred by males upon other males. **Women** had no role in the code except as adjuncts to masculine ties. One respected a woman, yes, but a woman's approval of an action of honor was irrelevant.

CODY, IRON EYES (1907–1999). For years Iron Eyes Cody's face was the most recognizable **Native American** face on television. During the 1960s, a long-running advertising campaign against littering ended its television commercials with a close-up of an aging Native American, Cody, looking over the countryside. A tear rolled down his cheek as he contemplated what humanity was doing to the environment. Cody's film career began in Cecil B. DeMille silents and ended with over 200 films to his credit. He nearly always played stereotypical Native Americans, although, as in *Perils of Nyoka* (1942) where he played the "Arab," he was also cast in other ethnic roles. By the 1940s and 1950s, Cody had assumed more substantial roles: *Sitting Bull* (1954), *The Great Sioux Massacre* (1965), *Nevada Smith* (1966), and *A Man Called Horse* (1970). Throughout his life, Cody maintained the fiction that he had been born in Oklahoma of Native American heritage. In fact, he was born Espera DeCorti, a second-generation Italian-American. Nevertheless, the U.S. Native American community embraced Cody fully for his lifetime devotion to Native causes. *See also* SILENT ERA CINEMA.

COMIC NEGRO. Early **silent**- and **classic**-era Westerns reflected the culture's typical racist attitudes. A common stock character was the comic Negro, a term reflecting the inherent racism of these films. Invariably these characters were servants, "menial" help, or simply the easy butt of a few jokes by the dominant white class. They could be trusted to be kind and gentle but were never considered equal to any white person on the set. Often they were treated more like family pets than like people, even by the major, normative characters. Standard scenes portrayed these characters as lazy, shuffling about when they should be hurrying, easily frightened by ghosts, and showing pop-eyed expressions, the huge whites of their eyes standing out against their dark faces. Commonly, a scene called for these characters to hide in the dark, giving themselves away when they either opened their huge white eyes or smiled with large white teeth. Several comic Negro character actors such as **Stepin Fetchit**, Ernest Whitman, and **Willie Best** ("Sleep 'n' Eat") made long careers in these roles. Even as late as **John Ford**'s *The Searchers* (1956), in Mose Harper (Hank Worden) we see a kindly black man who is naturally religious to the point of superstition. As the whites get ready for an **Indian** attack, Mose looks up and says, "That which we are about to receive, we thank thee, O Lord." Female roles were similarly offensive, with large **African American** women playing the kindly "mammy" or housemaid and nurse for white children.

Fortunately, these characters disappeared from films after the **civil rights** movement of the 1960s empowered African Americans to express their deep offense at such degrading racial images. Many re-release versions of early films cut scenes with these characters, out of respect for African American sensibilities. *See also* CLICHÉS.

COMMUNITY VERSUS THE INDIVIDUAL. One of the most common motifs in Western as well as mainstream fiction, the community-versus-individual theme pervades cinema Westerns even more than Western novels: "Among film makers—and it is easier on film—**John Ford** has an unrivalled ability to make us see the individual within the collective, and the collective beyond the individual" (Calder 1975, 5). *Stagecoach* (1939), for example, presents a collection of individuals isolated from their communal ties as they make the desperate trek to Lordsburg. Through the course of the film, these individuals must construct their own communal ties within the small group on the stagecoach.

CONNERY, SEAN (1930–). On a temporary leave from filming his James Bond movies, Sean Connery, the famously Scottish actor, played the lead in his only Western, *Shalako* (1968), a film based on a **Louis L'Amour** novel. Connery's love interest is played by **Brigitte Bardot**, the famously French female actor, in her one Western. Although Connery played an experienced frontiersman, he maintained his Scottish accent. The movie was filmed in Great Britain and in Germany.

COOPER, GARY (1901–1961). Born in Montana, Gary Cooper had a long career in Hollywood, starring in nearly every film genre. He was nominated for five Academy Awards and won two. He was also awarded an Honorary Academy Award just months before his death in 1961. Cooper began his career in the **silent era** and played a bit part in *The Vanishing American* (1925), but his first major film was *The Virginian* (1929), one of the earliest sound Westerns. This film, based on Owen Wister's 1902 novel, has one of the most famous lines in any Western. In a saloon, Trampas (Walter Huston) calls the Virginian (Cooper) a "son of a bitch." Cooper whips out his gun and slowly drawls, "If you want to call me that, smile."

Most agree, however, that Gary Cooper's greatest Western was *High Noon* (1952), the great cold war Western. Cooper's character, sheriff Will Kane, finds himself alone in a desperate attempt to save the town from Frank Miller and his boys, who are out to exact revenge after years in prison. Everywhere he turns, Kane is rejected: His wife leaves him. His deputy abandons him. People at the church simply pray. The saloon crowd jeers. Meanwhile the clock ticks down to noon when, by himself, Kane faces the outlaws. Cooper won one of his Oscars for this role.

Gary Cooper is known for his solid, masculine persona—a man of few words. Essentially, he represents the stereotypical strong and silent **cowboy hero** of the **classic Western**. Perhaps his tendency toward few words results from his role as mediator between peace-loving townspeople and violent savages outside the town. Sometimes it appears that Cooper has fewer words in the script than anyone else. "Like his gun, language is a weapon the hero rarely uses, but when he does, it is with precise and powerful effectiveness. In addition, the hero's taciturnity reflects his social isolation and his reluctance to commit himself to the action that he knows will invariably lead to another violent confrontation" (Cawelti 1999, 41). *See also VERA CRUZ; THE VIRGINIAN.*

CORBUCCI, SERGIO (1927–1990). Often referred to as "the other Sergio" (to **Sergio Leone**), Italian director Sergio Corbucci developed some of the most innovative Westerns of the 1960s and 1970s. While his **spaghetti Westerns** may not enjoy the critical reputation of Leone's, Corbucci was more prolific and in many ways more attuned to prevailing attitudes of the time.

He began his career as a movie critic, but he soon became an assistant director on several Italian comedies and then moved on to directing low-grade comic spoofs of recent box office successes and, eventually, "peplums," or historical muscle movies, such as *Duel of the Titans* (1961), a Steve Reeves movie. ***Django*** (1966) was his first significant Western, a film as important to the direction of spaghetti Westerns as Leone's **Dollars Trilogy** in that it reflected the spirit of mid-century absurdist drama.

The Great Silence (1968), however, may be Corbucci's masterpiece. The cold, barren, **landscape** (supposedly in Utah) proves as menacing as the desert landscape of his other films. Silence (Jean-Louis Trintignant), a mute gunfighter who had his throat cut in childhood, is hired by Pauline (Vonetta McGee) to exact revenge for the death of her husband. It is an unconventional and pessimistic film with serious political implications, much less comic than the Django Westerns.

In the 1970s, Corbucci began issuing what he called "proletarian fables" set in revolutionary Mexico. In *Companeros* (1970), Franco Nero, Corbucci's favorite lead, played the gringo caught in the clash between the revolutionaries.

After the spaghetti and **European Westerns** lost popularity, Corbucci returned to comedy for his last films. He even brought **Terence Hill** and Bud Spencer to modern times in the slapstick film *Super Fuzz* (1981) about a cop with superpowers. *See also* CINECITTÀ STUDIOS, ROME; TRINITY SERIES.

CORRIGAN, RAY "CRASH" (1902–1976). Born Raymond Benard, Crash Corrigan first gained a reputation for his athletic physique, beginning his career as a **stunt** double. At one time he doubled for Johnny Weissmuller of Tarzan fame. As a Western star, Corrigan was best known for his roles as Tucson Smith in the **Three Mesquiteers** series and Crash Corrigan in the Range Busters series. By the 1950s, with the **B Western** era over, Corrigan's film career ended as well. He attempted a television show, the Crash Corrigan Show, for one season in 1950. One of his last movie roles was that of the gorilla in *Bela Lugosi Meets a Brooklyn Gorilla* (1952). After his acting career ended, Corrigan became a successful businessman renting out location property to movie studios.

COSTNER, KEVIN (1955–). Born in California, Kevin Costner is an actor and director who is never satisfied with just one film on a given subject, whether it be sports, political issues, or Westerns, and his three Westerns have been hugely influential. *Dances with Wolves* (1990) helped shift the emphasis of Westerns from merely replaying the traditional Western **myths,** instead providing an alternative view to the ways we have thought of **Native Americans** in the West. *Wyatt Earp* (1994) set out to document precisely and objectively the life of this historic lawman and his family. Costner's most recent Western, *Open Range* (2003), attempted to be a **classic Western** in the traditional sense, and thus proved disappointing—but only when compared to *Dances with Wolves*, an unfair comparison. Occasionally some critics worry about the demise of the Western genre, but Kevin Costner has done as much as anyone to keep Westerns alive.

COSTUMES. Over time, costuming in cinema Westerns has reflected changing perceptions about the **myth of the West** and about what a Western ought to be. In the earliest Westerns, production staff probably costumed all characters in what they perceived to be the current dress for Western people. In *The Great Train Robbery* (1903), costumers make no attempt to distinguish the characters as particularly Western as opposed to rural. Early silent stars such as **Broncho Billy** and **William S. Hart** deliberately affected what they considered authentic working cowboy costumes that reflected the dark visions of their films. **Tom Mix,** however, began the trend in the early sound era toward stylish costuming that branded the star and displayed fashion rather than any sense of authenticity. Stars of **B Westerns,** then, developed specific costumes that immediately identified them with their audiences. **Spaghetti Westerns** of the 1960s and early 1970s reacted against fashion and returned to what some **Sergio Leone** fans probably thought of as realism, but realism usually meant dirty as opposed to clean-cut. Nevertheless, spaghetti stars such as **Clint Eastwood** and Franco Nero were still branded by their specific costume fashion. **Alternative Westerns** since the 1980s have attempted to return to historical authenticity in their costumes, but the **historical authenticity**

of **Kevin Costner**'s costumes differs markedly from the historical authenticity of the silent stars' costumes.

One specific element of the cowboy costume that has changed through the years is the use of chaps. The first screen cowboy, **Broncho Billy Anderson**, regularly wore large sheepskin chaps, yet this kind of chaps is almost never seen again, except in comic scenes to brand someone a tenderfoot. In *Buck Benny Rides Again* (1940), comedian Jack Benny goes West and wants to appear "authentic," so he dresses in great big sheepskin chaps just like Broncho Billy, but here they are a signal for laughter. Ken Maynard, **Buck Jones**, and Tom Mix frequently wore leather chaps, but in the film Western tradition, chaps are downplayed, probably because **cowboy heroes** in cinema Westerns rarely actually work for a living out on the ranch.

Another part of working-cowboy costumes rarely seen in Westerns is leather cuffs. Again, Broncho Billy's and William S. Hart's costumes featured these cuffs; they were an essential part of working-cowboys' equipment. As they roped cattle, real cowboys would dig their boot heel into the ground to provide a firm anchor and loop their rope around the cuff, which provided the protection from friction and rope burns. Authentic or not, cuffs were apparently too cumbersome for the movie cowboy, and apart from Anderson and Hart, they never quite caught on with Western leads. Rather cuffs seemed limited to actors playing villains or old-timers; for example, a lesser villain, Earl Dwire (in films such as *Six Shootin' Sheriff* (1938), frequently wore cuffs, and Raymond Hatton, playing a grizzled old-timer in several Western series, especially the Rangers series with **Jimmy Ellison** and Russell Hayden, used them as an integral part of his costume. Hatton's cuffs "seemed to be the real article, for they were well scarred with rope burns" (Fenin and Everson 1962, 183).

The cowboy hero's hat has also undergone considerable modification due to changing styles. William S. Hart wore a black hat with a flat brim and high, pointed crown—a style rarely seen on later heroes, except possibly in **William Boyd**'s costume. Tom Mix and **Tim McCoy** continued the tradition of very large hats with tall crowns, but later B Western stars wore much less prominent hats. **Roy Rogers** set the style for many with his low-crown white hat and sharply upturned side brim. **Gene Autry**, **Rex Allen**, and other B Western stars wore highly stylish hats. Most mainstream Western stars wore hats that clearly showed their wear. Hats worn by **John Wayne** and **Randolph Scott** were not primarily for fashion; grease lines showed up occasionally. But the biggest change to hat style came with the spaghetti Westerns. Clint Eastwood's low, flat crown and flat brim clearly differentiated his character from all who had come in the past.

If B Western stars were prone to wear showy costumes that bore no resemblance to historical Western outfits, they were succeeded by late-20th-century fashion-conscious Western stars. The stars of *Young Guns* (1988) and *American Outlaws* (2001) wear outfits evidently straight off the racks of fashionable Western wear stores. When Sharon Stone strides down the street of Redemption in *The Quick and the Dead* (1995), she wears a stylish duster, fancy stitched boots, a low-brimmed hat, and designer sun glasses.

Women's costumes have changed from decade to decade, more in response to fashions at the time of production than to reflect historical accuracy. High, understated bodices and long skirts typify the **silent era**, while more practical tops and shorter skirts emerged in the 1920s. From the 1920s on there has been no hesitation to show well-shaped legs and curves. **Pants roles** abound in Westerns of the 1930s and 1940s. *The Outlaw* (1943), starring a sultry Jane Russell, has often been seen as the film that began exploiting sex through revealing female costumes, standard features in most Westerns today.

Costuming **Native Americans** has generally paralleled the move from stereotyping to an attempt to treat the tribes authentically. Early silent Westerns and even many **classic Westerns** show Native Americans in costumes derived more from dime novels and comic books than history. **Indian** chiefs, for example, did not wear full-sized war bonnets while charging down a hill in pursuit of white settlers, except in cinema Westerns. **Alternative Westerns** have attempted to replicate historical dress to a greater degree than the past. *See also* GUN BELTS; HISTORICAL AUTHENTICITY.

THE COVERED WAGON (1923). James Cruze (director). Based on a novel by Emerson Hough, *The Covered Wagon* was one of the first epic Westerns, containing grand panoramic scenes of standard formula features such as **Indian** attacks, buffalo hunts, and crossing of dangerous rivers. These scenes became possibly the movie's most important contribution to later Westerns as they provided **stock**

footage in low-budget films for years. The popularity of the film proved that larger-budget Westerns were marketable. *See also* FORMULAS, CLASSIC WESTERN.

COWBOY HERO. The center of every **classic Western** is the cowboy hero, such as **Shane,** who at the edge of the frontier mediates between the coming civilization and the innate savagery of the wilderness. The cowboy hero inhabits two worlds: he can live in the town and work among those who represent civilization, but he can also read sign (follow tracks), use firearms, and fight the forces of savagery, whether **Indian** or **outlaw**, on their own terms. He is a man who abides by a strict **code** of behavior, prefers the life of men to that of women, rides a **horse** rather than a buggy, wears a six shooter and can draw quick as lightning, is a man of action rather than a man of words, and yet knows his days are soon to be over. The term *cowboy hero* distinguishes this character from the generic cowboy characters who abound in Westerns.

Real cowboys of old were low-paid, migrant agricultural laborers. In Hollywood movies, however, the cowboy hero in Westerns is rarely depicted as working. His connection with agrarian labor—and at that, only with horses and cattle—is mostly symbolic in that it relates him to traditional masculine intimacy with the land. We associate the cowboy hero with our **nostalgia** for a time when all work revolved around farm and ranch work and the laboring animals. But on film the hero rarely settles down and, instead, maintains a desire to keep moving. While he may talk of someday finding a ranch of his own to work, seldom does he actually take up ranching. Instead, while he somehow maintains enough income to keep ammunition in supply and to take care of his horse, the typical film cowboy hero is quintessentially a man of leisure. He does not pursue classic American virtues of work, enterprise, and success.

While the cowboy hero is invariably a loner, one who knows the West and himself, he also knows he does not want anything to do with the civilizing, feminizing forces coming from the east. Of course, he is a man—usually a young man—so despite the dominance of male forces in his world, the cowboy hero must inevitably deal with his need for female companionship beyond the occasional prostitute or **dance hall girl**. Cinema Westerns often develop this issue as a subplot. Usually the hero shuns marriage because it limits his freedom. Thus, for example, Johnny (**James Ellison**) in *Hop-Along Cassidy* (1935) falls deeply for Mary Meeker (Paula Stone), but just when it looks like a wedding will soon occur, Johnny hears that Hoppy and Red are heading to Montana to begin a new ranch. As "The End" appears on the screen, we see Johnny riding to catch up with the boys.

When marriage does occur it usually comes only at the end of the film and is usually only implied. The hero is most comfortable with a woman who is his gender complement. Those with criminal reputations are attracted to women who are also social outcasts, as with Ringo (**John Wayne**) and the prostitute Dallas (**Claire Trevor**) in *Stagecoach* (1939). The virtuous **Wyatt Earp** (**Henry Fonda**), on the other hand, is attracted to the virtuous Clementine (Cathy Downs) in *My Darling Clementine* (1946). Uncomfortable, or mismatched, relationships require one partner or the other to subsume his or her masculinity or femininity to the other. Will Kane (**Gary Cooper**) in *High Noon* (1952) and Amy (**Grace Kelly**) can make their marriage work only if Amy becomes more masculine and kills in order to save her man's life and if Will becomes more feminine and repudiates the **code of the West,** which says he must assert his masculinity or suffer the consequences. On the other hand, Ysobel (**Dale Evans**) can never marry **Roy Rogers** in *Cowboy and the Senorita* (1944), and most of the other films she makes with him, until she casts off her eastern feminist mores and assumes a degree of Western masculinity. *See also* HOMOEROTICISM.

CRAWFORD, JOAN (1905–1977). Nominated three times for the best actress Academy Award, winning the award outright in 1946, Joan Crawford was one of Hollywood's greatest stars. In life she defined what American culture considered ultimate glamour. In death, with the posthumous publication of her daughter's tell-all biography *Mommie Dearest* (1978), Joan Crawford transcended traditional Hollywood stardom. While Crawford is rarely associated with Westerns, her 1954 *Johnny Guitar*, regarded as a mediocre film when produced, today is considered one of her finest films and, by many critics who usually scorn Westerns, one of the 1950s finest artistic Westerns.

This early **feminist Western** pits a strong, independent business-woman, Vienna (Crawford), against her rampaging community. She already owns most of the town and is poised to make a fortune when the railroad comes through, but her ambitions reach far beyond the town. She gets framed for a stage holdup, however, and the sister (Mercedes McCambridge) of a murder victim becomes a powerful enemy leading the town against Vienna. Both **women** dominate the town and the men in it. Thus, Joan Crawford's Western reverses gender roles. "She's more of a man than a woman," one of the saloon gamesmen observes of her. Evidently Crawford's jealous rivalry with McCambridge carried over beyond the script and, according to Christina Crawford in *Mommie Dearest*, Crawford treated McCambridge cruelly throughout the filming.

CROWE, RUSSELL (1964–). Australian Russell Crowe has developed a career as one of the best actors of the 21st century, having three Academy Award nominations and one award for best actor. But Crowe's first film in the United States was a Western. He played Cort, the gunslinger-turned-pacifist clergyman in *The Quick and the Dead* (1995). Sharon Stone delayed production of the film until the relatively unknown Crowe could take the part. The 2007 remake of *3:10 to Yuma* has Crowe playing the outlaw Ben Wade in the role **Glenn Ford** made famous.

CRUZE, JAMES (1884–1942). Born Jens Vera Cruz Bosen in Utah, James Cruze was involved in some production or acting role in over 100 films of the **silent era**. He first began work in films with the New York–based Lubin Company in 1910. In 1922 Cruze directed *The Covered Wagon*, one of the early silent screen epics. He followed with another epic, *The Pony Express* (1925), which, however, was not a success. The film seemed static compared to its predecessor and the plot was clearly contrived. It starred Betty Compson, Ricardo Cortez, and **Wallace Beery**. Cruze was married to actors Marguerite Snow and Betty Compson.

CULT-OF-THE-INDIAN WESTERN. The cult-of-the-Indian Western refers to a kind of **alternative Western**, sometimes called counterculture Westerns. The term originates with Richard Slotkin. Throughout the history of the Western, **Native Americans** have mostly been treated unfairly and stereotypically. However, beginning in the 1960s, several films began to treat Native American culture not just sympathetically or nostalgically, but as morally superior to the dominant white culture, both of frontier history and of the contemporary moment. *Cheyenne Autumn* (1964), *The Great Sioux Massacre* (1965), and *A Man Called Horse* (1970) are considered cult-of-the-Indian Westerns. The earliest prototype, however, is probably *Soldier Blue* (1970), with its portrayal of the historic Sand Creek Massacre of 1864 being a cultural parallel to the My Lai Massacre in Vietnam (1968). *Little Big Man* (1970) also developed an antihero character in Jack Crabb (Dustin Hoffman), who deflates one Western stereotype after another. The Native America idealized in *Little Big Man* is, essentially, the American counterculture of the late 1960s.

The appearance of these 1960s and 1970s films coincided with a national reevaluation of Native American culture in such academic and popular works as Leslie Fiedler's *Return of the Vanishing American* (1966) and Vine Deloria's *Custer Died for Your Sins* (1969) and in the emergence of the politically aggressive American Indian movement.

Perhaps the most significant cult-of-the-Indian Westerns, however, are **Kevin Costner**'s *Dances with Wolves* (1990) and Walter Hill's *Geronimo: An American Legend* (1993), as they are based on **new Western history**.

CULT-OF-THE-OUTLAW WESTERN. This term, first used by Fenin and Everson as well as Richard Slotkin, refers specifically to the large number of films based on **outlaw** stories, such as those of **Jesse James**, produced in the 1930s and 1940s. This "new deal" period, grounded in progressive ideology, portrayed outlaws as victims of overwhelming economic forces or perhaps as saviors of the common people from robber baron kinds of evil. *Jesse James* (1939) and *I Shot Jesse James* (1949) are typical examples of this style, as is the *The Outlaw* (1943), based on the **Billy the Kid** legend. Later **alternative Westerns**, such as *American Outlaws* (2001), often return to cult-of-the-outlaw ideologies.

CURTIS, KEN (1916–1991). Born Curtis Wain Gates in Colorado, Ken Curtis made his fame playing the cornpone, one-eyed deputy Festus Haggen on the **television Western** series *Gunsmoke* from 1959 to 1975. Prior to that, however, Curtis had a long career in film and music. He began his entertainment career as a singer and even sang lead for the Sons of the Pioneers from 1948 to 1952. In 1952 Curtis married **John Ford**'s daughter, Barbara, and became a member of the John Ford Stock Company, playing roles in such major Westerns as *Rio Grande* (1950), *The Searchers* (1956), *The Horse Soldiers* (1959), *Two Rode Together* (1961), and ***Cheyenne Autumn*** (1964).

CUSTER, GENERAL GEORGE ARMSTRONG (1839–1876). The legendary 7th Cavalry commander has come to stand for all that was wrong with American **Native American** policy. He met his end at the **Battle of Little Big Horn** in June 1876. The defeat at the hand of Crazy Horse and his Sioux warriors was seen as a humiliation for the cavalry. Buffalo Bill's famous Wild West show always featured an act involving Custer's Last Stand. The popularity of that act carried over into the earliest days of film, and there were numerous treatments of Custer's career in the **silent era**.

Among the many films recounting the "glorious martyrdom" of General Custer's career are *Custer's Last Raid* (1912), starring Francis Ford; *The Plainsman* (1936); and *They Died with Their Boots On* (1941), starring **Errol Flynn**. Beginning with *The Great Sioux Massacre* (1965) and continuing with the **antimyth** *Little Big Man* (1970), Westerns have become critical of Custer's treatment of Native Americans.

The essential details of General Custer's life portrayed in Westerns include his flamboyant dress, his heroism in battle, his reputation for insubordination, and his death at Little Big Horn. Custer adopted colorful dress during his days at United States Military Academy at West Point, where he finished last in his class. During the Civil War, however, Custer was given a battlefield promotion to brigadier general due to bravery, and he returned home to Michigan a war hero. After the war, Custer rejoined the army with the rank of lieutenant colonel and was given command of the 7th Cavalry. Throughout his career, Custer was a controversial figure, usually in trouble one way or another with his military superiors.

In what was once called the Indian Wars, Custer became a hero with his victory over the Cheyenne in 1868 at the Battle of Washita Creek in **Indian Territory**. Today that battle is usually interpreted as a massacre of the Cheyenne by Custer. At the time, however, the battle was considered the first great victory in the final conquest of the West after the Civil War. Unfortunately, the hero of the first battle led his 7th Cavalry into an ambush at Little Big Horn in 1876, and Custer and all his men were killed.

– D –

DANCE HALL GIRLS. Saloons in early **silent** and **classic Westerns** often have several **women** employed who merely encourage cowboy customers to buy them drinks and have a little company. Since the West of these cinema Westerns is overwhelmingly masculine and dedicated to a **code** of virtue, dance hall girls as character types are a coded acknowledgement of the true nature of the Wild West and the pervasive role of prostitution in frontier society.

Sympathetic dance hall girls can be dark and mysterious, as is Helen Ramirez (**Katy Jurado**) in *High Noon* (1952), but they may also be blonde and vivacious, as is Frenchy (**Marlene Dietrich**) in *Destry Rides Again* (1939). Ruby (Ann Sheridan) in *Dodge City* (1939) probably defines the unsympathetic type as she collaborates with the evil saloon owner (Bruce Cabot) to destroy the sheriff, Wade Hatton (**Errol Flynn**). Other notable dance hall girls have been Feathers (**Angie Dickinson**) in *Rio Bravo* (1959), the playful and likeable pal of Dean Martin's and Ricky Nelson's characters, and Dolly (Louise Glaum) in *Hell's Hinges* (1916), **William S. Hart**'s vamp-like temptress.

Dance hall girls can be virtuous fallen women with hearts of gold, or they can be women of power who are trying to assert some sort of independence and control in a masculine world. The most memorable cinema characters tend to be the latter. Most **post-Westerns** and **alternative Westerns** openly acknowledge the role of prostitution in Western saloons.

DANCES WITH WOLVES (1990). **Kevin Costner**, Mary McDonnell, Graham Greene, Kevin Costner (director). Costner's **alternative Western** ushered in a new era of Westerns after the **antimyth Westerns** of the 1960s through the 1980s had played out their course and made their point in counteracting the **classic Western** tradition. *Dances with Wolves* did not merely attempt to overturn classic Western **clichés** and dominant **plot formulas**. Based upon premises of the **new Western history** that came to dominate Western historical studies in the late decades of the 20th century, Costner's film portrays more directly than previous Westerns the evils of **Manifest Destiny** and the depredations, not of the red man, but of the white man. It departed from previous Westerns—**silent**, classic, and antimyth—by "making a group of **Native Americans** the sympathetic protagonists and by showing the United States Cavalry as an aggressive and brutal invader the film, reversed the Western's mythical polarity between savage **Indians** and civilizing pioneers" (Cawelti 1999, 105).

The plot revolves around a Union soldier, Lieutenant Dunbar (Costner), ordered by choice to a remote frontier outpost on the **Great Plains** during the Civil War. His encounter with Sioux tribal members reenacts the first encounters with Native peoples in the New World centuries before. They are not familiar with each other's culture, and Dunbar must learn the Sioux language. He discovers a white woman in the tribe, Stands-with-a-Fist (McDonnell), who was captured as a child and is now fully adopted into the tribe, recently widowed yet content. She only vaguely recalls her native English language, and the film shows her progress of recovering the language along with long-suppressed memories. Dunbar becomes a willing captive and he is adopted by the tribe, taking on the name Dances-with-Wolves. Thus, the film reverses the traditional **captivity narrative** plot. Stands-with-a-Fist had been captured long ago and had suffered the most dreaded "fate worse than death" of classic Westerns. In *The Searchers* (1956), Ethan Edwards tries to kill Debbie when he finds her despoiled by the evil chief, Scar, because he thinks she would be better dead than an Indian. But in this film, the white captive is accepted by her adopted people and she has made a good life for herself. Dunbar seeks a similar life change. Eventually, however, Dunbar must face the invasion of whites coming into the territory, including the U.S. Cavalry. Told from inside the tribe, this Western portrays the invasion and destruction of a way of life from the Native American perspective. This film is not about winning the West but about losing it.

Dances with Wolves was nominated for 12 Academy Awards and won 7, including best picture, best director, and best music (by John Barry). McDonnell was nominated for best supporting actress and Costner for best actor. *See also* FORMULAS, CLASSIC WESTERN.

DANDRIDGE, RUBY (1900–1987). Ruby Dandridge was an African American actress of the pre–civil rights era who primarily played **comic Negro** roles. She was the mother of the much more famous screen star of the 1950s, Dorothy Dandridge. Ruby Dandridge usually played a white actress's childlike serving woman, cook, or some other menial role. In **Republic**'s *Home in Oklahoma* (1946), **Roy Rogers** (as himself) is trying to solve the murder of Sam Talbot. **Dale Evans** (Connie Edwards), out riding the dead man's horse, is thrown and the horse comes racing back to the ranch. At the same time, Devoria (Dandridge) hears a train whistle but thinks she hears Talbot moaning from his grave. She had heard the same noise the day Talbot was killed. Rogers solves the case when he figures out that Talbot had been killed much earlier than thought, namely when the train was making a scheduled run in the area. Devoria's fear reinforces typical white stereotyping of **African Americans in Westerns** of the period.

DARBY, KIM (1947–). Born Deborah Zerby in Los Angeles, California, Kim Darby will probably be forever remembered by Western fans for her role as Mattie Ross in Henry Hathaway's *True Grit* (1969). Mattie is a tomboy who sets out on a mission of revenge by hiring aging lawman Rooster Cogburn (**John Wayne**) to accompany her into **Indian Territory** after the outlaw who killed her father. Part of the film is a coming of age story for the young girl as the old lawman tries to keep her from growing bitter over what life has dealt her. John Wayne attempted to talk the popular singer Karen Carpenter into taking the role, and Mia Farrow was also suggested for the part. But Hathaway ignored other advice and recruited the young television actress. In later years, Darby recalled that Hathaway asked her on 10 separate occasions to take the role. She had just delivered a child and was going through a divorce, so she hesitated. In the end she agreed and brought her newborn daughter to the set each day. Her short stature and cherubic face allowed Darby to play teenagers well into her twenties, and the contrast between the young tomboy and the six-foot-four Wayne is a feature of the film. While *True Grit* was Darby's only Western, she maintained a distinguished acting career and now teaches acting at the University of California at Los Angeles as well as in her own studio.

DARK COMMAND (1940). **Claire Trevor**, **John Wayne**, **Roy Rogers**, Walter Pidgeon, **Gabby Hayes**, Raoul Walsh (director). **Republic Studios** was known primarily for making low-budget **B Westerns**, but it did occasionally have a major success. At its release, *Dark Command* was the largest budget movie Republic had made to date. It was also nominated for two Academy Awards and had a major director, Raoul Walsh. It was Wayne's and Trevor's next movie after *Stagecoach* (1939) and also featured B Western steadies Roy Rogers and Gabby Hayes. While Hayes played his usual character, Rogers showed he could act out of character—and he doesn't sing in this film.

Dark Command is the story of a Kansas schoolteacher **William Quantrill** (renamed Will Cantrell for some reason) who becomes a Southern partisan ranger during the Civil War. Will Cantrell (Pidgeon), in love with the banker's daughter, Mary (Trevor), is frustrated with his lowly position in life. He runs for town marshal. Unfortunately, at about the same time, Bob Seton (Wayne) comes to town, drifting in with Doc Grunch (Hayes) from Texas. Seton is also a frustrated young man, seeking his way in the world. He, too, is smitten by the charms of the banker's daughter, and he, too, runs for marshal. Though Cantrell is heavily favored, Seton wins the hearts of the townspeople as well as their votes and becomes the new marshal. As a result, Cantrell becomes bitter and vows to rise to the top and run Kansas no matter what it takes. When Mary's younger brother, Fletch (Rogers), gets in trouble for shooting an unarmed man, Cantrell takes advantage of the situation and raises a band of toughs who intimidate the jurors into declaring the boy innocent. Mary, not knowing of Cantrell's strong-arm tactics, marries him out of gratitude. The sheriff now looks foolish. The Civil War begins, and Cantrell's men begin wearing Confederate uniforms and raiding the countryside. Fletch and Mary are with him. Just before the legendary sacking of Lawrence, Kansas, Seton convinces Mary and Fletch of Cantrell's perfidy, and they flee with Seton to warn the town. The burning of the town and the death of Cantrell end the film. Mary now is free to marry Seton. Thus, Claire Trevor and John Wayne marry and head south in two consecutive movies.

Dark Command is surprisingly complex. Each main character is well developed. Symbolic characters appear at key intervals. Cantrell's mother (Marjorie Main), for instance, serving as Cantrell's conscience, constantly upbraids him. (Ultimately, at his darkest moment, he kills her.) The film also bypasses politics. Good people as well as bad are on both the Northern and the Southern sides. *Dark Command* was nominated for two Academy Awards.

DARNELL, LINDA (1923–1965). Born Monetta Eloyse Darnell in Dallas, Texas, Linda Darnell was often described as "the girl with the perfect face." Trained as a dancer, she also became a studio model where she was discovered by Hollywood. In her first film, *Hotel for Women* (1937), a non-Western, Darnell played a seductive young model; she was only 15 at the time. Her Westerns include *The Mark of Zorro* (1940), *Buffalo Bill* (1944), *Two Flags West* (1950), and *Dakota Incident* (1956). Her most famous role is probably that of Chihuahua, the sultry **dance hall girl** and mistress to **Doc Holliday** (Victor Mature) in *My Darling Clementine* (1946). While the film's main plot revolves around **Wyatt Earp** (**Henry Fonda**) and Doc and their rivalry with the Clantons, the main subplot consists of the female relationships. Holliday is torn between two **women**—Clementine (Cathy Downs), representing eastern goodness and purity, and Chihuahua, representing frontier feminine savagery and sensuality. Wyatt, meanwhile, wishes Clementine would pay attention to him. Linda Darnell's two most famous scenes are in this film: one is set in the saloon, where she sings "10,000 Cattle" as if she is mocking Wyatt; the other is when Chihuahua is shot by Billy Clanton (John Ireland). In the latter scene, Doc is forced to bring out his long-neglected medical bag, sober up, and operate. Clementine assists in the operation, but Chihuahua dies on the table, though not before admonishing Doc to straighten up and lead a clean life.

Linda Darnell had a lifelong phobia of fire. Scenes involving fire were always difficult for her to make. In 1965, while watching a rerun of one of her old movies, her house caught fire, burning over 90 percent of her body. She died the next day. Darnell had recently completed her final film, the Western *Black Spurs* (1965), with **Rory Calhoun**.

DAVIES, DELMER (1904–1977). After graduating from Stanford University with a law degree, Delmer Davies began working in the film industry almost immediately; he worked on the set of *The Covered Wagon* (1923) during these early years. After serving in numerous behind-the-scenes positions, he began directing in 1943. *Dark Passage* (1947), starring Humphrey Bogart and **Lauren Bacall**, is usually seen as Davies' masterpiece, but he also developed a close association with Westerns, all produced in the 1950s. While Davies is usually given much less prominence than his contemporaries **Anthony Mann** and **Budd Boetticher**, his Westerns often break from the traditional formulas and provide dark but revealing character contrasts. He stretched the limits of cultural expectations, as with *Broken Arrow* (1950), one of the first **cult-of-the-Indian Westerns**, in which the United States' policies toward **Native Americans** were questioned. Davies had a close association with **Glenn Ford** and worked with him in three Westerns: *3:10 to Yuma* (1957), *Jubal* (1956), and *Cowboy* (1958). Delmer Davies' reputation for Westerns mainly rests on *3:10 to Yuma*, a **noir Western** that has little action and is almost purely character driven. Davies' last Western, *The Hanging Tree* (1959), is remembered for its Oscar-nominated theme song; it was **Gary Cooper**'s last Western as well. *See also* FORMULAS, CLASSIC WESTERN.

DAVIS, GAIL (1925–1997). Born Betty Jeanne Grayson, Gail Davis played female leads in numerous low-budget Westerns of the late 1940s and early 1950s. In her early work with such actors as Charles Starrett, Tim Holt, and **Roy Rogers**, she played typical passive, dependent female roles. But in a number of late **Gene Autry** films, such as *Blue Canadian Rockies* (Columbia, 1952), Davis played independent **women**, often businesswomen, who could handle their own problems. When **television Westerns** replaced budget Westerns, Davis played the lead in the Annie Oakley series.

DEAD MAN (**1995**). Johnny Depp, Billy Bob Thornton, Iggy Pop, **Robert Mitchum**, Alfred Molina, Gary Farmer, Jim Jarmusch (director). *Dead Man* is the essential Western of the **postmodern** era. Variously billed as an anti-Western or **punk Western**, it takes the **Western moment** shared by all Westerns and strips away as many characteristics of Westerns as possible in an attempt to create a new **myth of the West** more in line with other areas of popular culture such as comic books, music videos, and, to a degree, video gaming. Pitched in the middle is a cowboy star from the past, Robert Mitchum, whose career began in **Hopalong Cassidy** Westerns.

Bill Blake (Depp), a displaced loner, descends into hell in the town of Machine, located at the end of the rail line. He is emasculated in the factory full of huge gears, wheels, and levers. He confronts and is humiliated by the cruel factory owner (Mitchum). Killing the factory owner's son liberates Blake to set out upon a spiritual **quest** for salvation. He meets Nobody (Farmer), a **Native American** shaman figure, who informs him that in reality he is William Blake, the late 18th-century English visionary poet. They take peyote together. Blake then goes on his spiritual journey, finally leaving the nastiness and filth of **John Ford**'s West to be reunited with the spiritual realm.

The black and white cinematography, the rock music by Neil Young, the rapid-cutting, music video–style of pacing take this Western far beyond anything previous and look forward to cinema Westerns of the 21st century.

DEADWOOD, SOUTH DAKOTA. This historical town has nearly always been associated with two things in cinema Westerns: the gold rush in the Black Hills that precipitated the Sioux uprisings of the 1870s and the murder of lawman **Wild Bill Hickok**. Hickok was playing poker in a saloon and holding the dead man's hand—a hand of aces and eights—when he was shot in the back. *See also* TELEVISION WESTERNS.

DE HAVILLAND, OLIVIA (1916–). Born in Japan, Olivia de Havilland is one of the most acclaimed female film stars of the 20th century. Her sister was the female actor Joan Fontaine. De Havilland won the Academy Award for best actress twice. She costarred with **Errol Flynn** in nine films, three of which were Westerns: *Dodge City*

(1939), *Santa Fe Trail* (1940), and *They Died with Their Boots On* (1941). The first two were directed by Michael Curtiz, who directed the other Flynn-de Havilland films. In each film, de Havilland played the faithful and beloved partner to Flynn's swashbuckling character. The films in which Flynn costarred with de Havilland are probably his greatest, but de Havilland managed to break through the character type and move on to numerous feisty, strong, and independent-**woman** roles. For a time, Flynn and de Havilland were romantically involved off-screen. In later years she joined **Ronald Reagan** in his Hollywood anticommunist crusade.

***DESTRY RIDES AGAIN* (1939). Jimmy Stewart, Marlene Dietrich**, George Marshall (director). *Destry Rides Again* is one of three films based on the same novel by **Max Brand**. Unlike the version made five years earlier, starring **Tom Mix**, this version bears little resemblance to the novel other than the title and the last name of the main character.

Bottleneck is a town out of control. The sheriff has just been killed by a corrupt racketeer. The equally corrupt mayor appoints the town drunk as sheriff. However, the new sheriff does have enough wits about him to wire Thomas Jefferson Destry (Stewart) to come help him out. Destry's father had been a gunfighter of repute. Destry arrives, but he does not wear guns, and instead of wielding any power, he simply tries to smooth talk all troublemakers into giving up. Meanwhile, the local saloon singer, Frenchy (Dietrich), has been ordered to win Destry over. She finds her work more than she can handle. Eventually, when Bottleneck is lulled into complacency, Destry's guns come alive with a fury, and the "silly" deputy sheriff tames the town. The film is unfortunately dated by its inclusion of a stereotyped **African American**—the maid, Clara (Lillian Yarbo), who quivers with terror every time a gun goes off.

While not in the same category as later comic Westerns such as *Blazing Saddles* (1974), *Destry Rides Again* does, nevertheless, contain comic elements, many of them surrounding Frenchy and her work in the saloon; in fact, Madeline Kahn parodies Dietrich's role in her part as Lili Von Shtupp in *Blazing Saddles*. Comedy aside, Dietrich's deep, sultry Germanic voice makes for some great music in this Western masterpiece. Jimmy Stewart's role of the "aw shucks" pacifist deputy fits the persona he cultivated in many of his popular non-Western films but is a far cry from his later personae in the **Anthony Mann** Westerns. *See also* COMIC NEGRO.

DETERRITORIALIZATION. Classic Westerns identify directly and intimately with the **landscape** of the West. Deterritorialization, a term originated by Paul Bleton, refers to the trend in **post-Westerns** toward separation from traditional Western settings. Western landscapes in post-Westerns often do not represent geographic space conventional to classic Westerns, such as **John Ford**'s use of **Monument Valley**, but may represent bizarre Mexican terrain or the terrain of fantasy. As often as not, the actual landscape used in shooting the film is not located in the United States or even in Mexico, as post-Westerns have been filmed all over the world. Deterritorialization has helped resurrect the Western film genre and has expanded and reconfigured the cinema Western as mythic terrain beyond the limits of history. *See also* ANTIMYTH WESTERNS; GENRE FILMS AND WESTERNS.

DEVINE, ANDY (1905–1977). Andy Devine came to Hollywood after a successful college football career. The heavyset actor was inevitably typecast in comic roles, often as **sidekick** for **Roy Rogers** and other cowboy stars of the 1940s. His most important role was probably that of Buck the stagecoach driver in *Stagecoach* (1939), providing comic relief during the tense ride across **Monument Valley** to Lordsburg with **Apaches** on the warpath. "If there is anything I do not like, it's driving a stagecoach through Apache country," Buck mutters at one point.

DE WILDE, BRANDON (1942–1972). Who can forget the last lines in *Shane* (1953)—"Shane! Come Back!"—yelled by Joey (De Wilde) as he runs after his hero who is riding off over the mountain? Brandon De Wilde played perhaps the most famous child's role in a Western when, at age 11, he played Joey Starrett, a boy who idolizes his gunfighter hero even while trying to understand his father, who does not wear guns, and his mother, who he knows sees much in Shane. As Joey, De Wilde displayed exactly the right amount of bright-eyed, coming-to-awareness facial expressions accompanied by a tone of voice that perfectly expressed incredulity at what he saw in Shane and adoration, if not worship, of his hero. For his role in *Shane*, De Wilde was nominated for a best supporting actor Academy Award.

That look of bright-eyed innocence in *Shane* came from a seasoned actor who had appeared in 492 performances on Broadway in *The Member of the Wedding*, which he reprised in the film version in 1952, a film that also received Academy Award nominations. After these two films, De Wilde was given his own television series, *Jamie*. As he moved through his teenage years, De Wilde developed a modest reputation as a 1960s teen idol, starring in several popular teen movies. He died in an automobile accident in Denver at the age of 30.

DICAPRIO, LEONARDO (1974–). Born Leonardo Wilhelm DiCaprio in Hollywood, California, DiCaprio played "The Kid," a classic young **gunfighter** with an itchy trigger finger, in *The Quick and the Dead* (1995). The Kid brags unendingly about how fast he is. To the gunfighter Ellen (Sharon Stone), he claims, "I'm so damned fast I can wake up at the crack of dawn, rob two banks, a train and a stage coach, shoot the tail feathers off a duck's ass at 300 feet, and still be back in bed before you wake up next to me." The Kid is Herod's (**Gene Hackman**) son and has never lived up to his father's expectations. It turns out that The Kid is not as fast on the draw as he thought: "Damn, that is fast!" he exclaims as he falls dead at his father's hand, the loser of a quick-draw shootout with Ellen. DiCaprio has been nominated for Academy Awards three times, all for non-Western roles. See also CROWE, RUSSELL.

DICKINSON, ANGIE (1931–). Born Angeline Brown in North Dakota, Angie Dickinson turned a beauty contest to an entry into a film career. While she had played various small roles, including several Westerns, before 1959, *Rio Bravo* proved to be her big break. In the film, which starred **John Wayne** and Dean Martin, Dickinson played Feathers, the sexy **dance hall girl** who helps her two partners defeat the plans of a gang to break one of their own out of jail. As sexy as any saloon girl character since **Marlene Dietrich**'s Frenchy, Feathers purrs at one point, "Hey, sheriff, you forgot your pants." After *Rio Bravo*, Dickinson went on to a long career in film and television.

DIETRICH, MARLENE (1901–1992). Everything about Marlene Dietrich's early life was shrouded in a mystery created by press agents and herself, including her age and her parentage. Early biographies list her birth name as Maria Magdelena Dietrich von Losch and have her being born in 1904, but she was actually born Maria Magdelena Dietrich in Germany in 1901. She developed a very successful film and singing career in Germany before coming to the United States and playing in many popular non-Westerns throughout the 1930s and 1940s. Dietrich's first film after becoming a U.S. citizen was, fittingly, a Western—at the time, an American film genre. In *Destry Rides Again* (1939), opposite **Jimmy Stewart**, Dietrich played Frenchy, probably the most famous saloon girl in any Western.

What made Dietrich's Frenchy such a great character was the transference of the sultry Germanic Dietrich persona to the old West. In her first scene in the film, her back is turned as she is singing "Little Joe, the Wrangler" in her famous dark and husky voice. The soon-to-be-no-more town sheriff is in the audience. She turns and faces the camera directly, which happens to be the perspective of Kent, her boss and friend in villainy. She winks, rolls her cigarette, and then looks alluringly at the luckless sheriff, now listening to his death song. Soon after the song, a naïve Russian immigrant, Boris (Mischa Auer), pats her rear. She turns and slaps him, showing that she is no common **dance hall girl**. He worships her thereafter.

Later in the film, Frenchy sings "You've Got That Look (That Leaves Me Weak)" in as sultry a manner as anything seen in cinema Westerns. She wears a feather boa, which she uses to excite the saloon patrons. The camera cuts back and forth between Frenchy and Boris, who rolls his eyes backward, embraces a wooden column next to him, and kisses the column as if it is Frenchy. Another cowboy, turned on by Frenchy's performance, fires off his pistols in the air to symbolize his arousal.

Deputy Sheriff Destry (Stewart) sees through her completely but manages lots of good clean 1930s-style sexual byplay. Marlene Dietrich's Frenchy set the standard for future saloon girl characters and was so famous that Madeline Kahn parodied Dietrich in the 1974 Western spoof *Blazing Saddles* (directed by Mel Brooks).

Well into her mature years, Dietrich starred in one other Western, Fritz Lang's *Rancho Notorious* (1952), a **revenge Western** in which she attempts the Frenchy act one last time.

DJANGO **(1966).** Franco Nero, **Sergio Corbucci** (director). This **spaghetti Western** directed by "the other Sergio" redirected the Italian Western tradition toward what would be a nearly completely **European Western** tradition. **Sergio Leone**'s Westerns, beginning with the **Dollars Trilogy** and later culminating with *Once Upon a Time in the West* (1968), were **antimyth Westerns**—films that attempted to overturn the **classic Western myth of the West**. Sergio Corbucci's Westerns paid no attention to the classic Western tradition. Instead, they developed surreal scenes, bizarre plotting, and incredible amounts of **violence**—all projected in cheap **Techniscope**. Django, the first film in the **Django series**, is typical.

Franco Nero (Django) played a superhero figure in the middle of a rivalry between the red-hooded Ku Klux Klansmen (called the Fanatics), led by Major Jackson, and jovial sadists (called the Banditos), led by General Hugo Rodriguez. The town is a ghost town filled with unemployed prostitutes. Django carries around a coffin, which contains his gun of choice—a hip-model machine gun. From this basic premise, the film develops a series of linear episodes centered on various acts of brutal violence: Django's girl, a prostitute named Maria, is brutally whipped by the Banditos. The town preacher, a corrupt clergyman offering moral protection to the brothel, has his ear cut off. The Fanatics go on a killing spree of peons. Prostitutes fight bloody battles in the mud. Django's own hand is crushed by horses' hooves in order to demonstrate who is in power. At a certain point, Django waits near a tree stump on the street as the Klansmen parade through the streets. Suddenly, Django whips out his machine gun from the coffin and opens fire. In the final showdown, Django gets Major Jackson and the Fanatics together in a cemetery. His "hands have been crushed, so he rests his gun on a metal cross, and pulls back the hammer with his bloody stumps ('In the name of the Father and of the Son and of the Holy Ghost')" (Frayling 1981, 79). Because of its perceived excessive violence, *Django* was banned in Great Britain.

THE DJANGO SERIES. Beginning with **Sergio Corbucci**'s 1966 **spaghetti Western** *Django* and Slim Alone's *Django Always Draws Second* (1974), the Django series consisted of 20 Westerns. When, early in its filming, the series became hugely popular in Europe, several Westerns already in production changed the name of their main character to capitalize on the popularity, so the series is not actually coherent or consistent. Throughout the series various actors, such as Franco Nero, Glenn Saxson, and Gianni Garko, played the lead role of Django, and various directors besides Corbucci profited from the popular hero's capital.

DODGE CITY, KANSAS. After the Civil War, markets for Texas beef opened up in the Midwest and East. The Transcontinental Railroad was the early economic connection between East and West, making two cities in Kansas—**Abilene** and Dodge City—the nearest and most convenient rail centers for the Texas cattle drives. Dodge City became the most famous of all the cow **towns**. It consisted of one main business street running parallel with the Santa Fe rail line. One side of town was respectable and the other was virtually lawless. In Westerns, saloons are usually depicted as the main businesses of the town, and Dodge City was no different. **Wyatt Earp** and his brothers along with Bat Masterson were some of the town's historically famous lawmen. Dodge City gained its cinema reputation first from *Dodge City* (1939), starring **Errol Flynn** and **Olivia de Havilland**. Later films celebrating Dodge are *Tombstone* (1993) and *Wyatt Earp* (1994).

DOLLARS TRILOGY. This is a collective term for **Sergio Leone**'s three **spaghetti Westerns** starring **Clint Eastwood**: *Per un pugno di dollari* (1964); *Per qualche dollaro in più* (1965); and *Buono, il brutto, il cattivo, Il* (1966), all released in the United States in 1967 as *A Fistful of Dollars*; *For a Few Dollars More*; and *The Good, the Bad and the Ugly*. While the three films are usually associated as a trilogy because of their cinematic, thematic, and musical style and because they all star Clint Eastwood, they are actually unrelated to each other by plot. None is a sequel to the other. In each film, Eastwood played a character who has been dubbed "the Man with No Name" by fans and critics, but he is actually named in each film—Joe (*A Fistful of Dollars*), Monco (*For a Few Dollars More*), and Blondie (*The Good, the Bad and the Ugly*). Technically, Eastwood played a different character in each film, but he dressed with similar style and was consistently a man of few words from nowhere. All three films emphasize the antihero nature of the Man with No Name, and all three are characterized by **Ennio Morricone**'s hauntingly original music.

DOUBLE BILLING. Double billing, or presenting a double feature, was the common practice of movie houses throughout the 1930s and 1940s. Prior to this, in the **silent era,** the standard bill for all films, including Westerns, would be a feature (of various lengths) accompanied by a comedy short and perhaps a newsreel. Double bills usually consisted of a feature-length film at the top of the bill and a B movie (whether Western or not) at the bottom. As double billing became standard, a new market for low-budget Westerns opened, and small independent producers began developing quickly made, low-budget **B Westerns.** Double billing declined rapidly by the 1950s and virtually disappeared by the 1960s, thus closing the market for inexpensive cinema Westerns. Fortunately for the small producers, television supplied a new market as of the 1960s.

DOUGLAS, KIRK (1916–). Born Issur Danielovitch Demsky in New York, the cleft-chinned, intensely masculine actor has been a significant force in Hollywood film since he began his career in 1946. The Westerns of Kirk Douglas span the **classic Western** era and demonstrate the progression through the period. *Along the Great Divide* (1951), a Raoul Walsh film, looks back to the great epics of the 1940s with their emphasis on panoramic **landscapes** and the insignificance of humanity in the natural world. *Man without a Star* (1955), in which Douglas played opposite **Claire Trevor**, typifies 1950s introspective Westerns. Douglas played a cowboy torn between the needs of settlers and their barbed wire and the needs of the ranchers and open range. His Westerns of the 1960s, such as *The Way West* (1967) and *The War Wagon* (1967), which costarred **John Wayne,** show the 1960s' emphasis on action and maintaining traditional cultural values. Douglas's *Posse* (1975), which he also directed, shows the ambiguity toward authority that 1970s Westerns were developing. The marshal brings in the notorious outlaw only to find the town turning against him.

But Kirk Douglas's most famous Western character is probably **Doc Holliday** in *Gunfight at the O.K. Corral* (1957). Opposite Burt Lancaster's **Wyatt Earp**, Douglas portrayed a man who has little to live for, only finding purpose through loyalty to Earp. His treatment of Kate (Jo Van Fleet) is far more brutal than Victor Mature's Doc Holliday in *My Darling Clementine* (1946).

DUEL IN THE SUN (1946). Jennifer Jones, Joseph Cotten, Gregory Peck, Lionel Barrymore, Lillian Gish, King Vidor (director), David O. Selznick (producer). As with *The Outlaw* (1943), *Duel in the Sun* was intended to be as sexually provocative as the times would allow. David O. Selznick wanted to make a Western epic on the scale of the Civil War–epic *Gone with the Wind* (1939). He cast his own future wife, Jennifer Jones, as the sensual half-Hispanic temptress of two brothers—one (Joseph Cotten), a good man, refined of manners and gentle of disposition, and the other (a very young Gregory Peck), a savage brute who takes after their father (Lionel Barrymore), a cruel yet wealthy land baron and senator. Lillian Gish, nominated for her only Academy Award for this role, played a mother who desperately tries to mediate between the sons and between her husband and their sons. *Duel in the Sun* was one of the largest-budget Westerns of its time, and although it earned its way in the box office, the film has generally been seen as a critical failure. Selznick's ambitions were never acknowledged.

DUST. The old West was a dirty place. When a horse and rider came down the street of an old West town with its false front stores, dust flew everywhere. The Conestoga wagons in front of the wagon train produced huge quantities of choking dust for the wagons following. Cowboys riding drag on the trail wore bandannas over their faces to filter out the floating dirt. Dust was everywhere—except in most Western films. In most film Westerns, when the rider comes into town on the fly and pulls up to the sheriff's office, the picture is clear of any significant dust because the production crews had just run a water truck over the set prior to the shot. Directors long ago figured they would sacrifice a bit of realism for the sake of clear pictures. The exception is the Western films of **Thomas Ince** and his lead actor **William S. Hart**. In a typical Hart two-reeler, filmed on location in Inceville, California, dust covers everything out of doors—deliberately, for the sake of realism. Unfortunately, some scenes in the old silents are quite clouded over.

DUVALL, ROBERT (1931–). Robert Duvall has been a distinguished actor over a long film career that began in the 1960s. An actor in **television Westerns** early on, his first cinema Western was a supporting part in *True Grit* (1969). Since then he has played major roles in such Westerns as *Joe Kidd* (1972), *Geronimo: An American Legend* (1993), and **Kevin Costner**'s *Open Range* (2003). In 2006 he played the lead in the television movie *Broken Trail*, which was written especially for him. Duvall's combination of gritty earthiness and practical, everyday-living style of acting has brought him much acclaim. He has been nominated for six Academy awards and won best actor in 1984 for *Tender Mercies* (1973), a non-Western.

– E –

EARP, WYATT (1848–1929). Legend and numerous films detailing Wyatt Earp's exploits usually contain the following elements: Earp was a tough lawman who tamed **Dodge City** with the help of his brothers, Virgil and Morgan, as well as famous deputy Bat Masterson. After taming Dodge, Earp and his brothers moved on to Tombstone, Arizona, where they tangled with the Clancys at the famous gunfight at the **O.K. Corral**. **Doc Holliday**, a tubercular dentist and **gunfighter**, usually appears in movies about Earp. Among the many films starring the legend are *Frontier Marshal* (1939), with **Randolph Scott**; *My Darling Clementine* (1946), with **Henry Fonda**; *Gunfight at the O.K. Corral* (1957), with Burt Lancaster; *Tombstone* (1993), with Kurt Russell; and *Wyatt Earp* (1994), with **Kevin Costner**.

Like all legends, the Wyatt Earp story is open to scrutiny, and Earp himself perpetuated the mystery. He lived out his last years in California cultivating his legacy. He contracted with Stuart Lake on an authorized biography, the details of which have not stood the test of later research. Most of what early Hollywood took as history of the Earp era evidently came from the aging gunfighter's personal stories. Some would argue that Hollywood's version of the old West comes not so much from history as from perhaps the most influential historical consultant in film history, Wyatt Earp himself.

EASTWOOD, CLINT (1930–). Clint Eastwood is unquestionably one of the most important figures in the history of cinema Westerns. On numerous levels, his Man with No Name character in **Sergio Leone**'s 1960s **Dollars Trilogy** forever changed the concept of the Western **cowboy hero** and the **myth of the West**. In the 1970s and 1980s, a series of important films continued to redefine the Western genre. *Unforgiven* (1992), for which he received his first Academy Award as director, is arguably the best Western film ever.

His story has become Hollywood legend. Clint Eastwood came from a working-class family in San Francisco, California. After a series of common jobs and a stint in the army, he was signed by Universal, primarily based on his athletic build and good looks. A series of bit parts throughout the 1950s eventually led to the role of Rowdy Yates in the popular **television Western** *Rawhide*, which ran for seven seasons. At the time, Westerns were the most popular genre on television, and *Rawhide* consistently led the ratings. Rowdy Yates was a young daredevil ramrod to the older and wiser trail boss, Gil Favor. For the 1950s, the Yates character had immense sex appeal, and Eastwood became a popular American cowboy star in the **classic Western** tradition.

In retrospect, Eastwood's dissatisfaction with his television acting career was inevitable since he had already worked behind the scenes in scriptwriting and directing. However, CBS held a rigid contract with its actors and did not want to lose a top-draw series star to the movies. Through a few threats of walking out and other moves, Eastwood persuaded executives to allow him to spend time in Europe with **Cinecittà Studios** making cheap Italian movies. CBS most likely reasoned that these movies would be so bad that they would be a short-lived venture for Eastwood and would never be seen in the United States anyway.

Quite the opposite happened, however. Eastwood teamed up with Sergio Leone to make a series of three Westerns that would change Westerns permanently. The three films, known collectively as the

Dollars Trilogy were *Per un pugno di dollari* (1964); *Per qualche dollaro in più* (1965); and *Buono, il brutto, il cattivo, Il* (1966)—later released in the United States as *A Fistful of Dollars*; *For a Few Dollars More*; and *The Good, the Bad and the Ugly*.

The films were so successful in Europe that Cinecittà sought American distribution. All three films came out in one year. Reactions to the films were immediate and strong. *A Fistful of Dollars* was released in January 1967; *For a Few Dollars More* in May 1967; and *The Good, the Bad and the Ugly* in December 1967. Critics scornfully dismissed these films made in Italy (actually Spain) as "**spaghetti Westerns**." Many felt that these popular movies would destroy the Western genre, coming only a decade after the embarrassing (to them) **B Westerns** had finally faded away.

The most severe criticism of these films focused on Eastwood's character. All the usual stereotypes were overturned with this Man with No Name. Other than being a man of few words, Eastwood's character bore no resemblance to cowboys played by such stars as **Randolph Scott** or **John Wayne**. In *A Fistful of Dollars*, the Man with No Name enters town, backed by **Ennio Morricone**'s innovative soundtrack, riding a donkey, wearing a flat-brimmed hat and a serape, and chewing on a cigarillo. He bears loyalty to no one save himself, he ignores traditional morality, and he shuns legal authority as simply irrelevant or as part of the problem to be eliminated. The **violence** that ensued in these films was far in excess of anything from the *Rawhide* television series (to which Eastwood returned after filming in Italy) or other classic Westerns; a violence that might purify but it did not **regenerate**. When the Man with No Name stared down his victim and then squeezed the trigger, his stare turned from hatred to pleasure. With the Dollars Trilogy, the classic era of Westerns effectively ended. The new era would bring forth a spate of **antimyth Westerns**.

For Eastwood, the release of the Dollars Trilogy was timed perfectly. The children who had grown up watching **Hopalong Cassidy** and **Roy Rogers** Westerns now rejected the values of their parents and were ready to embrace anything that reinforced their new values. In the spaghetti Westerns, an old cultural artifact became new and reenergized, and Clint Eastwood became the hero for a new generation.

After the Dollars Trilogy, Eastwood returned to the United States and made an American spaghetti Western–style film, *Hang 'Em High*

(1968)—a solid Western similar to the Dollars films except that this time Eastwood played a lawman.

Then he began a series of non-Western characters, notably Dirty Harry, who simply brought Sergio Leone's Man with No Name up to date. Eastwood then worked with Lee Marvin on a musical Western, *Paint Your Wagon* (1969; directed by Joshua Logan), which, while a curiosity, nevertheless is probably the best Western musical to date. In the 1970s Eastwood returned to more classic Westerns, first with *Joe Kidd* (1972) directed by John Sturges, who had directed the classic Western *The Magnificent Seven* (1960). While for Eastwood this Western was a reconnection with real American Westerns, for Sturges it proved quite a departure. The following year Eastwood directed his first Western, *High Plains Drifter* (1973), a film that owes much to **William S. Hart**'s *Hell's Hinges* (1916). He directed again in *The Outlaw Josey Wales* (1976), perhaps his most savagely violent film to that point. In 1985 Eastwood directed *Pale Rider* and played the Preacher, a man who lulls a ruthless mining baron and his thugs into complacency reminiscent of *Destry Rides Again* (1939).

For the 1992 film *Unforgiven*, Eastwood won his first Academy Award for best director and the film won best picture. In this film Eastwood seemingly overturns his Man with No Name persona, playing a simple farmer who is trying to honor his deceased wife's request that he forsake his guns and bring up his small children correctly. In the end, however, he must take up his guns again.

Since the end of the classic Western era, fans and critics have debated the future of Westerns. Who knows whether Clint Eastwood will return to Westerns, but it is clear that throughout the post–classic Western era—the post–**John Wayne** era—he has been developing some of the best Westerns ever produced. The inevitable comparisons to Wayne persist. What Eastwood has done that John Wayne could never do was receive critical acclaim from the film industry, seen in his numerous Academy Awards, and also from academic film critics. Eastwood brought artistic respectability to the Western. *See also* RE-GENERATION THROUGH VIOLENCE.

ELAM, JACK (1918–2003). Elam's sagging face and slant-eye look made him perfect as one of the most famous bad guys of the 1950s and 1960s. He appears one way or another in many of the classics such as *High Noon* (1952), *Vera Cruz* (1954), and *The Man from*

Laramie (1955). In later years he was such a familiar Western **outlaw** that he began playing roles that spoofed his character. His role as the dim-witted Jake in *Support Your Local Sheriff* (1969) is perhaps his most memorable, but his role in **Sergio Leone**'s *Once Upon a Time in the West* (1968) probably displays his best acting. In this serious Italian Western, Elam (Snaky) is a ruthless killer, yet as he naps against the station wall awaiting the train, a fly buzzes him, and nothing he does shoos the fly away. At last, **gunfighter** that he is, Snaky pulls his gun and traps the fly in the barrel. Minutes later, he dies trying to get the drop on Harmonica (**Charles Bronson**) just off the train.

ELLIOTT, SAM (1944–). A mainstay in **television Westerns** since the 1970s, Sam Elliott has played in several late-20th-century Westerns, including *Molly and Lawless John* (1972), opposite Vera Miles, and *The Desperate Trail* (1995). His best acting, however, is probably displayed in his role as Virgil Earp in *Tombstone* (1993). Elliott is married to Katharine Ross, who starred in *Butch Cassidy and the Sundance Kid* (1969)—in which Elliott had a very small role. Sam Elliott has been the quintessential image of the American cowboy so much so that he even played the Marlboro Man in the comedy *Thank You for Smoking* (2005). *See also THE MAGNIFICENT SEVEN.*

ELLIOTT, WILD BILL (1903–1965). Born Gordon Nance in Missouri, Bill Elliott was associated with the character of **Wild Bill Hickok** for most of his career, playing the role in a 15-chapter serial, a feature film, and a series of budget films for Columbia with costar **Tex Ritter**. Elliott's Hickok character had the reputation of being a level head with the fastest gun, and his very name spread fear among the lawless. His trademark line was "I am a peaceable man" and his horse was Sonny. After his film career, Elliott became a spokesman for Viceroy cigarettes. He died of lung cancer in 1965.

ELLISON, JAMES "JIMMY" (1910–1993). Born James Ellison Smith, Jimmy Ellison is usually associated with **William Boyd**'s **Hopalong Cassidy** films. He starred with Boyd in *Hop-Along Cassidy* (1935), the first film in the series, and continued until 1937. Ellison played Johnny Nelson, a character from the popular Clarence Mulford Hopalong Cassidy novels. Johnny is a high-strung, handsome cowboy, ever loyal to Hoppy, and quick on the draw. Because William Boyd was somewhat older than the character from the novel, Jimmy Ellison's Johnny inevitably took on all the romantic roles in the series.

While **B Western** fans primarily remember Jimmy Ellison from the Hopalong Cassidy days, he later played Buffalo Bill beside **Gary Cooper**, as **Wild Bill Hickock**, and **Jean Arthur**, as **Calamity Jane**, in Cecil B. DeMille's *The Plainsman* (1936), a picture far out of the Hopalong Cassidy league. While Ellison played his part competently, he evidently displeased DeMille and only sporadically reached that level of Hollywood stardom thereafter, and never again in high-budget Westerns. His dashing, college-boy good looks typed him in youthful romantic roles, which he eventually outgrew.

END OF THE WESTERN ERA. In his frontier thesis, Frederick Jackson Turner famously declared that the frontier was officially closed by 1890. Indeed, after the last major historical event of the old West, the Oklahoma Land Rush of 1889, most Westerners believed the West to be crowded and finally settled. Almost immediately a sense of **nostalgia** developed, and it became important for America's collective cultural consciousness that the **myth of the West** be preserved. The days of covered wagons were no more. **Indian Territory**, for years a notorious "no man's land," was now settled. North Dakota, South Dakota, Washington, and Montana became states in 1889. Geronimo was safely on a reservation, and while there would still be problems with Native Americans into the 1890s, nevertheless, by 1890 "the Western hero was safely down on paper" (Calder 1975, 6). *See also* FRONTIER THESIS, TURNER'S.

END-OF-THE-WEST FILMS. One of the most common subgenres of Westerns looks back nostalgically on a West that has gone forever. What is lamented is not so much a passing of time as a passing of a way of life. In one sense, all Westerns yearn for a return to the days of yesteryear, but end-of-the-West films such as *The Shootist* (1976) and *Butch Cassidy and the Sundance Kid* (1969) are typically situated in the period between the end of the old era and the beginning of the new century. Often the heroes are characters who lived their lives fully in the old days and are trying to cope with the new ways. *See also* END OF THE WESTERN ERA.

EPIC MOMENT. The epic moment is the usually brief time in the development of a civilization when the forces of chaos and stability are both evident and the founders of the culture rise up to subdue chaos. For the ancient Greeks, it was the period of the Trojan War celebrated by Homer. For the Romans, it was the period of the conquest of Italy celebrated by Virgil. For the United States, it was the **Western moment** celebrated by cinema Westerns and popular Western fiction.

ESSANAY FILM MANUFACTURING COMPANY. In 1907 **George M. "Broncho Billy" Anderson** and George K. Spoor established Essanay Film Manufacturing Company, the first major film studio, in Chicago. Essanay went on to produce films of Charlie Chaplin, Gloria Swanson, **Tom Mix**, Broncho Billy, and many others. The company dissolved in 1916.

ETHNIC MALE COMPANIONS. A commonplace facet of American fiction is that the hero's closest male companion is a person of another race; thus we have Leatherstocking and Chingachgook of James Fenimore Cooper's frontier tales, and Huck and Jim of Mark Twain's *Huckleberry Finn.* Cinema Westerns continue this pairing. The Lone Ranger (Clayton Moore) and Tonto (**Jay Silverheels**) of *The Lone Ranger* (1956) are perhaps the most familiar pair, but Ethan (**John Wayne**) and Martin (Jeffrey Hunter) of *The Searchers* (1956) continue the tradition. The ethnic companion ordinarily possesses skills and social characteristics that complement the hero and make the pairing a completed whole. These relationships are often so close-knit that for all practical purposes, the men are joined in a sexless marriage. Speculations on the **homoerotic** nature of Western male companionships are common. *See also* HOMOEROTICISM.

EUROPEAN WESTERNS. As early as 1909—with the Great Northern Film Company's production of a very early Danish Western, *Texas Tex* (Fenin and Everson 1962, 56)—Westerns were a part of European films being made, often, to imitate American films. We know that by the later **silent era**, Westerns were well-liked in Europe. **Joë Hamman** was an early German cowboy star. As Westerns became increasingly popular in Europe during the early sound era, production companies were in a quandary about how to market English-language films in those countries.

An early solution was to shoot a film two ways at the same time—one for American audiences and one for European audiences. Both productions would use the same scripts, sets, action scenes, and stunts but have different casts. Raoul Walsh's *The Big Trail* (1930) was one such film. **John Wayne** made his credited film debut in the film, but an alternate version with a completely different cast was made at the same time. The dual production system did not last long as Hollywood eventually figured out how to overdub speech and market subtitled films.

Very early French Westerns betrayed a lack of understanding of what the West was like. In Jean Durand's *Hanging at Jefferson City* (1910), the set only slightly suggests the American frontier West. Much of the film takes place in a minimally saloon-like barroom. Characters wear French farm clothes with large cowboy hats. Two lawmen actually wear uniforms, rather than the usual Western wear, and they have enormous badges pinned to their chests.

The middle of the 20th century saw an enormous growth in production of cinema Westerns, particularly in Italy with **Cinecittà** and other studios' **spaghetti Westerns**. *See also* LEONE, SERGIO.

EVANS, DALE (1912–2001). Born Lucille Wood Smith, in Uvalde, Texas, Dale Evans's parents changed her name in infancy to Frances Octavia Smith.

Evans began her entertainment career as a vocalist during the big band era, first performing on radio in Memphis, Tennessee, where she changed her name to Dale Evans. From Memphis she moved to Chicago and from there to New York, where she sang at the Coconut Grove nightclub.

With her newfound celebrity, Evans was asked to audition for a role in *Holiday Inn* by 20th Century Fox. The role did not materialize but a one-year contract did, and Evans began playing minor roles in Fox films. Her popularity grew steadily, and she was given increasingly better roles. The ultimate turning point of her career came when she was cast as costar to **Roy Rogers** in *Cowboy and the Senorita* (1944). Herbert Yates of **Republic Studios** had seen the musical *Oklahoma* on Broadway and had the idea to change Rogers's **singing cowboy** pictures to replicate Broadway musicals, and Evans fit the role. On New Year's Eve 1947 she married Rogers, "the King of the Cowboys," and thereafter she was known as "the Queen of the Cowgirls."

Onscreen, Dale Evans's persona was that of a spunky, independent-minded woman out to make her way in the world, with or without the help of men. In *Home in Oklahoma* (1946), she played a reporter from back East who has come to investigate rumors that ranch owner Sam Talbot might have been murdered and not killed in a horse accident as assumed. In this film Rogers and Evans worked a common plot variation of the East versus West **binary**. The woman reporter is an easterner who comes West on a professional matter. The **cowboy hero** must show her that the West is a special place. Her eastern upbringing gets her into trouble because she cannot appreciate western ways. At the same time, however, she brings to the West the idea that a **woman** can be just as tough as a man in her own domain. Thus, she solves problems that thwart the westerners. Evans and Rogers worked this plot device repeatedly in the 28 movies they made together.

Evans continued making non-Westerns up until their marriage in 1947. It was her fourth marriage, all others ending in divorce, and his second marriage, his first ending after his wife's death. The Rogers built a large family through the years, and their personal tragedies became the subject of several inspirational memoirs.

EVANS, MURIEL (1910–2000). Born Muriel Adele Evanson, Muriel Evans—sometimes blonde, sometimes brunette—played opposite **Buck Jones**, **Tex Ritter**, and **John Wayne**, but is perhaps best known for her roles as the passive yet virtuous love interest to **Jimmy Ellison** in **William Boyd Hopalong Cassidy** films. In *Three on the Trail* (1936), for example, she played an out-of-work schoolteacher hired by a rogue to be the bookkeeper for the Bar 20 ranch. This rogue seeks to take advantage of her as he accompanies her to the ranch, and the Bar 20 cowboys must rescue her twice from the clutches of evil men.

– F –

FARMING. The great Westward movement of the 19th century was in one sense a movement that broke the soil and planted farms all over the trans-Mississippi West. Even in ranching country there were plenty of small farms side by side with the ranches. The Homestead Act of 1862 allowed anyone to claim 160 acres of free land as long as they improved it in specific ways within five years. Thus, toward the **end of the Western era**, farms were everywhere in the West—everywhere but in the movies. But, as Scott Simmon writes, while the Hollywood Western wants to idolize farmers in a Jeffersonian way, "it cannot abide depicting farmwork" (2004, 134). **Cowboy heroes** ride horses and move cattle, if they work at all. The reason is that ranching and cattle drives work themselves out cinematically better than farming. Panoramic shots of large stretches of unbroken land show a romantic West that would be spoiled by patchworks of farms. In a film like *Shane* (1953), even though the homesteaders farm for a living, we actually see very little farming.

FEMINIST WESTERNS. This term is often used loosely to refer to any Western in which **women** dominate, but it applies most directly to Westerns in which gender roles are reversed and the female characters play male roles and the male characters are subservient to the females. An early anomalous **classic Western** often labeled feminist is *Johnny Guitar* (1954) in which two women dress and act like men while squaring off for a traditional showdown. The trend for such feminist Westerns naturally accelerated after the women's movement of the 1960s, and from the late 20th century to the present, certain movies have appeared that have clearly intended to make a feminist statement. *The Quick and the Dead* (1995), for example, has a woman **gunfighter** who bests all her male opponents. *The Ballad of Little Jo* (1993) tells the story of a woman who is disgraced by nice society and forced to live her life disguised as a man. Some films like *Bad Girls* (1994) and *Gang of Roses* (2003) revolve around gangs of women gunslingers who band together for strength and protection. In *The Missing* (2003), a mother tracks across treacherous desert in search of her daughter who had been captured by **Apaches**. In all these movies, the male characters prove ineffective and weak when confronted by strong women. *See also* ALTERNATIVE WESTERNS; GREENWALD, MAGGIE; PANTS ROLES.

FETCHIT, STEPIN (1902–1985). Born Lincoln Theodore Monroe Andrew Perry in Key West, Florida, Fetchit renamed himself after a racehorse that had won him some money. He played stereotypical **comic Negro** roles throughout the 1930s and 1940s. While Fetchit prospered in this capacity, he nevertheless serves as an unfortunate example of the severe white racism of the time. Fetchit was probably the most famous **African American** actor of his day, leading a lavish lifestyle from his film earnings. Eventually, however, he went bankrupt. In the 1970s, Fetchit converted to the Black Muslim faith.

Generally, his characters were childlike in their simplicity and lazy to the extreme. Fetchit perfected a slurred, mumbling speech pattern thought by whites to represent typical African American dialect. In *Wild Horse* (Allied, 1931) even the simplest of tasks baffle Stepin. One comic scene shows him attempting to make an old mule get up and obey him. In another scene, Stepin is told to post rodeo flyers around town. After he posts one to a barn wall, he leans back against the wall. When he walks away, the flyer is pasted to his back. Utterly baffled, Stepin walks around trying to figure out what happened to the rodeo flyer. His best acting role was in **Anthony Mann**'s *Bend of the River* (1952) in which his character, while still submissive, is not comic.

FINLEY, EVELYN (1916–1989). Evelyn Finley was one of the female leads of the late 1940s low-budget Westerns who represented the trend toward strong, independent **women** who could stand up to the villains as well as the **cowboy heroes**. In *The Sheriff of Medicine Bow* (1948), a **pants role**, Finley played Nan, the daughter of a rancher who is sent to prison unjustly. It is up to her to protect the ranch from villains. When **Johnny Mack Brown** comes to her rescue, Nan does not need him. Finley was an excellent rider and did much **stunt** work and doubling. *Ghost Guns* (1944), also starring Brown, features Evelyn Finley's equestrian abilities.

FISTFIGHTS. At some point in most Westerns, the action erupts into a fistfight. Low-budget affairs, such as *Hoppy Serves a Writ* (1943), occasionally feature an all-out fight in a saloon with smashed chairs and the obligatory cowboy falling over the railing from the second floor, but it would be difficult to find any major Western—*Shane* (1953), *Red River* (1948), *Unforgiven* (1992)—without the requisite slugfest. That is because the **code of the West** demands restrained violence, so the **cowboy hero** will fist fight with gusto, but never kill with his hands; he only kills with guns. Unlike his opponents, the cowboy hero never uses knives or hard objects in a fistfight. One particular kind of fistfight, the brutal all-out fight between two erstwhile male friends, is sometimes seen as having **homoerotic** overtones. In *High Noon* (1952), for instance, Will Kane has it out with his deputy in the stable, and perhaps the two derive masculine pleasure from the fight.

A FISTFUL OF DOLLARS (PER UN PUGNO DI DOLLARI) **(1964)**. **Clint Eastwood**, **Ennio Morricone** (music), **Sergio Leone** (director). This was, for practical purposes, the original **spaghetti Western**, released in Italy in 1964 and in the United States in 1967 as the first part of the **Dollars Trilogy**. The plot is based closely on Japanese filmmaker Akira Kurosawa's *Yojimbo* (1961). Ennio Morricone's haunting score integrated music with plot and theme in ways never done before in Westerns.

An unshaven Man with No Name (Eastwood) rides into a border town on a mule, wearing a serape and a wide, flat-brimmed hat, clinching a cigarillo in his teeth. Townspeople jeer at him. Soon he finds himself in the middle of a feud between the Baxters and the Rojos. The film is characterized by elaborate, interminable shifting stares among adversaries, and even among family and friends, and by one-sided duels in which no one besides the hero gets off a round. In the film's central scene, Eastwood's character rescues Marisol (Marianne Koch) by killing six men with five shots. Later, after he finally kills six Rojos with a loaded Colt .45, he releases the bound innkeeper with a miraculous seventh shot.

The town of San Miguel, in its stark bareness, serves almost as an allegorical cityscape of death. The landscape and the cityscape seem to represent dryness, sterility, and death—with absolutely no redeeming features. In the last scene, Eastwood's character emerges from a cloud of dust to face the Rojos in a final confrontation. In the end, Leone completely rejects the **classic Western** concept of **regeneration through violence** as the Man with No Name rides away from the town after eliminating the Rojos without having made the town better off. He has not saved the town in the way Will Kane saves his town in *High Noon* (1952).

FLYNN, ERROL (1909–1959). Born in Australia, Errol Flynn, distinguished in speech and manner, starred in four big-budget Westerns in the 1930s and 1940s. He first made his reputation in swashbuckler films like *Captain Blood* (1935), *The Charge of the Light Brigade* (1936), and *The Adventures of Robin Hood* (1938)—all with **Olivia de Havilland** as his love interest. The pair continued their work together with three Westerns. While the impossibly handsome and athletic Flynn worked well in swashbuckling, **costume** films, he usually appeared an anomaly in his Westerns. In *Dodge City* (1939), for instance, he played a Texas cattleman (with a gentlemanly accent) who brings order to the lawless cow town. His character gets in a saloon fight more reminiscent of *Captain Blood* days than the usual Western barroom brawl. In *Santa Fe Trail* (1940), he played Jeb Stuart, who, along with George Custer (**Ronald Reagan**), is hunting down abolitionist John Brown just prior to the Civil War.

In his last Western, *They Died with Their Boots On* (1941), Flynn played **General Custer**. This biographical film traces the famous general's career from West Point through his battle exploits in the Civil War to his marriage with Libby (de Havilland) and the Indian battles culminating in the **Battle of Little Big Horn**. Flynn's Custer is flamboyant yet noble in pursuit of patriotic ideals; Flynn was perfect for the role. For many, Errol Flynn defined gentlemanly masculinity, dominating action movies for a short period of Hollywood history. He was certainly the most refined of Hollywood's **cowboy heroes**. Flynn died of a heart attack at the age of 50.

FONDA, HENRY (1905–1982). Born in Nebraska, Henry Fonda was a Hollywood celebrity for over 50 years, starring in some of the most memorable films of all time, including quite a few great Westerns. Beginning with *Jesse James* (1939), nearly every film and Western Fonda made was a major motion picture, and with each he gained a new image that was remembered through the years: young **Jesse**

James, thin and good-looking, with the troubling look of a man searching for a black and white answer to problems that have no solution; Gil Carter in *The Ox-Bow Incident* (1943), a simple cow puncher caught up in a mob thirsty for blood; **Wyatt Earp** in *My Darling Clementine* (1946), an honest lawman dedicated to justice and peace, in love with **Doc Holliday**'s intended; Colonel Thursday in *Fort Apache* (1948), a racist Indian hater.

Fonda played psychologically complex characters and could not be pinned down to a specific persona. He often played the clean, wholesome American hero caught up in situations beyond his control. Sometimes he played the simple-minded but decent guy just trying to do right. But he could also play the psychotic bent on evil, as in *Fort Apache* and, late in his career, the **spaghetti Western** *Once Upon a Time in the West* (1968), directed by **Sergio Leone**. In the latter, Fonda played the gunfighter Frank, ruthless, yes, but worse, just plain mean. A famous image from the film is Leone's trademark close-up of the eyes—Fonda's eyes, in this film—glazed over with pure evil. Fonda said later that *Once Upon a Time in the West* was his favorite Western.

FOR A FEW DOLLARS MORE (*PER QUALCHE DOLLARO IN PIÙ*) (1965). **Clint Eastwood**, **Lee Van Cleef**, **Ennio Morricone** (music), **Sergio Leone** (director). This is the second of Sergio Leone's **Dollars Trilogy**, following *A Fistful of Dollars* and preceding *The Good, the Bad and the Ugly*. Clint Eastwood's Man with No Name character is back in action, this time as Monco, with Van Cleef playing Colonel Mortimer. The two are **bounty hunters** seeking the same bandit but for different reasons. Through the desert, into El Paso, and deep into the Mexican wilderness, the antiheroes chase their outlaw. As with the other Leone Westerns, the film combines extreme, dirt-and-grime realism with action scenes straight out of fantasy. Monco confronts his foe in a saloon, then realizes the two exits are covered by his enemies. He whips out two huge guns, and with three quick shots solves the problem. Eastwood's character does not ask many questions about what is right or wrong in a given situation, but close-up after close-up of Van Cleef's eyes after his killings reveal an utterly evil soul. The haunting music of **Ennio Morricone** pervades nearly every scene. *See also* SPAGHETTI WESTERNS.

FORAN, DICK (1910–1979). Born John Nicholas Foran and the son of a U.S. senator, Foran began his career as Nick Foran, a radio and big band singer. He was Warner Brothers' only **singing cowboy** and a response to the immediate popularity of **Gene Autry**; Foran's *Moonlight on the Prairie* (1935) was released just two months after Autry's *Tumbling Tumbleweeds*. Foran's films were more directly aimed at the youth audience than the early Autry films, and his image tended to be that of a sentimental and loveable older brother. While Foran's films, mercifully, were free of the low comedy common to **B Westerns**; nevertheless, they used the unfortunate and distracting gimmick of puppets to make a point for children. The action in his films came from **stock footage** from old Ken Maynard silents. Foran was probably a better singer and actor than Autry, and the songs in his films were more organic to the plot than Autry's production numbers tended to be. What is widely considered his best Western came after his days as a singing cowboy—*Heart of the North* (1938), a full-budget, near epic feature film. Long after his singing cowboy days, Dick Foran did well-regarded character acting well into the 1960s.

FORD, GLENN (1916–2006). Born Gwyllyn Ford, Canadian actor Glenn Ford had an acting career spanning seven decades. Known for his manly bearing, boyish grin, and unassuming, natural acting style, Ford played a wide range of roles, including those in Westerns. He always appeared utterly at home outdoors, on a horse, and with a gun. Nearly all his Westerns include significant love interests: Rhonda Fleming in *The Redhead and the Cowboy* (1951), Felicia Farr in *3:10 to Yuma* (1957), and Maria Schell in *Cimarron* (1960). *3:10 to Yuma* will probably be remembered as Ford's best performance in a Western, where he plays the **outlaw** Ben Wade being held for the train to prison. *Cimarron*, an epic of the Oklahoma land run and its aftermath, is one of his more underrated Westerns. He played Yancey, the patriarch of a family who makes their fortune with their newspaper. A tumultuous relationship with his Lady Macbeth–like wife (Schell) provides the film with necessary dramatic tension. Off-screen, Ford evidently had as much romantic charisma as on-screen, maintaining rumored intimate relationships with such film stars as Bette Davis, Rita Hayworth, **Brigitte Bardot**, Connie Stevens, and Maria Schell. *See also* MANN, ANTHONY.

FORD, JOHN (1894–1973). Born John Martin Feeney in Maine, John Ford began his career in film by working bit parts in the films of his brother (Francis Ford) and others. Among his earliest bit parts was that of a Klansman in **D. W. Griffith**'s *The Birth of a Nation* (1915). Much of Ford's early life and background have become Hollywood legend. For example, "Jack" Ford is known for celebrating his Irish roots in his films. Tradition has it that he took his last name from the Model T. He often claimed to have been given early opportunities to direct one- and two-reel silent Westerns because he could "yell real loud."

Ford's first significant film as director was *The Iron Horse* (1924), which tells the story of the building of the Union Pacific Railroad across the West. Typical Fordian Western themes are evident in this film: human progress is equated with technological progress, and the frontier belongs to the whites not the Native Americans, who cause problems at every turn.

The 1930s is usually seen as the time when the **silent era** of Westerns ended, talking pictures became established, and **B Westerns** dominated the theaters. A few higher-budget Westerns were made in the 1930s, such as *The Plainsman* (1936) and *Dodge City* (1939), and the time was right for Westerns to return to the top of the theater bill. Thus, with *Stagecoach* in 1939, John Ford helped establish a new kind of Western, and a new era of Westerns began— the classic era. According to Cawelti (1999), the major difference between most Westerns of the 1930s and the new **classic Western** as seen in *Stagecoach* was that Ford "emphasized the theme of regeneration through the challenge of the wilderness, using spectacular forms of the Western landscape to give symbolic background to the drama" (90). *Stagecoach* was Ford's first film set in the spectacular **Monument Valley** in Arizona. The contrast between the tiny stagecoach, traveling in a straight line across the floor of the valley, and the enormous buttes and mesas towering above developed a clear symbolic meaning of both the redemptive power of landscape and its destructive potential, particularly when populated by savages. As with the **Native Americans** in Ford's earlier Westerns, the **Apaches** of *Stagecoach* are merely representative. They have no human significance. The film began Ford's long association with **John Wayne**.

Throughout the 1940s, Ford devoted much of his attention to Westerns. *My Darling Clementine* (1946)—with its account of the ultimate Western hero, **Wyatt Earp**—is one of the few Ford Westerns to depict actual historical events and people. John Wayne returned to Westerns as the center of Ford's post–World War II **Cavalry Trilogy**: *Fort Apache* (1948), *She Wore a Yellow Ribbon* (1949), and *Rio Grande* (1950). In these films the director began to explore major cultural themes similar to the ways he had in his non-Western films such as *The Grapes of Wrath* (1940), *How Green Was My Valley* (1941), and particularly the combat film *They Were Expendable* (1945).

Ford's films of the 1950s continue a series of critical examinations of contemporary American society and its concept of its past. *The Searchers* (1956) explores the nation's problems with racism in the pre–civil rights era, distancing the issue of black-white relations by treating them through the frontier conflicts between whites and Native Americans.

Throughout these years, Ford's productions took on the aura of a repertory dramatic company as he worked with a fairly stable group of actors in one film after another. John Wayne dominated the top of the credits, but **Henry Fonda** and **Jimmy Stewart** came in and out. **Ward Bond, Harry Carey Jr.**, and **John Carradine** could usually be counted on as well. In fact, Carey dubbed the group the John Ford Stock Company.

Ford's films of the 1960s are nostalgic **end-of-the-West films**. *The Man Who Shot Liberty Valance* (1962) is framed around the death of aging gunfighter Tom Doniphon in the early years of the 20th century. Congressman Ransom Stoddard (Jimmy Stewart) returns to Shinbone, the scene of the turning point in his life many years before, and he finds that his whole life was based on an elaborate deception. The film shows a West that is no more. Another **end-of-the-Western-era** film, *Cheyenne Autumn* (1964), was Ford's attempt at a revisionist Western as he, at the end of his career, portrays Native Americans sympathetically.

As the turbulent decade of the 1960s called into question everything he stood for, John Ford, like his close friend John Wayne, became adamant in his support of nationalistic policies that were unpopular with the majority of the American public. One of his last projects was a documentary urging steadfastness in the war in Vietnam. As a result, John Ford and his Westerns came to represent everything wrong with America. What Ford and Wayne stood for was what the **antimyth Westerns** of **Clint Eastwood** and **Sergio Leone** were repudiating. Ford, then, was to witness the end of the classic era of Westerns that he helped develop. See also DE HAVILLAND, OLIVIA; FLYNN, ERROL.

FORMALIST WESTERNS. Formalist Westerns, a type of **alternative Western** that began appearing after the 1970s, ultimately derive from the **spaghetti Westerns** of **Sergio Leone** and others. The term originates from Richard Slotkin, who identifies **Clint Eastwood**'s *Joe Kidd* (1972) and *High Plains Drifter* (1973) as chief examples. The type features fanciful plots, gunfighter heroes, and bizarre landscapes with little geographical significance or reality. Normative characters play against the stereotypes of **classic Westerns.**

FORMULAS, CLASSIC WESTERN. *The Great Train Robbery* (1903), along with early popular novels such as Owen Wister's *The Virginian* (1902), quickly established the basic formulas for **classic Westerns**. Since the beginning, cinema Westerns, like popular Western novels, have depended heavily on standard formulas to convey the directors' and screenwriters' intended effects. The minute the audience realizes that the film is a Western, it will, because of the standard classic Western formulas, have certain assumptions and expectations about the film. The audience can assume, for example, certain kinds of settings, stock characters, action, plots, and heroes and heroines. Typical formula plots consisted of **revenge** plots, **Chase-and-pursuit** plots, and conflicts between groups (pioneers versus Indians and ranchers versus farmers, for example). The basic elements of the classic Western formula generally consist of the following:

1. Characterization: In the classic Western formulas, the protagonist, or **cowboy hero,** partakes of both the civilized life and the unrestrained life of nature. He is always placed in conflict with antagonists who represent lawlessness, savagery, and evil, and he is always male. Any female interest is always secondary, even when romance is part of the plot. In fact, entertaining romance is usually seen as a weakness in the hero. All important characters on the hero's side are either white or acceptably close to being white. Minorities (**Native American** and Hispanic primarily) are on the antagonist's, or villain's, side. Benign minorities (**African Americans** and Asian Americans) serve in submissive roles.

2. Plot: The classic Western formula plot always begins with action pitting the cowboy hero against a major dilemma that defines his character; it tests his manhood, his moral character, and his commitment (with mixed emotions) toward civilization. Inevitably, there is a **chase-and-pursuit** scene and a showdown. The plot always concludes with a happy ending or at least one in which all conflicts are resolved satisfactorily.

3. Setting: There are not many choices for formula settings. The films are primarily set on the uncivilized frontier, prairie, mountains, or desert. Westerns may also be set in small **towns** or on ranches, but they are never set primarily in the large city, on farms, in pastures (herding sheep), or at the seashore.

Some Westerns fulfill all formula expectations while others, even some classic Westerns, deliberately counter audience expectations, at least to a degree. The formulas also allow one film to resonate with echoes from previous Westerns or previous kinds of Westerns. An appropriate understanding of **Sergio Leone** Westerns or, later, **Sam Peckinpah** Westerns requires a knowledge of classic **John Ford** Westerns.

Antimyth and **alternative Westerns** have worked actively to overturn traditional plot formulas of classic Westerns, arguably because the formulas of the past had become such **clichés** that the Western was in danger of stagnating. *See also* FRONTIER AS ESCAPE FROM THE CITY; BASIC PLOT FORMULAS.

FRENCH CRITICISM. French critics have consistently seemed more appreciative of American cinema Westerns as serious art than have American critics. The French were the first to "write about the Western hero as a frustrated man, who finds needed satisfaction, the 'safety valve,' in releasing charges of his gun, atypical phallic symbol" (Fenin and Everson 1962, 21). They were also some of the first to study the Western as a genre—to identify its characteristics as an art form. Jean Louis Leutrat, in his study of Westerns of the 1920s, claims that the genre did not become pure, or strictly identifiable, as a Western until it broke away from the earlier modes of dramatic presentation—such as melodrama, burlesque, comedy, and so forth—in 1929 with Victor Fleming's version of *The Virginian* (1929). *See also* SUR-WESTERN; *THE VIRGINIAN.*

FRONTIER AS ESCAPE FROM THE CITY. As with other **binary oppositions,** cinema Westerns pose a tension between life in the city, particularly eastern cities, and life outdoors on the frontier. Looming always as a subtext in Westerns is the existence of those cities back East. A **cowboy hero** such as John Bernard Books (**John Wayne**) in *The Shootist* (1976) only comes into the city when he is about to die after spending his life on the frontier. Since most normative characters in Westerns are situated in the lower middle classes, the threat of a return to the city also means the possibility of a return to the ghetto where most frontier types would be if they were part of the city. The frontier serves as an escape from squalid urbanity.

FRONTIER MARSHALS. From 1942 until 1947, **PRC** ran this **Trigger Trio** series with Lee Powell, Bill Boyd, and Art Davis as the marshals. Boyd and Davis were **singing cowboys**, and the movies were heavy on music and light on action. Only six episodes were made. The series ended when Powell went into the military, eventually dying in action in 1944.

FRONTIER THESIS, TURNER'S. The foundational interpretation of Western history through most of the history of cinema Westerns was based upon Frederick Jackson Turner's Frontier Thesis. Turner was a historian who made his reputation in 1893 with a paper delivered at the Chicago World's Fair in which he claimed that the **Western movement** was the single most formative influence upon the American character. Characteristics such as individualism, nationalism, and egalitarianism derived primarily from the frontier experience. Cinema Westerns up until the **post-Western** period, then, celebrated the connection of American character with the Western frontier. But Turner also claimed that the frontier had closed in 1890 and that American history was then forced to move on for the development of its national character. As a result of this concept of the closing of the frontier, Western directors, screenwriters, and novelists all treated the

West as a thing of the past. For their appeal, Westerns depended upon **nostalgia** for what had vanished in America. The **new Western history** of the late 20th century began the process of questioning the validity of Turner's Frontier Thesis. FRONTIER AS ESCAPE FROM THE CITY.

– G –

GAMBLER, PROFESSIONAL. This character type is instantly recognizable in Westerns and is seldom confused with the **cowboy hero**, who also shows skill at cards. The professional gambler, reminiscent of riverboat gamblers prior to the Civil War, dresses and acts like a fine Southern gentleman. He wears a long frock coat and collared shirt with cravat, has a modicum of education, and knows how to treat a lady. Hatfield (**John Carradine**) in **John Ford**'s *Stagecoach* (1939) defines the type. He shows himself to be a ladies' man, and he is treated with respect by Lucy Mallory (Louise Platt), the officer's wife and the one real lady onboard. Nevertheless, something is never quite right with Hatfield and he can only be trusted to a point. John Carradine made a career playing professional gamblers. *See also* CARD PLAY AND THE COWBOY HERO.

GAMES, WESTERNS AS. Following early studies in game theory by such writers as Johan Huizinga, critics have frequently associated Westerns with games, and the old children's game of cowboys and Indians reinforces the theory. Westerns, the premise goes, are played out on an elaborate playground laid out with specific boundaries. The playground is the trans-Mississippi **Great Plains**. The basic game is played out by designated participants: the **cowboy hero** (designated by a white hat); the **outlaw** nemesis (designated by a black hat); savage Indians; townspeople; and dark-haired **dance hall girls** and blonde, virtuous women (both of whom seek in different ways to emasculate the hero). The game is played according to clearly understood rules based on the intricacies of the **code of the West**. The cowboy hero is strictly bound to the rules and must win the game by playing by those rules. The outlaw nemesis and the savage Indian are under far fewer restraints, though even the outlaw may begrudgingly refuse to draw first and the Indians never attack at night. The game is subject to endless variations in cinema Westerns. *See also* INDIANS.

GANG OF ROSES (2003). Jean-Claude La Marre (director). This **postmodern Western**—or as La Marre calls it, a revisionist, hip-hop Western—revolves around four tough, fast-shooting **women**, three **African Americans** and one Asian, setting out on the trail of vengeance for a gang who murdered Rachel's (Monica Calhoun) sister. The women have a history of robbing banks and are known as the gang of roses. The plot matters little, however, since the focus is on the urban style with which the women carry themselves. Popular hip-hop singer Lil' Kim plays one of the gang members and hip hop plays on the soundtrack. The film is usually associated with *Brothers in Arms* (2005), also directed by Jean-Claude La Marre. *See also* HISTORICAL AUTHENTICITY; PUNK WESTERNS.

GARNER, JAMES (1928–). Born James Baumgarner in Oklahoma, James Garner developed a persona in the 1960s as a devilishly handsome, worldly wise **cowboy hero** with a suave yet cynical sense of humor. Whatever role he took, Garner inevitably turned it to laughs. He began his career in Westerns with the highly popular **television Western** *Maverick*. Garner's best film Western was probably the comedy *Support Your Local Sheriff* (1969), which was followed a few years later with *Support Your Local Gunfighter* (1971). When Mel Gibson reprised Garner's old television role in the film *Maverick* (1994), Garner played a prominent role in the film. James Garner has made a long career in film and television and is still very active in numerous film projects.

GENRE-BASED MYTHOLOGY. This term originates with Richard Slotkin and refers to the way a genre, such as Westerns, through repeated formulaic depictions, contributes to a cultural mythology. Westerns, which have developed their own codes, stock characters, standardized plots, and cinematic and narrative conventions, and which bear only an indirect relation to authentic history, nevertheless have created the accepted meta-narrative of the old West. This meta-narrative has influenced U.S. foreign policy during the Ronald Reagan and both Bush presidencies and has become foundational to the

American public image. Yet virtually all of this mythology is based not on history but on interpretation of history through, primarily, cinema Westerns.

GENRE FILMS AND WESTERNS. The **classic Western** differs from other popular genre films in several ways. It differs because of the symbolic **landscape** in which the Western takes place and because of its influence on the character and actions of the hero. Detective or gangster fiction is usually characterized by the quality of the action. Romance and horror fiction, on the other hand, is usually characterized by the quality of the mood. Classic cinema Westerns, in contrast, are characterized by the protagonist's action in relation to the symbolic landscape.

GERONIMO: AN AMERICAN LEGEND **(1993).** Wes Studi, Jason Patric, **Robert Duvall**, **Gene Hackman**, Matt Damon, Walter Hill (director). Although Walter Hill's *Geronimo* did not do as well at the box office as it deserved, this **alternative Western** film is a major contribution to the Western genre. For the first time, the legendary story of Geronimo is told through **Apache** eyes. Wes Studi played the famous warrior in what was probably his best acting role. Gene Hackman played the infamous General George S. Crook who, despite being a lifelong **Indian** killer, has in the end developed a measure of respect for the Apache chief, at least the respect of one warrior for another. The Apaches fight ferociously to avoid being shipped to a reservation in **Indian Territory**. Only with the help of renegade Apache scouts can the U.S. Cavalry finally hunt down Geronimo and pressure him to surrender. The United States promises the Apaches a reservation in central Florida instead of Indian Territory, and as soon as the Apaches surrender, they are rounded up along with the renegade Apaches who cooperated with the army. Unfortunately for the Apaches, the U.S. government finds that the Florida land is too valuable for Indians and ships them to Indian Territory after all. John G. Cawelti sees this film as a more complex treatment of **Native American** history than *Dances With Wolves* (1990) because it "suggests that the destruction of the Apache culture was not only a betrayal but a historical tragedy" (1999, 108). *See also* INDIANS.

GIBSON, HOOT (1892–1962). Born Edmund Richard Gibson in Nebraska, Hoot Gibson developed a persona of a lighthearted, folksy cowboy who could ride like a rodeo champion—because he was a rodeo champion, having been declared World's All Around Champion Cowboy in 1922. He worked very much in the **Tom Mix** tradition. *Chip of the Flying U* (1926), in fact, is a remake of a Mix film of the same title, both based on B. M. Bower's best-selling novel. In *A Man's Land* (1932), Gibson played a ranch foreman who has inherited a half share in the Triple X ranch. Marion Shilling played the daughter of the original owner who owns the other share. **Adele S. Buffington**'s script keeps Gibson's character on his toes as he must deal with rustlers as well as his new partner's eastern ideas of ranch life. As with other early Western stars, Gibson continued acting in character roles long after his days at the top of the bill. His last Western was **John Ford**'s *The Horse Soldiers* (1959).

GLANCE (AIMLESS GLANCE OF COWBOY HERO). This term originates with Umberto Echo and refers to the stylistic convention of the hero's laconic facial expressions in the face of danger. **Clint Eastwood** in particular, in the **Sergio Leone** Westerns, casts about that expressionless look in which all emotion is conveyed by a certain glint of the eyes. But nearly all the regular **cowboy heroes,** from **William S. Hart** to the **singing cowboys** to **Kevin Costner** in *Open Range* (2003), take that short pause before the camera for a sideways look at the implications of the moment. The glance is not to be confused with the **male gaze**, for the glance is something the actor does while the gaze is something the audience does.

***THE GOOD, THE BAD AND THE UGLY (BUONO, IL BRUTTO, IL CATTIVO, IL)* (1966).** **Clint Eastwood**, Eli Wallach, **Lee Van Cleef**, **Ennio Morricone** (music), **Sergio Leone** (director). This is the final film in the **Dollars Trilogy**, preceded by *A Fistful of Dollars* and *For a Few Dollars More*. Three men—Blondie (Eastwood), Angel Eyes (Van Cleef), and Tuco (Wallach)—search for hidden gold during the Civil War, eventually squaring off in a graveyard. Each represents, respectively, the good, the bad, and the ugly. This **spaghetti Western** continues Sergio Leone's redefinition of the

Western myth, particularly as it relates to ideas of heroism, moral **regeneration through violence**, good and evil. The only thing that matters is the different ways in which killing is accomplished; *why* one kills is not important. Against the confusion of the Civil War, the three characters seek only self-enrichment. Loyalty to anything outside themselves does not exist. Morality is based solely on the attitude of the killers: the look of satisfaction "on the face of Van Cleef as he murders, and the impassivity of Clint Eastwood's expression as he does the same" (Calder 1975, 33). *See also* DOLLARS TRILOGY.

GRAND NATIONAL PICTURES. After **Mascot Pictures'** success with **Gene Autry** and the new **singing cowboy** movies in the early 1930s, Edward F. Finney, a film publicist with a lengthy résumé, decided to capitalize on the emerging trend of musical Westerns for the new Grand National Pictures company. After scouting and screen testing, Finney settled on radio singer **Tex Ritter** as his new singing cowboy and signed Ritter to a five-year contract of eight films a year at $2,400 per film. The company had a very short existence, from 1935 to 1940.

GREAT PLAINS, SYMBOLIC SIGNIFICANCE OF. Classic Westerns have generally preferred settings on the Great Plains of the United States, the area that extends east and west between the Mississippi River and the Rocky Mountains, and north and south from the Dakotas to central Texas. If **landscape** in general is used in cinema Westerns to isolate and intensify conflicts between order and lawlessness, then the plains fit the cinematographer's dream. The vast stretches of arid land inhospitable to any kind of life, wildlife as well as human, provide perfect visual **symbolism. Towns** are isolated and railroads stretch for miles without interruption.

THE GREAT TRAIN ROBBERY **(1903).** Edwin S. Porter (director). Essentially, this was the first narrative film—the first moving picture that related a fictional story—and it was the first Western. It was produced by Edison and Company. Perhaps the most memorable moment of the film occurs at the end of the last scene. The robbery is completed. The bandits are caught. Suddenly, on-screen and looking directly at the audience, one of the **outlaws** points a gun at the audience and fires. For the original audience, this action probably had the same effect that I-Max films have today when they send us on roller coaster rides or drop us out of airplanes. Even this early in the **silent** film era, the last scene is color tinted.

Among the curiosities of this production is the fact that Porter would have considered a Western for the subject of this experimental film. After all, it was 1903 and he filmed a "Western" from an eastern perspective. There is nothing about this film that is Western, other than the suggested geographical setting, which is actually New Jersey. What makes this more than just a very recent train robbery in New Jersey?

As far as the film's narrative goes, it is purely a vignette. There is no character development, no motivation. Despite the fact that the money being stolen from the train presumably belongs to corporate interests, the ordinary folk seem deeply concerned that the robbers be caught, which says much about the political focus of the film. After all, why should it matter to the townspeople? The robbery also involves a murder, but one might wonder if Porter has the passenger killed primarily to deflect sympathy. Nevertheless, with this film, cinema Westerns were invented. *See also* ANDERSON, BRONCHO BILLY; *BUTCH CASSIDY AND THE SUNDANCE KID*; FORD, JOHN; STUNTS.

GREENWALD, MAGGIE (1955–). Since the 1980s, Maggie Greenwald has worked behind the cameras in numerous roles. Her work is unapologetically feminist and her **feminist Western**, *The Ballad of Little Jo* (1993), sought to change the way Westerns portray **women**. The film examines the unspoken facts of life for women in the West. A woman with a tarnished reputation had no chance for survival except as a prostitute. Jo Monaghan (**Suzy Amis**), banished by her family after being raped, becoming pregnant, and delivering an out-of-wedlock child, determines another route of survival: she cross-dresses and succeeds in passing as a man in a frontier community for many years. Greenwald, whose directing has been mainly for television, presents a domestic tale set in the West that has little of the grand panorama expected from a **classic Western**. *See also* FRONTIER AS ESCAPE FROM THE CITY.

GREY, ZANE (1872–1939). Zane Grey was one of the earliest writers of Western fiction to publish best sellers on a regular basis. Building on the tradition of **formula Westerns** established by Owen Wister, Grey wrote over 90 popular novels, mostly Westerns. For many, Zane Grey's name was synonymous with pulp Westerns for much of the 20th century. Not surprisingly, many of his novels were made into films. Four versions of *Riders of the Purple Sage*, Grey's most popular novel, have been made—in 1918, 1925, 1931, and 1996. Grey's direct involvement with the film industry came in 1919 when he formed Zane Grey Productions, a short-lived company that was a forerunner of Paramount Pictures. Perhaps the most famous Zane Grey film, Fritz Lang's 1941 *Western Union*, which was billed as "Zane Grey's *Western Union*," is actually based on an original studio screenplay. No book had been written, and Grey himself had died two years earlier. The studio adopted the Zane Grey name for marketing purposes. After the film's release, a novelization of the film was also marketed as if written by Grey himself. About 55 films are based on Grey novels, the most recent in 1996.

GRIFFITH, D. W. (1875–1948). Griffith is often seen as the inventor of cinema mythographic narrative with his epic *The Birth of a Nation* (1915). Prior to 1915, however, Griffith made numerous one- and two-reel Westerns: "The scores of one- and two-reel films Griffith produced between 1908 and 1914 (including several Westerns) were technically inventive and increasingly sophisticated in form, but as narratives they were little more than kinetic dime novels" (Slotkin 1992, 238). *The Birth of a Nation*, while not a Western, was the first great cinema epic and as such showed how cinema could be used for portraying the grand myths of the nation. Unfortunately, Griffith's film is nearly unwatchable today due to its extreme racist content. Equally unfortunate is the fact that the film was instrumental in establishing a theme that would be foundational to the developing **myth of the West**—the idea that in one sense the struggle between whites and **African Americans** is a struggle to save the body of a white woman from the inevitable sexual depredations of black men, a struggle against "a fate worse than death." In *The Birth of a Nation*, when a white woman is raped by a black man, her only recourse is to commit suicide. Westerns after the **silent era** often substitute the black-white struggle with the Indian–white man struggle. *See also* INDIANS; *THE SEARCHERS*.

GUN BELTS. Through the years, the cowboy star's gun belt has changed very little—a single gun in its holster with a full supply of cartridges. The leather thong across the hammer holding the gun in the holster was almost never seen on film until more recent **alternative Westerns**, despite the fact that pistols do not stay in their holsters during deadly **fistfights** and **stunt** horse-riding feats. **William S. Hart** always wore a Mexican sash under his gun belt. Fred Thompson wore an all-white affair. **Bill Elliott** wore his pistols butt forward, facilitating a spectacular cross draw.

Some **symbolism** of the gun belt has developed through the years. A string or cord holding the holster to the leg, making a quick draw a bit faster, usually signals a professional **gunfighter**. The **cowboy hero**, however, eschews the tie-down because it indicates a bit too much willingness to kill. Whether a hero wears one gun or two guns sometimes indicates proficiency and seriousness of purpose. Left-handed gun belts often code masculine **homoeroticism**.

***GUNFIGHT AT THE O.K. CORRAL* (1957). Burt Lancaser, Kirk Douglas**, Dennis Hopper, Jo Van Fleet, Dimitri Tiomkin (music), John Sturges (director). By 1956 the **classic Western** had about run its course, though it would not die easily. This high-budget Western with huge star power is the quintessential Western story, but it is also a textbook model of the decayed classic Western. There are no shades of right and wrong here (Lancaster does wear a black hat, however), and every **cliché** that all the **B Westerns** ostensibly exploit winds up in this film as well: saloons, gamblers, easily provoked gunfights, **dance hall girls**—there is little in this film that is not a cliché.

Wyatt Earp (Lancaster) is a clean-shaven, slim, athletic town marshal for the civilized side of **Dodge City, Kansas**. He runs a clean town: no guns allowed under any circumstances. Across town, however, is utter chaos and anarchy—visualized in one scene as **Doc Holliday** (Douglas) rides down a street full of saloons, gun shots in the air, and prostitutes everywhere. Wyatt is the bulwark against confusion. At one point, rowdy cowboys led by Shanghai Pierce (Ted de Corsia) burst into a civilized church dance. Chaos threatens order but the "preacher" (Wyatt's nickname) manages to get the upper hand and restore order. Even among the good, however, it is possible for life to spin out of control. Thus the subplot, which concerns Doc and his hacking cough, a **professional gambler**, and Doc's girl (Van Fleet). In Fort Griffin Doc gets in trouble and Wyatt saves his skin. Later Doc comes to Dodge and despite situations that call into question every ounce of his masculinity (at one point, Johnny Ringo [John Ireland] throws whisky in his face and taunts him), Doc keeps his pledge to Wyatt to avoid gunplay.

Into the peaceful town comes Laura (Rhonda Fleming), a female gambler. Manly Wyatt jails her to protect the town from such women, but everyone falls in love with her—including Wyatt, thereby threatening his manhood. Wyatt resigns his post and packs his things for California. But word comes from his three brothers in Tombstone, Arizona; they need him desperately. Laura begs him not to go, and he must choose—loyalty to his brothers or loyalty to a woman, his fiancée. He makes the right choice by **code-of-the-West** standards, and heads for Arizona, Doc accompanying him.

Wyatt and Holliday land in Tombstone, and after some preliminary scrapes, they eventually shoot it out at the corral against the Clantons, Johnny Ringo, and the McLowerys (including **Jack Elam**)—four against six. Young Billy Clanton (Dennis Hopper) has a good heart and is ready to reform, but as with Wyatt and his brothers, he must choose family loyalty over all else. Wyatt regretfully plugs young Billy to finish the fight. All is reconciled and Wyatt again heads to California. He hopes Laura will be waiting for him; the audience knows she is.

One unexplainable element of the plot is Doc's girl—Kate Fisher (not Kate Elder as in other versions). She is a lush who is frantically, desperately dependent on Doc, who treats her—as he says himself—like trash. He abuses her horribly, but she still remains loyal to him at the end. Ultimately, we must ask whether she is any different from Wyatt's much more respectable girl. Kate is played by Academy Award–winner from the previous year, Jo Van Fleet, who nearly steals the show with her superior acting performance.

This is a feel-good movie. Good triumphs over evil once again. Men must do their duty and women must accept that; it is very reassuring. The soundtrack with its famous theme song by Dimitri

Tiomkin has probably become more memorable than the movie itself.

GUNFIGHTER, SOCIAL ROLE OF. Gunfighters are an essential part of the culture of the world of cinema Westerns, but their social role is always suspect, always ambiguous. In **classic Westerns**, gunfighters are always men. The **code of the West** justifies gun fighting if played according to the rules: (1) the gunfighter must never draw his gun first; (2) he must never shoot another without giving the person a fair, fighting chance; and (3) he always looks the other in the eye when he draws. The gunfighter is not an outlaw. However, all Westerns look to the future and to the steady encroachment of **civilization**—to the day when men and women cannot live by the code of the West. In the new order, the gunfighter is taking the law into his own hands. He is a man torn between the old order and the new.

In film after film, the **town**, which one day will criminalize the gunfighter's activities, needs him badly. The gunfighter himself often has an ambivalent attitude toward his role. Some like Shane regret that they used to live by the gun. Others such as Will Munny (*Unforgiven*) feel like they had no choice in their role. Whatever the case, the town's reaction toward the gunfighter is always, first, repulsion, and then tentative acceptance. Usually, though, there is little gratitude for his services. *See also HIGH NOON; SHANE; UNFORGIVEN; GAMES, WESTERNS AS.*

– H –

HACKMAN, GENE (1930–). Born in California, Gene Hackman has made his reputation in Westerns playing some of the nastiest villains imaginable. After beginning his career in television, he got his break in Hollywood playing Clyde's brother in *Bonnie and Clyde* (1967), for which he was nominated for an Academy Award. The 1990s was the decade for all of Hackman's Western roles. He won his second Academy Award for his role as Little Bill Daggett in **Clint Eastwood**'s *Unforgiven* (1992). Daggett is a petty, vicious, corrupt sheriff who rules his town as a tyrant. In *Geronimo: An American Legend* (1993), Hackman played U.S. Cavalry general George S. Crook, a role in which he can sympathize with the plight of Geronimo. In *Wyatt Earp* (1994), Hackman played Earp's overbearing father, and in *The Quick and the Dead* (1995), he reprised his role from *Unforgiven* as Herod, Redemption's town boss who, again, rules as a tyrant. Altogether, Gene Hackman has been nominated five times for Academy Awards and has won twice.

HAMMAN, JOË (1885–1974). Joë Hamman was a longtime French actor and director. Early in his career, Hamman played the popular cowboy called Arizona Bill in French **silent** Westerns. In *Pendaison à Jefferson City (Hanging at Jefferson City)* (1910), Bill dismounts a huge horse and walks into a saloon wearing a small-billed hat that he could have worn anywhere around the French countryside. Everyone is dressed in simple peasant clothing. Very little in the film indicates that it is a Western.

HARRIS, RICHARD (1930–2002). Even though he has been associated primarily with non-western roles, such as King Arthur in the musical *Camelot* (1967) and Dumbledore in the Harry Potter films, Richard Harris, twice nominated for the best actor Academy Award, was prominent in Westerns throughout the last half of the 20th century. In *A Man Called Horse* (1970), Harris played an English aristocrat forced through captivity to adopt the ways of the Sioux—probably his best performance in a film involving some of the most brutal scenes of torture and initiation rites of any Western ever made. In **Clint Eastwood**'s *Unforgiven* (1992), Harris plays English Bob, a pulp writer trying to glamorize the West. He meets his end in another exceptionally violent episode. Harris's other Westerns include *Major Dundee* (1965), *Man in the Wilderness* (1971), *The Deadly Trackers* (1973), *The Return of a Man Called Horse* (1976), *Triumphs of a Man called Horse* (1982), and *Silent Tongue* (1994).

HART, MARY (1919–1978). Born Lynne Roberts in El Paso, Texas, Hart is probably best remembered as the first of **Roy Rogers**'s leading ladies in **Republic** films, appearing in seven Rogers pictures from 1938–1939. She began making films under her own name in 1937, appearing in a **Three Mesquiteer** film, among others. But when she was paired with Rogers, Republic changed her name from

Lynne Roberts to Mary Hart in order to bill the films as Rogers-Hart films, based on the much more famous Broadway composers' names.

In all seven Rogers films, Hart generally played traditional, submissive roles. Rarely were her characters integral to the plot. Like other female stars of **B Westerns**, her main function was visual—to be the central shot while Rogers was singing. Only in one film, *Billy the Kid Returns* (1938), did her character actually have a job—as a clerk in her father's store. In *Rough Riders' Roundup* (1939), Hart's character defies her father's will and elopes, but in so doing, she merely changes from dependent daughter to dependent wife.

Hart's best acting, however, was not in a Roy Rogers film, and she performed the role under her real name, Lynne Roberts. In *Eyes of Texas* (1948), Hart broke away from the traditional roles of her previous films and played a strong-willed, independent woman—a nurse not concerned with pleasing the males in her life. Her role was integral to the plot as her character undergoes a treacherous mission and helps capture the villains of the film. Thereafter Lynn Roberts/Mary Hart appeared in several non-Westerns, making her last film in 1953.

HART, WILLIAM S. (1864–1946). After **Broncho Billy Anderson**, William S. Hart was the second great Western star, and he had an influence on the genre far beyond the **silent era**. Born in New York, Hart set out early to travel the West and learn from the quickly fading frontier. Returning to New York, he began his acting career at age 19 and quickly developed a reputation as a Shakespearean actor; legend had it that his middle initial stood for Shakespeare (it actually stood for Surrey). Roles on the New York stage included *The Virginian* and *Trail of the Lonesome Pine*, but what brought Hart his break was his role as Messala in the stage version of *Ben Hur*. In 1907 he reprised the role on film. By 1915 **Thomas Ince** was putting Hart in his Westerns, and Hart made the move from New York to Hollywood with Ince's company. Eventually, he directed and oversaw all production of his own films. Fritz, his faithful cowpony, was part of Hart's team from the beginning in *The Bargain* (1914).

Hart's own experiences in the West motivated him to portray an authentic West with real cowboys, not the streamlined version of the West he saw in films being made at the time. Gritty reality was what he pursued, and what one notices today when watching an old Hart

Western is the dark interiors lit by flaming lamps (easily and often ignited) and **dust** all over the streets and exterior scenes. Hart tried as often as practical to have actors with real experience, so he hired **Native Americans** to play Indians, and he sought out real **gamblers**, **dance hall girls**, and prostitutes.

Hell's Hinges (1916) is usually considered Hart's finest film, certainly his most complex. Though it is an early film, *Hell's Hinges* displays the persona that Hart would carry throughout his work—that of the good badman. He nearly always played a character who at the beginning of the film was considered an outlaw, a desperado, or, as in *Hell's Hinges'* Blaze Tracy, just a flat-out bad man. Yet no one is so depraved that he or she cannot be redeemed. And in a Hart film, redemption for the hero is found at the hands of a beautiful woman. Blaze Tracy's salvation comes not from the preacher but from the preacher's beautiful yet virtuous sister, Faith Henley (Clara Williams). In *The Toll Gate* (1920), Black Deering's (Hart) redemption comes at the hand of a child and his mother. The desperado on the run knows that if he stays to rescue a child from drowning he will be caught. He saves the child and the mother pledges her gratitude to him just as the posse arrives. *Tumbleweeds* (1925), Hart's last film and probably his most ambitious, takes place during the Oklahoma Land Rush. Scenes from the wagons, horses, and settlers racing across the prairie were raided for **stock footage** countless times throughout the ensuing decades.

Hart was a visionary filmmaker, exercising complete control over all his productions, and he had as his goal to promote a philosophy in the essential goodness of humanity. He did this by portraying a dark, grim picture of the frontier as a force that can destroy or build character. Each of his films developed from early scenes of tension to increasingly more violent scenes, culminating with a final shootout. The gunplay was much more realistic than would be seen in Westerns for many decades, and the violence was pure; it redeemed the hero and it redeemed the world of the film. For Hart, the masculine **code of the West** was a definitive code of behavior. No deviation from the code was ever acceptable.

Historical authenticity was Hart's trademark. He had lived in the West. He knew what the real old West was like, or so he claimed. **Wyatt Earp** and **Al Jennings** were consultants on his films. His **cos-**

tumes were what real cowboys wore—sparse, dirty, and practical. Occasionally he wore a frock coat that was dispensed with early on. Pants held up by braces were unglamorously stuffed into the tops of scuffed working boots. Beneath his gun belt he wore a Mexican sash, the belt itself slung low with huge revolvers protruding outward. But above all else was the William S. Hart grim look of determination that defined his character. Underneath a large black hat with high crown and wide, flat brim was that sparse, lean face with parallel lines and the most forbidding facial features of any of the later Western stars.

Westerns in the succeeding decades went in several directions. Streamlined **B Westerns** dressed up the West in strange and utterly inauthentic ways. **Classic Westerns** asserted the glorious American ideals of **Manifest Destiny** and masculine supremacy. Hart's dark vision, though, reemerged in the late classic Westerns of **Anthony Mann** and **Budd Boetticher** as well as in the **alternative Westerns** at the end of the century.

Hart never tried to move from the silents to the talkies. By the time of his last film in 1925, his popularity was being eclipsed by **Tom Mix** and a new breed of cowboy stars. But in 1935 Hart finally talked to his fans. The occasion was the re-release of *Tumbleweeds*, the silent picture showing once again in theaters to fans now accustomed to sound. At his Newhall ranch in California, Hart filmed a prologue in which he addressed his fans directly. He came forward walking Fritz, paused, and then began his thank you to his fans of old. As Hart introduced the film, he reasserted his basic vision of the redemptive powers of the West. Then he waved goodbye as he and Fritz walked away over the horizon. *See also* DUST; FRONTIER AS ESCAPE FROM THE CITY; REGENERATION THROUGH VIOLENCE; STUNTS; *THE VIRGINIAN*.

HAWKS, HOWARD (1896–1977). Born in Indiana but raised in Southern California, Howard Hawks, along with **John Ford**, was one of the most dominant film directors of the 20th century. His education at Cornell, was in engineering, and during World War I he flew planes for the U.S. Army. Both experiences helped form his interests behind the camera. He worked in a variety of off-set capacities throughout the 1920s and began directing in 1926. While Hawks directed some of the finest Westerns ever, he also worked in a wide range of genres. He assisted in directing Westerns such as *Viva Villa!* (1934) and ***The Outlaw*** (1943) before directing what many consider his most famous Western ***Red River*** (1948), with **John Wayne**. Wayne also starred in most of Hawks's other Westerns, including *Rio Bravo* (1959), *El Dorado* (1967), and *Rio Lobo* (1970). Reportedly, Hawks was so disgusted with the success of ***High Noon*** (1952)—because of its pro-communist tendencies and because it lacked masculinity—that he responded with *Rio Bravo* (1959).

HAYES, GEORGE S. "GABBY" (1885–1969). For most older fans of Westerns, Gabby Hayes epitomized what a **cowboy hero**'s **sidekick** was all about. Gray haired, bewhiskered, toothless, and prone to saying plenty of "Gosh, darns"—this pretty well sums up Hayes's role in over 200 Westerns. He actually began his career playing the heavy and occasionally appeared as the villain well after the sidekick roles began. As a heavy he was usually clean shaven and was billed as George Hayes. Despite his on-screen persona as a comic old-timer, Hayes in real life cultivated an opposite image—a man of educated, sophisticated tastes. For that reason, perhaps, Hayes commonly played a character who suddenly becomes rich and then, in the next scene, dresses up and carries on snobbish airs, as in *Bad Man of Deadwood* (1941).

The character of Gabby Hayes evolved over a period of years. Early on George Hayes appeared opposite Ken Maynard, Bob Steele, and **John Wayne**, but he had yet to find a very distinct persona. Later he became Windy Holiday for several **Hopalong Cassidy** pictures, and the Gabby Hayes look started to take shape. Then he teamed with **Roy Rogers,** beginning in *Wall Street Cowboy* (1939), and became Gabby Whittaker, Rogers's sidekick, through 1946. Throughout the 1940s Hayes was ranked as one of the top-ten Western money makers by *Motion Picture Herald*. Raymond E. White notes, "While Hayes' popularity was based on 'Gabby,' it was also tied to Roy Rogers. The two actors made more than 40 films together, and in the stories 'Gabby' Hayes enlarged upon Roy Rogers' role as a Western hero, often attributing superhuman qualities to him. Hayes enhancement of Rogers' heroic attributes in the films in turn amplified Rogers off-screen image as an American Cowboy Hero" (Yoggy 1998, 84).

George Hayes did play in several A Westerns. His best acting performance was in Cecil B. DeMille's *The Plainsman* (1936). After the end of the **B Western** era, like others he turned to **television Westerns** and even had his own show for several years. For a time he advertised Popsicle treats, making a prominent popping noise with his mouth.

HELL'S HINGES (1916). William S. Hart, Charles Swickard (director). Usually seen as Hart's most complex film, *Hell's Hinges* follows the standard Hart formula of a bad man being redeemed by a virtuous woman. The story follows a preacher of weak character sent West with his sister to Hell's Hinges, a town desperately in need of saving. Blaze Tracy (Hart) leads the bad element of the town in making life miserable for the preacher and his new church. The preacher succumbs to every temptation, but his sister, Faith (Clara Williams), persists in the vision to establish the church. In the end, as the purifying flames destroy Hell's Hinges, Blaze and Faith ride away to another day. The film, then, is a "fable of redemption through immersion in the wilderness that lies at the heart of the Myth of the Frontier" (Slotkin 1992, 246). *See also* MYTH OF THE WEST; REGENERATION THROUGH VIOLENCE.

HICKOK, WILD BILL (1837–1876). James Butler Hickok was one of the most colorful lawmen in the old West, celebrated in numerous Western films. The real Wild Bill knew how to develop an image and a persona as well as any of the film stars who later played his part. Nearly every fan of cinema Westerns knows the Hickok image: the long flowing hair over the shoulders, the handlebar mustache, the frock coat, the oversized Ned Buntline specials low slung in his **gun belt**. Hickok was a town-taming lawman, first taming **Abilene, Kansas**, at the height of the cattle boom, then moving down to **Dodge City**. Hickok was a showman himself, actually teaming up with Buffalo Bill Cody in a touring theatrical company for a while. **Calamity Jane** is usually associated with Wild Bill in most versions of the story. His death in **Deadwood, South Dakota**, on August 2, 1876, is one of the most famous in Western lore. He was sitting in a saloon playing poker, holding aces and eights—the dead man's hand—when Jack McCall walked up behind him, placed a gun to his head, and fired. Many film versions of Wild Bill's life have been produced through the years. Perhaps the most notable is *The Plainsman* (1936) with **Gary Cooper** as Wild Bill.

HIGH NOON (1952). Gary Cooper, Grace Kelly, Katy Jurado, Lloyd Bridges, Tex Ritter (theme song), Fred Zinnemann (director). Released in 1952 at the height of anti-Communist paranoia in the United States, *High Noon* was almost immediately associated with those who were unpatriotic. Will Kane (Cooper), former sheriff, has just married Amy (Kelly), a young Quaker girl and, hence, a pacifist. The wedding is barely over when word comes that Frank Miller (Ian MacDonald) has been released from prison and is returning to town on the noon train—to get the sheriff. However, Kane is no longer sheriff, so others will have to take care of the problem. Kane leaves on his honeymoon with Amy, but at the edge of town he stops the buggy, thinking it is not right for him to leave. Amy begs him to continue, but Will cannot. Everything about who he is as a man says he cannot back down from Frank Miller. So he rejects his bride and returns to town to try to gather a citizens group to help. He goes to the church. He goes to the saloon. He asks old friends. But no one will help him, not even his young deputy. The music becomes more intense. Time is running out, and it looks like Will Kane will have to face Miller and his rowdies (including **Jack Elam**) alone at high noon. The film plays out, and everywhere Will goes he sees a clock ticking down the minutes. The subplot involves Kane's former lover Helen (Jurado) deliberately inflaming Amy's jealousy so that Amy will help her husband. *High Noon* is probably the best of the cold war Westerns. *See also* CODE OF THE WEST.

HIGH PLAINS DRIFTER (1973). Clint Eastwood, Verna Bloom, Marianna Hill, Clint Eastwood (director). A small **town** in the far North is beset by a band of **outlaws**. The townspeople turn to The Stranger (Eastwood) for protection, a man who has ridden into town out of nowhere. He sneers at their desperate pleas for help but eventually agrees to prepare the town—but only on his own terms. It turns out that years before, The Stranger had been a victim of both the gang coming in from prison and the town itself.

High Plains Drifter was Clint Eastwood's first Western as director. Unlike his **spaghetti Westerns** set in Mexican deserts replete with images of **dust** and desolation, this film is set in the northern desert at the base of snow-capped mountains. It is a classic **revenge Western**. The Stranger, still a Man with No Name, is consumed with unexamined lust for revenge against both the townspeople who hire him and the gang that humiliated him in the past. Eastwood leaves no question that the town deserves the complete destruction wrought on it at the end. All townspeople are hypocrites; the whore is no worse than the preacher. Only the hotel owner's wife represents normative values, but hers is a minor role and we never know if her values are the same as The Stranger's. The destruction and purification of the town by fire is reminiscent of ***Hell's Hinges*** (1916). *See also* FORMALIST WESTERNS; HART, WILLIAM S.

HILL, TERENCE (1939–). *See* TRINITY SERIES.

HIRED GUNS. Perhaps the most common villain in Westerns is the gunslinger who works for hire, usually at the behest of a wealthy patron who needs to clean out some undesirables. ***The Wild Bunch*** (1969) and ***The Magnificent Seven*** (1960) represent films in which groups of hired guns work together. Italian films such as **Sergio Leone**'s *Once Upon a Time in the West* (1968) exploit the character as all sides of the conflicts are peopled by hired guns. Typically, the character is mercenary, ruthless, and efficient in his killing ability. The twist on the character comes in films about retired hired guns, films like ***Shane*** (1953) and *The Shootist* (1976), where the gunman tries to hang up his guns but cannot.

HISTORICAL AUTHENTICITY. From the time of Buffalo Bill's Wild West show to the present, the relationship between dramatic presentations and the facts of the historical West has been problematic. Westerns in cinema have been around for far longer than the historical post–Civil War "western" period, which roughly lasted from 1865 to 1890. Questions naturally arise as to how much of what is perceived as authentic history really comes from conventions established by cinema Westerns through the decades. **Wyatt Earp**, for example, lived out his last years in Hollywood, dying in 1929, and he regularly served as a consultant on Western films. But the facts of the Earp legend, as well as details about characters such as **Doc Holliday**, the Earp brothers, Tombstone, **Dodge City**, and the gunfight at the **O.K. Corral,** are murky because nearly all that we assume we know comes from the one source—Wyatt Earp—who had a reputation to build and spin a tale when it suited him.

But other questions of authenticity arise as well. The relationship of the Western to history is perhaps more important in defining what a Western is than even geography. We are always aware as we watch a Western that we are witnessing events that ostensibly transpired in the **Western moment**. The degree to which a film is historically authentic regarding geography, **costume**, politics, weaponry, and other matters often becomes, for some, a major factor in evaluating the quality of a film. Directors such as **William S. Hart**, **John Ford**, and **Kevin Costner,** in their respective periods, tended to emphasize authenticity. **B Westerns** and **spaghetti Westerns**, on the other hand, rarely respected authenticity.

Authenticity, however, should not be confused with **realism**. A Western film such as *Hondo* (1953) might be relatively authentic yet not be realistic. Authenticity is often a superficial replication of known history and may bear little relation to the realism of human nature.

HOLDEN, WILLIAM (1918–1981). Born William Franklin Beedle Jr., William Holden early on played the stereotypical good-looking **cowboy hero** types, several times with **Glenn Ford**, but in his later and better films he played mature, worldly-wise, and ambivalent roles. In **Sam Peckinpah**'s *The Wild Bunch* (1969), for example, his Pike Bishop character is the main protagonist, yet he is ruthless, lawless, and cruel. His first Western was *Arizona* (1940), with **Jean Arthur** as his love interest. But his best Westerns were ensemble films where he was the leader of a group of men with some objective, films such as *The Horse Soldiers* (1959), *The Wild Bunch*, *Wild Rovers* (1971), and *The Revengers* (1972). William Holden was nominated three times for best actor and won the award once.

HOLLIDAY, DOC (1851–1887). John Henry (Doc) Holliday was a **gunfighter** and friend of **Wyatt Earp** and his brothers. As portrayed in Western movies, the basic elements of Doc's story usually have him as a dentist who came West due to his poor health. He is dying of tuberculosis and in most films has a tell-tale cough. His relationship with Wyatt is usually stormy, but they remain friends to the end. His girl is Big Nose Kate, or sometimes Katie Elder (though not the Katie Elder of *The Sons of Katie Elder* [1965]). He usually is associated with the Earps in **Dodge City, Kansas**; Fort Griffith, Texas; and Tombstone, Arizona, where he helps the Earps defeat the Clanton gang at a shootout at the **O.K. Corral**. Important films featuring Doc Holliday include **John Ford**'s *My Darling Clementine* (1946), John Sturges's *Gunfight at the O.K. Corral* (1957), *Tombstone* (1993), and **Kevin Costner**'s *Wyatt Earp* (1994).

HOLT, JENNIFER (1920–1997). Born Elizabeth Marshall Holt, Jennifer Holt was the sister of cowboy star **Tim Holt**. Most of her work was with Universal and **PRC** during the 1940s. Holt generally played independent and aggressive **women** opposite such male leads as Eddie Dew, **Johnny Mack Brown**, and Eddie Dean. She never appeared in a film with her brother. Perhaps most unique for Holt were the roles in which she played the female **outlaw**. In *The Hawk of Powder River* (1948), she played the title role as a vicious outlaw chief who, to those around her, appears virtuous and respectable and beloved of the sheriff's son. Yet she really robs stagecoaches and works her feminine wiles to control unsuspecting men. In *The Old Chisholm Trail* (1942), Holt's character gets into a vicious **fistfight** with Mady Correll.

HOLT, TIM (1918–1973). Born Charles John Holt III in Oklahoma, Tim Holt starred in numerous **B Westerns** in the 1940s. His father, Jack Holt, was a prolific actor in **silent** Westerns as well as early talkies, and his sister, **Jennifer Holt**, was a popular star of B Westerns at the same time as her brother. Holt's best work was in supporting actor roles in full-budget films such as *Stagecoach* (1939) and *The Treasure of Sierra Madre* (1948).

HOMOEROTICISM. Were there gay cowboys in the old West? Undoubtedly. Do Western movies portray gay cowboys? Of course, the **modern Western** *Brokeback Mountain* (2005) addresses the subject directly. Recent critics have been going back to the **classic Westerns**, reevaluating the issues of masculinity that dominate these films and examining questions of "coding" homoerotic elements of the **myth of the West**. In literature of the past, gay men were often signaled as left-handed. **Billy the Kid** is nearly always portrayed as a left-handed **gunfighter**. Was Billy the Kid gay? In *Cattle Queen of Montana* (1954), **Ronald Reagan**'s character is a left-handed gunfighter. Was that simply a goof in the movie, given that the former president was actually left-handed?

What about close male bonding? In Westerns the male attachment is often stronger than the male-female attachment. In *Hop-Along Cassidy* (1935), a very typical Western, why does Jimmy, who has been courting Mary during the whole movie, leave Mary behind and head off to Montana with Hopalong and the boys at the end of the movie? How do we interpret one of the greatest fight scenes in the history of Westerns, the one in *Red River* (1948) between Tom and Matt? Unlike most slugfests, this fight involves very close, intimate holding and groping that causes nearly every viewer to do a double take. Are these two close male rivals signaling to the audience their true homoerotic desires? Viewers and critics are very much concerned with this issue in the 21st century. *See also* FISTFIGHTS.

HONDO **(1953). John Wayne**, Geraldine Page, John Farrow (director). Usually remembered now as one of the only 3-D Westerns, this film brought novelist **Louis L'Amour** to national fame, though his role in the origin of the story has since been questioned. Hondo came out a few months after *Shane* (1953), and the resemblance is striking. Hondo Lane (Wayne), a gunman riding through, stops at a farm house. Only a small boy (Lee Aaker) and his mother (Page) live there. The husband turns out to be a scoundrel wasting away in town. Hondo kills him not knowing the connection. The **Apache** chief Vittorio befriends the boy and his mother as well. Geraldine Page was nominated best supporting actress for her role.

HOPALONG CASSIDY SERIES. William Boyd played Hopalong Cassidy in nearly 70 films, followed by a radio show, the first dramatic network television show, comic books, lunch pails, and an entire industry based on the "Hoppy Craze" during the 1950s. Thus

Hopalong Cassidy was by far the most successful series of Westerns ever.

The character of Hopalong came from a popular series of novels written by Clarence E. Mulford. The original Hopalong was a young, red-haired cowboy with a hot temper who cussed and chewed tobacco and who would shoot anyone who made fun of his lame leg. The novels were popular and were prime material for Hollywood. But when Harry Sherman of Paramount formed the character, he smoothed over the rough spots. Instead of young, red headed, and hot tempered, the Hopalong of the film version was a middle-aged, white-haired, mild-tempered, white-horse-riding jovial cowboy played by Boyd. The early films in the series followed Mulford's original plots fairly closely, eliminating just the adult material, but eventually the films borrowed the novel titles and not much else. Nevertheless, due to their grounding in the best-selling novels, Hopalong Cassidy Westerns tended to be superior to most **B Westerns**.

Boyd was not a horseman, so he had difficulty developing into the famous cowboy star. While making the first film, *Hop-Along Cassidy* (1935), Boyd sprained an ankle riding, so he is never seen riding close up and he actually walks with a limp, earning the nickname Hopalong. Never again in the series does Boyd limp. Cliff Lyons did all the riding in the early films for Boyd. **James Ellison** and **Gabby Hayes** also partnered with Boyd for the first film and for many after.

All Hopalong Cassidy films worked off the same **formula**. There would be a slow buildup to the action, with an obligatory **fistfight** (rarely involving Boyd), and then a leather-burning chase scene across the prairie with quick-cutting **running inserts**, all to thunderous music such as "Dance of the Furies" from Christoph W. Gluck's *Don Juan* (used several times). In theaters, audiences of young people would wait for these moments and then, just as in some cult movies of the 1990s, would leap to their seats and chant as the chase ensued.

The image of Hopalong Cassidy became an icon for B Westerns. Boyd always began the film in a solid black suit and large black hat with a high, rounded crown. He wore an intricately stitched double **gun belt**. His pistols were chrome plated and finely engraved. Like the other cowboy stars, he had a trick **horse**, the solid white Topper, whose saddle and bridle were also finely stitched. Although he was often pictured on milk cartons and bread wrappers roping calves, Hopalong Cassidy never roped anything in the movies.

As with other cowboy stars such as **Gene Autry** and **Roy Rogers**, William Boyd had a special creed of behavior for his young fans, Hopalong Cassidy's Creed for Boys and Girls:

1. The highest badge of honor a person can wear is honesty. Be mindful at all times.
2. Your parents are the best friends you have. Listen to them and obey their instructions.
3. If you want to be respected, you must respect others. Show good manners in every way.
4. Only through hard work and study can you succeed. Do not be lazy.
5. Your good deeds will always come to light. So, do not boast or be a showoff.
6. If you waste time or money today, you will regret it tomorrow. Practice thrift in all ways.
7. Many animals are good and loyal companions. Be friendly and kind to them.
8. A strong, healthy body is a precious gift. Be neat and clean.
9. Our country's laws are made for your protection. Observe them carefully.
10. Children in many foreign lands are less fortunate than you. Be glad and proud you are an American.

The Hopalong Cassidy films under Harry Sherman's guidance were perhaps the highest quality films of the B Western era. In fact, several of the early films had feature running times and budgets equal to many full-budget Westerns. Perhaps the best of these, besides the first one of the series, are *Bar 20 Rides Again* (1935) and *Hopalong Cassidy Returns* (1936). The late films in the series, after Harry Sherman left, did not keep up the quality and aimed almost exclusively at the juvenile market. *Strange Gamble* (1948), with Andy Clyde as sidekick, was the last William Boyd Hopalong Cassidy film. After that, Boyd moved production to television.

However, that was not the last Hopalong Cassidy film. Christopher Coppola's *Gunfighter* (1998) brought back the cowboy one more time starring rodeo cowboy Chris Lybbert as the young Cassidy and

Martin Sheen as the old Hopalong Cassidy. This film, which had no box office success at all, is a **postmodern Western** based more on the original Mulford novels than on the William Boyd movies. *See also* TELEVISION WESTERNS.

HORSE (COWBOY HERO'S HORSE). From the beginnings of the Western genre, the **cowboy hero**'s special relationship with his horse and the essential value of the horse have been emphasized. When a cowboy is forced to sell his horse, as occurs in Owen Wister's *The Virginian*, he loses his sense of dignity and worth. Horse thieves in Westerns naturally deserve to be hanged.

From a psychological perspective, the cowboy's close relationship to a specific horse, a named horse, is sometimes seen as a substitute for the male's need for female companionship, unavailable in historic myth because of the scarcity of **women** on the frontier or unavailable in the post-code Western due to cultural restrictions on women's roles. Thus, the **symbolism** of a cowboy astride his beloved horse becomes clear. Horses provide the cowboy hero with a sense of nobility reminiscent of knights-errant and their steeds. They also differentiate the masculine independence of the hero who rides his solitary horse while assorted other male characters in town are confined to buggies and wagons—thus denying their manliness.

Antimyth Westerns often counter the usual horse symbolism. The Man with No Name, or Joe (**Clint Eastwood**) in *A Fistful of Dollars* (1964), rides into town on a burrow, not a noble steed. Lee Marvin in *Cat Ballou* (1965) is discovered drunk atop his drunken horse, leaning, horse and all, against a building.

William S. Hart was one of the earliest Western stars to identify himself with a specific horse, his beloved Fritz, who follows him through numerous films and is celebrated by Hart's farewell to Westerns in his sound prologue to the 1939 reissue of the silent *Tumbleweeds* (1925). Especially throughout the 1930s and 1940s, **B Western**–period cowboy stars often gave top billing to their horses. **Roy Rogers**'s **Trigger** was billed as "the Smartest Horse in the Movies." **William Boyd**'s image was inevitably associated with his horse Topper. Some horses, such as **Tom Mix**'s Tony were associated with their **stunt** and trick ability. While some later Western stars called horses by name, for example, **John Wayne** and his horse Dollar, named horses—and their cowboy owners—were primarily associated with lower-budget Westerns. Some of the most famous movie horses and their stars are as follows:

Apache (Bob Baker)
Black-eyed Nellie
  (**Smiley Burnette**)
Black Jack (Rocky Lane)
Brownie (Bob Steele)
Buttermilk (**Dale Evans**)
Cactus (**Sunset Carson**)
Champion (**Gene Autry**)
Cyclone (**Red Barry**)
Dollar (John Wayne)
Flash (Eddie Dean)
Fritz (William S. Hart)
Koko (**Rex Allen**)
Lightnin' (Monte Hale)
Lucky (Jimmy Wakely)
Mike (George O'Brien)
Pal (**Bob "Tex" Allen**)
Pie (**Jimmy Stewart**)
Raider (Charles Starrett)
Rebel (Pete Russell)
Ringeye (Smiley Burnette)
Rocky (Kermit Maynard)
Rush (Lash La Rue)
Rusty (Tom Keene)

Scout (Jack Moxie)
Scout (Tonto)
Shamrock (Robert
  Livingston)
Sheik (**Tim Holt**)
Silver (**Buck Jones**)
Silver (The Lone Ranger)
Silver Bullet (**Whip Wilson**)
Silver King (Fred Thomson)
Smoke (**Dick Foran**)
Sonny (**Betty Miles**)
Sonny (**Wild Bill Elliott**)
Starlight (**Tim McCoy**)
Stardust (**Randolph Scott**)
Sultan (**Ray Corrigan**)
Target (**Gail Davis**)
Tarzan (Ken Maynard)
Thunder (**Wild Bill Elliot**)
Tony (Tom Mix)
Tony, Jr. (Tom Mix)
Topper (**William Boyd**)
Trigger (Roy Rogers)
White Flash (**Tex Ritter**)
White King (**Fred Scott**)

HORSE OPERA. A disparaging colloquial term often used, along with **oater**, to refer to any Western, but especially the **B Westerns,** produced from the 1930s to 1950s. The term is not used by serious cultural or film critics.

HOUSTON, GEORGE (1896–1944). George Houston was one of the **singing cowboys** coming out of the opera tradition and responding to the popularity of Nelson Eddy rather than the country tradition of **Gene Autry**. Houston was a graduate of Julliard and sang with the

American Opera Company before entering movies in 1935. Through a series of 11 films, he played The Lone Rider for **PRC** with Al St. John as his comic **sidekick**. Houston never seemed comfortable in his role as singing cowboy, and St. John probably carried the series. Like most PRC Western productions, Houston's films were made on the cheap and hastily put together. Two years after the end of The Lone Rider series, Houston died of a heart attack.

– I –

INCE, THOMAS (1882–1924). Thomas Harper Ince was one of the early inventors of the Western film. After a brief sojourn on the Broadway stage, Ince began a long career in the film industry with **Biograph** beginning in 1910. After moving to California the next year to direct Westerns for **D. W. Griffith**, Ince helped create what is today known as Hollywood.

Ince is compared to his original mentor, D. W. Griffith, as an early film pioneer. But Griffith devoted himself much more to creating films from the basics up whereas Ince concerned himself more with the general matters of production. In reality, Ince directed few films but produced many, and his ultimate contribution to film lies in his role as producer. It is through Ince that the movement to the producer-director system of filmmaking began.

As a maker of Western films, Ince attempted to authenticate his films through spectacle based on Wild West shows of the pre-film era. In 1911 he hired the Miller Brothers 101 Ranch Wild West show from Oklahoma for the two-reeler *War on the Plains*, which *Motion Picture World* considered the most authentic Western produced to that point. *Custer's Last Fight* (1912) further authenticated Ince's vision of reality by insisting that the actors and company were working cowboys who had experienced life on the vanished frontier. Essentially this film cinematically replicated the famous reenactment of Custer's Last Stand from one of Buffalo Bill's Wild West.

In 1915 Ince, with Griffith and Mack Sennett, formed the Triangle Film Corporation, forerunner of United Artists. Because of his shared passion with Griffith for realism based upon location, Ince developed Inceville, his elaborate outdoor studio in the foothills around Hollywood, at the mouth of Santa Ynez Canyon—still a part of the untamed Western frontier.

While early Ince films tended to be mere spectacle, in later films plot became superior to action. Today's viewers are often baffled by the pre-code morality in films such as *The Woman* (1913), where bigamy and suicide are casually condoned. Ince's **women** often undergo radical transformations from good to evil or evil to good, frequently as a result of molestation. Either way, the result is usually tragic. In *The Woman*, the widowed Anne Little (Leona Hutton) becomes a **dance hall girl** and marries a gambler but later discovers that her first husband is still alive. The gambler comes home to find her dead, holding a note asking forgiveness for the wrong she has caused him. A simple dichotomy of good versus evil usually prevails, with the good inevitably being associated with the church and the evil with the saloon. Ince films tend to heavily promote prohibition.

But it is as a pioneer in early film production rather than through his films that Thomas Ince is remembered. Simple but effective ways of moving the crew and cast from one shooting to the next, now taken for granted, were first developed by Ince. Scripts for his silent films show meticulous detail to facial expression, lighting, film tinting, positioning—all eventually becoming commonplace. But perhaps Thomas Ince's greatest historical contribution to Westerns is his development of **William S. Hart** into the greatest cowboy star and director of the silent era.

In November 1924 Thomas Ince died under mysterious circumstances while attending a party—along with Marion Davies, Charlie Chaplin, and other celebrities—aboard William Randolph Hearst's yacht off the Southern California coast. When the yacht returned to dock, Ince's body was removed, with heart failure resulting from severe indigestion being ruled as the official cause of death. Hollywood rumors, however, have persisted through the years to the effect that Ince was shot after making a pass at Davies or after arguing with Chaplin for making a pass at Davies. *See also* HISTORICAL AUTHENTICITY.

INDIANS. The very phrase *cowboys and Indians* conjures up an automatic image of **Native Americans** being, first, "the Other" and, second, "the Enemy." For most of the United States' history, the word

Indian has carried negative connotations. Only recently has there been any significant effort in American culture to accept that whites deliberately planned and attempted genocide against Native Americans in the 19th century. Remember General Philip Sheridan's reputed assertion: "The only good Indian is a dead Indian." The blindness to or denial of this genocide dominates the way **silent** Westerns and **classic Westerns** have depicted Native Americans. The dawning of recognition affects the way Native Americans are depicted in **alternative** and **postmodern Westerns**.

Indians as characters hardly exist in most 20th-century Westerns. Instead, they exist as a faceless group or as stereotypes. As a group, Indians nearly always represent the savage enemy. "We"—the assumed viewer as well as the normative characters in the film—exist in towns, civilization. "They" exist somewhere out there in the wilderness. We are civilized; we are normal. They are savage; they are the Other. We revile them as the red menace. They exist as something to be mastered and conquered. They exist as an impediment to **Manifest Destiny** and **savage war** is essential to purify the plains. Thus, they are not seen as human. For example, when the **Apaches** attack the stage in *Stagecoach* (1939), they are not humans attacking but savages. None has individuality. In fact, the Indians in the movie are subhuman. Real Native Americans would have simply shot the horses out from under the stagecoach and taken their time with the slaughter. Then again, real Native Americans rarely attacked stagecoaches for the pleasure of attacking them.

When Indians are depicted individually, as in *The Searchers* (1956), they are either monsters (the Comanche chief, Scar) or buffoonish (Martin's squaw, Look). Only occasionally, as with *Hondo*'s (1953) Apache chief Vittorio, is there a possibility of individualizing and humanizing the Indian character, although one could argue instead that the white boy adopted by Vittorio is becoming dehumanized instead of the Indian becoming more human.

Thus, stereotypes of Indians abound in 20th-century Westerns. At the fort there are always a few serving as props, hunched over in their blankets. As the whites down below make their way across the valley, the camera pans up to the ridge where we see a whole line of Indians poised for the attack. They sit on their horses, immobile. A camera moves in to a close-up of a motionless face streaked with war paint, a cruel glint in the eye. A sudden movement of the chief's pony, and the horde descends on the hapless settlers.

Even when most 20th-century filmmakers attempted to portray Native Americans positively, they inevitably resorted to harmful stereotypes. For example, there is the Indian as noble savage, a creature from a simpler time, a more innocent time, who can commune directly with basic nature in ways civilized humanity cannot. There is also the vanishing American, the Indian at the end of the trail looking nostalgically backward. There is the Indian princess, the beautiful maiden who longs for the white hero but who can never be approached because of racial differences. Or there is the squaw, the Indian woman condemned to a life of servitude in ways white women have shed. All such stereotypes dehumanize Native Americans. In the world of the film, such dehumanization justifies whatever cruelties the normative characters wish to inflict. For the audience, such dehumanization justifies the figurative erasure of a significant subculture in the United States.

The issues for recent filmmakers, then, are many when it comes to dealing with Native American themes. *Little Big Man* (1970) was one of the earliest Westerns to challenge previous assumptions about Native Americans and U.S. actions toward them, including the activities of **General George Armstrong Custer** in his Indian campaigns. The turning point in the history of cinema Westerns, however, probably came with **Kevin Costner**'s *Dances with Wolves* (1990). This film not only portrayed Indians sympathetically, but it portrayed Indians as normative and the oncoming white hordes as the Other, the savage. This film was a tremendous box office success as well as a runaway winner at the Academy Awards. Its influence cannot be overestimated. *Geronimo: An American Legend* (1993) continued the trend of presenting an alternative view of the Western **myth** and is generally considered the best Native American film to date.

Another important issue that has affected the filming of Westerns is the casting of white actors in Native American roles. Jeff Chandler made a career playing Cochise, and Burt Lancaster once played Masai, the Apache warrior. In fact, prior to the 1960s, it was very rare to have Native Americans portray significant roles in films. They were often used as extras but rarely in speaking roles. Today it is unthinkable to portray a Native American with a white actor in the same way that it is no longer acceptable for a white actor to dress up in black-face and portray an **African American** the way **Gene Autry** did early in his career. *See also* RACIAL OTHERS AS THREATS TO WHITE WOMEN; *THE VANISHING AMERICAN.*

INDIAN TERRITORY. Historically, as the Westward Movement progressed after the Civil War, more and more territory of the **Great Plains** was opened for settlement. But the U.S. government knew that it would eventually have to find a permanent place for the displaced **Native American** tribes. As a result, the territory south of Kansas and north of Texas was designated Indian Territory. White settlers were not allowed. Inevitably, Indian Territory became a "no man's land" where only the roughest of outlaws holed up. It was a land beyond the reach of the law. **Jesse James**, the Dalton gang, and **Belle Starr** were just a few of the famous outlaws calling Indian Territory home. As Native American tribes were subdued, they were moved here, usually with great resistance.

A reference in a Western to Indian Territory typically means that it is the place to escape to if the law is in pursuit. Films as diverse as *True Grit* (1969) and *Hoppy Serves a Writ* (1943) are based on this premise. Films sympathetic to Native Americans do not usually portray Indian Territory favorably. **John Ford**'s *Cheyenne Autumn* (1964) shows the Cheyenne tribe desperately trying to escape its reservation in Indian Territory because of the unbearable climate, terrain, and resultant living conditions. The **Apaches** in *Geronimo: An American Legend* (1993) fight fiercely against General Crook, not because they may be forced to live on a reservation but because they will be forced to live in Indian Territory. They finally surrender when they are promised a reservation in central Florida. They no sooner settle in Florida than they are forced to move back to Indian Territory.

Even Indian Territory could not remain unsettled by whites forever, and the last Western territory made available for settlement was Indian Territory. It was opened through a series of land runs, the most famous being the Land Run of 1889, depicted in numerous Westerns including *Tumbleweeds* (1925) and *Cimarron* (1960), in which thousands of settlers lined up at the boundary set by the U.S. cavalry, and at noon, after the starting shot was fired, they all rushed into the new territory. The footage of the land run in *Tumbleweeds* was used in numerous Westerns thereafter. In 1907 Indian Territory became the state of Oklahoma. *See also* INDIANS.

ITALIAN WESTERNS. *See* SPAGHETTI WESTERNS; EUROPEAN WESTERNS.

– J –

JAMES, JESSE (1847–1882). Of all the **outlaws** in the old West, perhaps only **Billy the Kid** has appeared in as many Western films as Jesse James. The basic details of the Jesse James story that occur in most film versions include the following: Jesse and his brother, Frank, fought with the Confederacy during the Civil War and at one point rode with **William Quantrill** in Kansas. After the war they returned home to find the railroad companies forcing families out of their homes. At this point, versions of the story differ. Some portray Jesse and the James gang as vicious outlaws on expeditions of murder and rapine. Others portray the James gang as Robin Hood types who were simply taking the part of the common people against evil robber barons. The James gang often allied with Cole Younger and his brothers, whose specialty was robbing trains although they also robbed banks. Frank was usually considered the gentler of the two brothers. Jesse married Zee Mims (or Cobb) and moved to Florida at the end of his career and changed his surname to Howard. One day in 1882, Bob Younger, a former gang member, sneaked up behind Mr. Howard and shot him in the back. An old song came out of the episode: "That Dirty Little Coward who Shot Mr. Howard." *I Shot Jesse James* (1949) shows Bob Ford (John Ireland) watching Jesse through a window (Reed Hadley) as he hangs a picture. Ford shoots him in the back.

All these parts of the legend have been disputed or modified at one time or another, but anytime Jesse James is mentioned in a film, it is generally assumed the audience will possess this minimal knowledge. Some of the stars who have played Jesse James include Tyrone Power in *Jesse James* (1939), Colin Farrell in ***American Outlaws*** (2001), and Brad Pitt in *The Assassination of Jesse James by the Coward Robert Ford* (2007).

JANUARY, LOIS (1912–2006). Although Lois January appeared in many non-Western Universal films in the 1930s, she also worked in **B Western** roles with male actors such as **Tim McCoy** and Bob Steele. Typical for the 1930s, the redhead usually played the pretty young female in need of male leadership and guidance. A typical Lois January film is *The Roaming Cowboy* (1937), with **Fred Scott**. January's character almost succumbs to the pressure to deed over her ranch to an evil land grabber, but Scott rescues her just in time. At the end we see her sitting on a swing with her **cowboy hero**, watching the sunset and dreaming of their future together.

JEFFRIES, HERB (1911–). Known as the Bronze Buckaroo, Herb Jeffries was a **singing cowboy** who starred (as Herbert Jeffrey) in a string of Westerns in the 1930s, including *Harlem Rides the Range* (1939), *The Bronze Buckaroo* (1939), *Two-Gun Man from Harlem* (1938), and *Harlem on the Prairie* (1937). He was the only **African American** to star in his own series of Westerns. Before his film career, Jeffries was a big band singer and after films he returned to his singing career.

JENNINGS, AL (1863–1961). The last of the old-time **outlaws**, Al Jennings was born Alfonso Jackson Jennings in Tazewell County, Virginia, but spent his early adult life in El Reno, Oklahoma, as an attorney who eventually went bad and formed his own outlaw gang, the Jennings gang. For a short time Jennings and his gang developed a reputation as train robbers, and Jennings himself, despite his five-foot-one-inch frame, became a notorious **gunfighter**, killing 18 men ("I always shot 'em in the throat so they could not talk back") and even standing down **Jesse James** at one time. At least, these are the legends Jennings cultivated through the years. After serving his prison term and receiving a presidential pardon, Jennings entered the film business when it was in its most primitive state.

In 1908 Jennings the reformed outlaw collaborated with legendary sheriff Bill Tilgman in making *A Bank Robbery*, filmed on location in Cache, Oklahoma, a town that still had the classic old West look. The 19-minute film, with no story boards, shows the outlaw gang planning their holdup, then riding into town, entering the bank, shooting it up (we see the scene only from the outside), coming out, and riding down the street out of town. As they ride down the street, the camera pans the townspeople on the street. Several are waving at the camera.

The film was the beginning of an attempt by Jennings and Tilgman to establish the film industry in Oklahoma as New York was becoming impractical, especially for filming Westerns. In 1918 Jennings established his own production company, the Al Jennings Company, located in Tucson, Arizona. Thereafter, he had a long career in Hollywood, being associated with over 100 films, including non-Westerns, in various phases of the industry. Two film biographies of him were made, *Beating Back* (1914), starring Jennings as himself, and *Al Jennings of Oklahoma* (1951), starring Dan Duryea and Gale Storm. Jennings died at 98 in Tarzana, California, the last survivor from the old West.

Jennings's Hollywood career, as with the Hollywood career of **Wyatt Earp**, brings up the interesting question: How much of what Hollywood saw as the authentic West truly was historic? While most of Jennings's claims to gunfighter notoriety have been shown false, much of what early Westerns relied on for authentic detail was based solely on the testimony of Jennings and others who claimed to have lived through the legendary days of old. *See also* HISTORICAL AUTHENTICITY.

JOE KIDD (1972). **Clint Eastwood**, **Robert Duvall**, John Sturges (director). Robert Duvall played the classic evil land baron (Frank Harlan) out to dispossess Latinos from old Spanish land grants. Kidd (Eastwood) joins Harlan but quickly realizes that the evil Chama (John Saxon), leader of the **Mexicans**, is less evil than Harlan. This **antimyth Western** is a perfect mix-up of good and bad. Ultimately, no one except Chama's girl Helen (Stella Garcia) is normative. None have values or ideals beyond personal gain. Joe Kidd's values in particular are ambiguous. But that is the point. The Latino villagers are utterly helpless, utterly weak—totally passive. Harlan says he will kill five villagers in the morning and five in the afternoon and continue doing so until Chama shows up. (Chama plans to let Harlan kill them.) So Harlan's men, including Kidd, call out the villagers and tell five to come forward. Five walk out and stand stupidly waiting to be shot, listening as the bad guys take bets on whether they can hit a certain button on one of their shirts. The scene is probably intended to be symbolic, but what does it symbolize? If it is intended to be realistic, it is not. More likely, it is a messy plot point that Sturges or screenwriter Elmore Leonard did not consider important, perhaps reflecting some unexamined racism.

***JOHNNY GUITAR* (1954). Joan Crawford**, Sterling Hayden, Mercedes McCambridge, **Ernest Borgnine**, **John Carradine**, **Ward Bond**, and Nicholas Ray (director). This film is usually labeled a cult Western because while it was neglected for the most part in its own time, today it is viewed as a groundbreaking **feminist Western**. The main character is Vienna (Crawford), a strong-minded woman who can handle a gun and who has powerful ambitions. She owns a saloon out of the puritanical townspeople's domain, and she plans on using it to expand her own power once the railroad comes through. Her main rival is another strong woman, Emma (McCambridge). Gender roles are reversed as the men become mere supporting partners for the **women**, who eventually meet in a showdown. *See also* PANTS ROLES.

JOHNSON, BEN (1918–1996). Born in Oklahoma, Ben Johnson worked on ranches and wrangled horses before coming to Hollywood. There, he first served a long apprenticeship as a stuntman before turning actor as the affable Sergeant Tyree in *She Wore a Yellow Ribbon* (1949), a role he reprised in another of **John Ford**'s **Cavalry Trilogy**, *Rio Grande* (1950). In both cases, Johnson is the bright young enlisted man who was formerly a member of the Confederate army and now serves with no bitterness at all in the Union Cavalry fighting Indians.

Johnson's career in Westerns followed the trend of the genre throughout the last half of the 20th century. He played supporting roles in other **classic Westerns** such as *Shane* (1953) and *Cheyenne Autumn* (1964), but as the classic Westerns changed, Johnson changed as well. By 1968 he was playing with **Clint Eastwood** in *Hang 'em High*, and he was one of the bunch in *The Wild Bunch* (1969). His last Western film was the forgettable *The Outlaws: Legend of O. B. Taggart* (1994), opposite Mickey Rooney. Throughout his career, Johnson regularly played in **television Westerns** and made-for-television Western movies. His best performance was in the modern Western *The Last Picture Show* (1971), for which he won an Oscar for best supporting actor. *See also* STUNTS.

JONES, BUCK (1889–1942). Born Charles Frederick Gebhart in Vincennes, Indiana, Jones changed his name soon after making his first Western, *The Last Straw*, in 1920. Like other early Western stars, Jones started out with the Miller Brothers 101 Ranch Wild West show and other touring shows. He married one of the performers, Odelle Osborne, and for a while the couple toured with their own show. After settling in Southern California in 1917, Jones sought a steady income by working as an extra in the newly popular Western movies, including some of **William S. Hart**'s films. Throughout the 1920s, Jones found steady work in silent films for Fox Studios. Almost none of these films survive, so we must rely on the early reviews from such sources as *Variety* to learn that they were high on action and entertainment value and not much else. A dispute with Fox led to Jones's departure from Hollywood and an ill-fated venture with his own high-budget Wild West show. The project bankrupted Jones, and he was forced to return to Hollywood just as the transition to talkies was taking place.

Early producers assumed that Westerns, because they were mainly outdoor action films, would not work well as talkies, so they were reluctant to back them in the new format. One producer, Sol Lesser, took a gamble with Jones and signed him to a contract with Columbia for eight pictures at $300 apiece. The films were successful, and Jones's asking price increased accordingly from then on. In 1936 the *Motion Picture Herald*, a trade paper for distributors, ranked Buck Jones as the top box-office draw among Western actors. After a career with Columbia, Jones signed with Monogram in 1940 to film the **Rough Riders** series in which he costarred with **Tim McCoy** and Raymond Hatton. What most fans remember about these films is the stirring theme song, "The Rough Riders Ride Again," with which each film begins. Though Jones's move to share billing with two other stars might have been evidence of a career in decline, the series proved immensely popular and Jones was clearly becoming the dominant star—so much so that McCoy left the series after Jones was killed in the famous Cocoanut Grove nightclub fire in Boston in

1942. Jones was guest of honor at a dinner party when the fire broke out. He died of severe burns two days afterward.

Buck Jones's films defined the 1930s low-budget Western, especially in the days before the rise in popularity of the **Hopalong Cassidy** pictures and the **singing cowboy** pictures of, primarily, **Gene Autry**. When he had control of his pictures at Columbia, Jones, unlike most **B Western** stars, sought to vary his roles and not play himself primarily, though he still emphasized **stunt** work and action. His earliest films stretched conventional morality as far as they could in pre-code days. In *Timber Wolf* (1925), Jones forcibly abducts a **dance hall girl** (Elinor Fair) to prevent her from marrying the villain. He then tames her and marries her. Even in 1935 in *Stone of Silver Creek*, Jones played a saloon proprietor and professional gambler—roles not acceptable for cowboy stars of most B Westerns.

Jones described himself as "an old-time cowboy." He wore a very basic, practical **costume** and though he kept his white **horse**, Silver, through his best pictures, his horse never dominated the film. Whatever one makes of Buck Jones's career, he deserves notice for keeping the masculine cowboy tradition of **William S. Hart** alive for a few more years before the streamlined Westerns of the singing cowboys took over.

JORY, VICTOR (1902–1982). Canadian-born Victor Jory probably typified the classic Hollywood heavy as much as any other actor in a long career spanning 57 years. Tall and lean, with an oily face, constantly shifting eyes, and a rattling, insecure voice, Jory was perfect for these roles. Every time the camera was on him, every time he said anything, he was clearly thinking about something else, and what he was thinking was not good. He played a **Native American** in *Cheyenne Autumn* (1964).

Jory's sinister presence even in small roles was often a highlight of the film. In the first scene of **Budd Boetticher**'s *Seven Men from Now* (1956), ex-sheriff Stride (**Randolph Scott**) rides through the countryside in pouring rain (on a mission of revenge, we soon find out) and comes to a tent. Two men are inside, one being Jory's character (uncredited). There is a moment of idle talk over coffee as Jory shiftily considers what to do. We find out the sheriff is in pursuit of some murderers from Silver Springs. "Did they ever catch them fellas who did it?" Jory asks. "Two of them," the sheriff replies. The camera instantly shifts outside the tent as two gunshots are fired.

JURADO, KATY (1924–2002). Born Maria Cristina Estella Marcella Jurado de Garcia in Guadalajara, Mexico (her birth date is in dispute), Katy Jurado had a long career in Spanish-language cinema as well as in American and other national cinema. **Budd Boetticher** discovered her and cast her in one of his bullfighting movies. She also was closely associated with **John Wayne**. Very much a Hollywood insider throughout her long career, Jurado is probably most famous for her role as Helen Ramirez in *High Noon* (1952). Ramirez owns the saloon and once had a relationship with the newly married Sheriff Will Kane (**Gary Cooper**). She is dark, sultry, glamorous in an earthy way, and a woman who knows how the world really works, in contrast to Kane's new wife, a Quaker named Amy (**Grace Kelly**). At one point, confronting the passive new wife, Helen contemptuously asks, "What kind of woman are you? How can you leave him like this? Does the sound of guns frighten you that much?" Jurado's English was still in a primitive state when she filmed *High Noon*, so she had to learn all her lines phonetically.

Jurado went on to win an Academy Award for best supporting actress in *Broken Lance* (1954). Later Western roles included **Marlon Brando**'s *One-Eyed Jacks* (1961) and **Sam Peckinpah**'s *Pat Garrett & Billy the Kid* (1973). She was married to **Ernest Borgnine** for a while.

– K –

KELLY, GRACE (1929–1982). Grace Kelly, twice nominated for Academy Awards and winner once, was the leading female actor in such Hollywood classics as *High Society* (1956) and *The Country Girl* (1954) and in such Alfred Hitchcock thrillers as *To Catch a Thief* (1955), *Rear Window* (1954), and *Dial M for Murder* (1954). But Kelly actually got her film start in Westerns with her role as Amy, the new Quaker wife of Sheriff Will Kane (**Gary Cooper**) in *High Noon* (1952).

The newlyweds are on their way out of town when Sheriff Kane hears that Frank Miller (Ian MacDonald) is coming back after a long prison term, and he plans on revenge. Torn between his love for a woman and his duty as a man, Will Kane knows what he must do. Kelly's role highlights perhaps the most classic male dilemma in the Western **myth**: the tension between devotion to the world of **women** and the world of men. Speaking to the sultry Helen Ramirez (**Katy Jurado**), a former lover of Kane's, Amy makes one of the most famous statements in **classic Westerns** on this theme: "I've heard guns. My father and my brother were killed by guns. They were on the right side but that did not help them any when the shooting started. My brother was 19. I watched him die. That is when I became a Quaker. I do not care who's right or who's wrong. There is got to be some better way for people to live." Kelly's ingénue blonde good looks and vacant-eyed lack of comprehension of the ways of the world serves as a contrast to the dark-haired seductress Helen. In the end, though, it is Amy who is forced to a decision and must take up a gun to save her husband's life.

In a continuation of her fairy tale Hollywood life, Grace Kelly went on to marry Prince Rainer of Monaco in 1956 and became Princess Grace.

– L –

LADD, ALAN (1913–1964). Born in Arkansas, Alan Ladd is most remembered by Western fans for his role in *Shane*, the 1953 film directed by George Stevens. Shane is a mysterious figure who accidentally comes upon a farmstead owned by a family that he immediately comes to love. When trouble develops, it becomes clear that Shane is a man who knows how to use a gun. Though he was once a gunfighter, Shane wants to settle down and live like the Starrett family, maybe have a wife like Marian (**Jean Arthur**) and a son like Joey (**Brandon De Wilde**). Ladd was ideal for this role. Earlier in his career he had played heavies in non-Western films noir, and he had even appeared in a few Westerns such as *Whispering Smith* (1948) and *Branded* (1950). As Shane, however, Alan Ladd became one of the most revered characters of any Western. Young Joey Starrett idolized him. He and Marian give each other long looks, knowing that under other circumstances matters might have been different.

Yet, Shane respects Joe Starrett (Van Heflin) as well; there is never any real jealousy. Just as a side note, Arthur was 13 years older than Ladd at the time.

L'AMOUR, LOUIS (1908–1988). Born Louis Dearborn LaMoore in North Dakota, Louis L'Amour is one of the most prolific Western fiction writers of all time. His novels still dominate sales of paperback Westerns. Like other novelists, **Zane Grey**, **Max Brand**, and Clarence Mulford, many of L'Amour's novels became Western films. His novels are characterized by L'Amour's famous claim to **historical authenticity**, especially geographic authenticity. If the novel describes a character crawling down a gully toward a wash, you can be sure, L'Amour fans claim, that the author had climbed down that same gully at one time or another. Recent critics, while not disputing such claims, question the overall fictional authenticity of the novels. L'Amour novels that have been made into films include *Catlow*, *Shalako*, *Kid Rodelo*, *Taggart*, *Guns of the Timberland*, *Heller in Pink Tights*, *Apache Territory*, *The Tall Stranger*, *Utah Blaine*, *The Burning Hills*, *Blackjack Ketchum: Desperado*, *Stranger on Horseback*, *Treasure of Ruby Hills*, *Four Guns to the Border*, and *Hondo*.

It was *Hondo* (1953) that established L'Amour's reputation. The highly successful film, starring **John Wayne** and Geraldine Page (who won an Oscar for best supporting actress), was ostensibly based on L'Amour's novel *Hondo*. L'Amour was originally nominated for an Oscar for best writing, but the nomination was withdrawn when it was discovered that the film was not based on a novel but on L'Amour's short story "The Gift of Cochise," published in *Collier's* magazine. Recently, Lee Clark Mitchell has shown that even the novel, *Hondo*, L'Amour's first big seller, was actually an unauthorized novelization of the screenplay by James Edward Grant. L'Amour did eventually write an acknowledged novelization of the film *How the West Was Won* (1962).

LANDSCAPE. Part of what makes a Western a Western is the magnificent landscape that serves as an independent element of the film, almost like another character, and the relationship of the characters to it is basic to the premise. The clear message of all landscape shots is that the land is permanent while the inhabitants of the film and all their actions, ambitions, and failures are transitory. Large-budget Westerns such as *How the West Was Won* (1962) use the landscape to give significance and meaning to the film. **B Westerns** often use landscape merely as a backdrop. The camera naturally displays the splendor of the landscape. It is there all the time, ready to fill the screen with its vastness, and much of its splendor lies in its power to overwhelm us, to reveal humanity's insignificance. Many directors such as **Anthony Mann** isolate the emptiness, the solitude, the loneliness of life upon the Western landscape. For men, this life can be adventurous and rewarding. But for **women**, the landscape often means loneliness and ultimately ignoble death. The savage, naturalistic landscape in films such as *The Ballad of Little Jo* (1993) and *The Missing* (2003) serve merely as an impersonal agent of death or personal destruction for the female protagonists.

Behind all panoramic shots lies an unstated assumption that all the beautiful terrain across the horizon exists to be exploited, to make people rich. The rolling plains mean vast areas for raising cattle or for transporting cattle to market. Such cattle raising does not despoil the land so long as the range remains open. Mountain ranges hide gold and precious metals needing to be mined. Miners work hard and deserve their share of nature's worth. Miners and cowboys celebrate the earth. But land barons who fence off the range and push off legitimate homesteaders are the villains in Westerns, as well as mine owners who exploit labor for their own selfish ends. At the end of the movie, the protagonists and those they protect may grow rich, but they do so by using the land, not by exploiting it.

The critical issues regarding landscape usually revolve around its regenerative power on human character. Early writers and filmmakers of the **silent era** tended to see the West as an area of the country that was pure and that formed proper character and purged weakness. Filmmakers of the **classic** era emphasized the savagery (whether human savages or natural obstacles) of landscape that needed to be subdued. **Alternative Westerns** such as *Dances With Wolves* (1990) often condemn what humanity has done to the land. *See also* AMIS, SUZY; BLANCHET, CATE; COSTNER, KEVIN; FEMINIST WESTERNS; GREENWALD, MAGGIE; MYTH OF THE WEST.

LEONE, SERGIO (1929–1989). Born in 1929 in Rome, the son of a film director from the **silent era**, Sergio Leone superseded **John Ford** as the dominant maker of Westerns in the 1960s. His rise to fame and influence was completely unexpected. In Italy in the 1950s, Leone was making what were known as "sword and sandal epics," films like *The Last Days of Pompeii* (1959) and *The Colossus of Rhodes* (1961). A turning point in his creative life evidently occurred when he discovered the Japanese filmmaker Akira Kurosawa and decided to adapt *Yojimbo* (1961) as a Western. His first Western, *Per un pugno di dollari* (1964)—released in the United States as *A Fistful of Dollars* (1967)—owes not only its plot to Kurosawa but much of its cinematic style as well. But with this film as well as the others of the **Dollars Trilogy**, Leone gave the **spaghetti Western** respectability and started the trend in which Westerns question the underlying myths upon which John Ford, **Howard Hawks**, and others had based their **classic Westerns**.

Perhaps Leone's most doctrinaire Western questioning classic values is *Once Upon a Time in the West* (1968), filmed partly in the United States, featured **Henry Fonda** in the lead, a star associated with John Ford and classic Westerns. In this film, Fonda, who had played **Wyatt Earp** in *My Darling Clementine* (1946), played an enraged, cruel killer who takes pleasure at one point in killing a child.

Much of the appeal of Leone's Westerns came from his new style of filmmaking adapted for Westerns. First, he collaborated with **Ennio Morricone** to combine music and visuals in revolutionary ways to emphasize dramatic camera movements, extreme close-ups of the eyes of characters, and slow-building tension that increases to intense emotional peaks. Some of Leone's techniques had not been used since the days of silent films.

Perhaps the single element of Westerns that Leone changed most was the concept of **violence** and its purpose in relation to the Western **myth**. When **Lee Van Cleef**'s character in *Buono, il brutto, il cattivo, Il* (1966)—released in the United States as *The Good, the Bad and the Ugly* (1967)—kills, he enjoys it. When we look into his eyes through the extreme camera close-up at the moment of the killing, we see no questioning, no thought that killing is necessary but distasteful. Instead, we see pleasure and we see evil. Though the other characters do not have the same evil look while killing, there is little distinction between the way Van Cleef kills and the way Eli Wallach (the Ugly) or the way **Clint Eastwood** (the Good) kills. Violence serves no social purpose in Leone. It is only an assertion of the existential self. There are no heroes in Leone Westerns because for there to be a hero there would have to be some concept of external good and external evil based on its value to society. For Leone, only the existential self matters. Good may differ from evil but only in relation to self. Whether for this reason or others, it is notable that the French existentialist Simone de Beauvoir may have been a fan of Leone's Westerns. Writing in *Tout compte fait*, (1972), she said, "Some adventure films have kept me in suspense—some westerns, for example, including films made by the Italians such as *The Good, the Bad and the Ugly*" (Frayling 1981, 129).

LINCOLN, ABRAHAM (1809–1865). The president of the United States during the Civil War, Abraham Lincoln played a key role in the ending of the war and the beginning of westward settlement, a role that is an understood subtext of many Westerns. Although during the classic historical period of the **Western moment** several presidents significantly impacted the West—especially presidents such as Ulysses S. Grant and Rutherford B. Hayes—only Lincoln matters much for understanding Westerns. He appears in many cinema Westerns, such as *The Plainsman* (1936) and *They Died with Their Boots On* (1941), and always as a symbolic figure, sometimes in the background rather than as a real character. The things that are understood about Abraham Lincoln, though not necessarily historically accurate, are that he was responsible for freeing the slaves; that he agonized over how to restore the South to the Union as the Civil War was winding down; that he was assassinated in Ford Theater by John Wilkes Booth, a Southern sympathizer, just weeks after the war ended; that had he lived, peace and unity would have been achieved much more quickly than it was. He is nearly always played as a father figure who promised hope for a new West but whose untimely death caused great hardship for an ailing country.

LITTLE BIG HORN, BATTLE OF. On June 25–26, 1876, near the Little Big Horn river in Montana, **General George Armstrong Custer** and his 7th Cavalry were destroyed by a coalition of Lakota and Cheyenne Indians led by Crazy Horse. The battle represented the last high point of the Native American resistance to white invasion at the end of the 19th century. In U.S. history, the battle has always represented an especially humiliating defeat. Cinema Westerns have represented the battle many times. Usually the question for Westerns is whether to represent a sympathetic Custer, as **Errol Flynn**'s character in *They Died with Their Boots On* (1941), a film intended to inspire patriotism as World War II was approaching, or whether to represent Custer as **new Western history** usually interprets him—as a brutal Indian killer. *See also* INDIANS.

LONG SHOTS. Long shots and extreme long shots characterize the cinema style of Westerns. Long shots are camera angles of full figures with some background, and extreme long shots give a faraway, panoramic view of a scene merging character with the frontier **landscape**. Serious, character-driven films often emphasize close-up shots while comedies and Westerns emphasize long shots. A classic long shot is the one from *Shane* (1953) as the hero first rides onscreen from a distance, mountains in the background, a murmuring brook in the foreground from which a deer is drinking.

LUCKY LUKE **(1991). Terence Hill** (director). The Lucky Luke phenomenon is often unknown to American fans of Westerns, but Lucky Luke in all guises has been phenomenally popular in Europe and in French-speaking countries. The original Lucky Luke is a comic book cowboy who can shoot "faster than his shadow." In this film version, Terence Hill of the famous **Trinity series** played Lucky Luke and basically kept his Trinity character but with a little more energy. As sheriff of Daisy Town, Luke, and his talking horse Jolly Jumper (voice of Roger Miller), has his hands full when the Daltons come to town and stir up the Indians. Besides comics and movies, Lucky Luke has appeared in an animated television series.

– M –

THE MAGNIFICENT SEVEN **(1960). Yul Brynner**, Steve McQueen, **James Coburn**, Horst Buchholz, Eli Wallach, Elmer Bernstein (music), John Sturges (director). Along with ***Gunfight at the O.K. Corral*** (1957), this film has been considered one of John Sturges's "super Westerns"—blockbuster films with major stars and large budgets made at the end of the **classic Western** era. Unquestionably, *The Magnificent Seven* was a major movie event in its time. Today it is primarily seen as a vehicle for the great music of Elmer Bernstein. The theme later became the music for Marlboro cigarettes and the Marlboro Man. Bernstein's theme with its many variations throughout the soundtrack lend a sense of majesty to the **landscape** and to the adventure the Seven engage in. The film was the first Western based on a film by Akira Kurosawa, this one being *The Seven Samurai* (1954) about Samurai warrior-swordsmen defending a 14th-century village. **Sergio Leone** revisited Kurosawa works to make *A Fistful of Dollars* (1964) in the **Dollars Trilogy**. In retrospect, *The Magnificent Seven* can be seen as a precursor to the **spaghetti Westerns**.

A brutal bandit gang led by Calvera (Wallach) intimidates a small Mexican village for years. Fed up, the villagers pool all they have and send a delegation to the border to hire a **gunfighter**. Eventually, Chris Adams (Brynner) agrees, for his own purposes, and lines up six others to ride into Mexico and face Calvera. The Seven ride through brutal terrain and come across a small village that is regularly terrorized by the banditos. At one point or another, each of the Seven exhibits his own particular skills in killing.

While the film was a success financially, it never received the critical acclaim of Sturges's later work because once past the scenery and music and into the characters themselves, all we get are **clichés** among a grouping of actors that never quite works. James Coburn perhaps presages his later wonderful takedowns, but Yul Brynner is no cowboy or gunfighter. No explanation is given for his thickly affected accent. Horst Buchholz plays an Hispanic character, but he retains his German accent. Steve McQueen was always good in action films but, despite having a background in **television Westerns**, never did well in cinema Westerns. Eli Wallach's days as one of the great bad guys of Westerns had not yet happened. He gets little actual screen time here, but he makes the most of it as the embodiment of pure, unmotivated evil, the kind of evil U.S. audiences feared most in their own lives in 1960.

MALE GAZE. This common term for how we watch films originated perhaps with Mary Devereaux, although Lee Clark Mitchell developed its application to Westerns in particular. When we watch a movie, we watch it through the eye of the camera. What the camera sees is what we see. The camera eye is always from the male perspective simply because the male perspective dominated the original culture of both movie making and movie watching. Even if the cameraman or the cinematographer or the director is female, the point of view of the camera is male. So when the **cowboy hero** comes onto the screen, the camera gazes at him. It lingers over **Clint Eastwood**'s or **John Wayne**'s body, often deliberately panning slowly up and down, taking in the costume but also the body itself. We gaze in admiration. We want to be like him. When, however, the glamorous female lead such as **Claudia Cardinale** or Raquel Welch comes onto the screen and the camera begins its slow gaze, we look not in admiration, even if we are female, but we look as males and desire to dominate her. The male gaze is so natural that we never even notice it, yet it controls much of the way we interpret the film as a whole.

MANIFEST DESTINY. This term, which may have originated with John L. O'Sullivan's 1839 treatise *Manifest Destiny*, refers to a concept that is a basic subtext of all Westerns from the **classic** and **silent eras**: that because the United States was blessed and chosen by God to be a blessed nation, it was manifestly destined to march forth across the entire continent and transform the frontier from red savagery to white civilization. In virtually every instance of cinema contact between **Native Americans** and whites prior to *Dances with Wolves* (1990), it is assumed that the whites are right in subduing and displacing the Native Americans. Any character who aids Native Americans in their fight against whites is considered an evil person of the worst sort. Thus, gunrunners, as in *The Plainsman* (1936), *They Died with Their Boots On* (1941), or *The Man from Laramie* (1955), are automatically seen as despicable, while the white cavalry with its abundance of weaponry is hailed as heroic. *See also* FRONTIER AS ESCAPE FROM THE CITY.

MANN, ANTHONY (1906–1967). Born Emil Bundesmann in San Diego, California, Mann began his career on the New York stage both as actor and director. In 1938 he moved to Hollywood and worked behind the scenes as casting director, talent scout, and assistant director before directing his first films in 1942: *Dr. Broadway* and *Moonlight in Havana*. His first Western was *Devil's Doorway* (1950), followed be a string of successes throughout the 1950s, most starring **Jimmy Stewart**: *Winchester '73* (1950), *The Furies* (1950), *Bend of the River* (1952), *The Naked Spur* (1953), *The Far Country* (1954), *The Man from Laramie* (1955), *The Last Frontier* (1955), *The Tin Star* (1957), and *Man of the West* (1958).

Winchester '73 was Mann's first major success and one that secured his reputation. The film began Mann's reliance on Jimmy Stewart, established Mann's directing style, and began developing themes that would run throughout his Westerns. Much of Mann's work often moves through the human emotions, usually reaching a level of near insanity before the plot turns to normalcy. Often his plots treat revenge of one type or another. These **revenge Westerns** follow the progression of revenge from mild urgings to maniacal obsession. Thus, the typical Mann hero, as in *Winchester '73* and *The Man from Laramie*, sets out on a revenge **quest**, initially for revenge on others, but at some point the hero turns inward, sees the void inside, and seeks revenge upon himself instead. Mann's Westerns, while not short on plot, nevertheless are usually psychological films often associated with film noir. In fact, the term **noir Western** was evidently developed primarily with Anthony Mann in mind.

Anthony Mann's Westerns usually reach for the epic, portraying the **cowboy hero**'s struggle against himself but also his struggle against overpowering forces—first against the forces of community, but also, as in *The Naked Spur* (1953), against the forces of nature, the forces of the savage, barren Western **landscape**. In contrast, *Bend of the River* (1952) is set in the Northwest and here the forests, steep mountain slopes, and raging rivers are the natural hazards against which characters confront each other. McLyntock's (Stewart) final struggle occurs in the mountain river that kills and sweeps away its dead without remorse. For Mann, the landscape "become[s] part of the action" (Calder 1975, 14). Similarly, in *Winchester '73*, the final fight occurs on the barren rock that symbolizes the intense hatred of two brothers reduced to their most fundamental natures in brutal struggle.

Fittingly, Mann ended his career searching for the genuine epic, first with *Cimarron* (1960), the story of empire building in Oklahoma, and then outside the Western genre with *El Cid* (1961) and *The Fall of the Roman Empire* (1964).

THE MAN WHO SHOT LIBERTY VALANCE (1962). Jimmy Stewart, John Wayne, Andy Devine, John Carradine, Lee Van Cleef, Woody Strode, Lee Marvin, **John Ford** (director). Jimmy Stewart plays Ransom Stoddard, a young lawyer who has come to a rough town and is forced to humiliate himself by the **outlaw** Liberty Valance (Marvin). Ultimately, Stoddard must face Valance in a showdown in the street. There is no way the bookish lawyer from back East has a chance against the town's terror. Miraculously, though, the young lawyer shoots the villain dead and becomes the town hero. He is even elected to Congress and serves the town well for many years. The actual story takes place long years after the shootout on the streets when the eminent congressman comes back to town for the funeral of an old gunfighter (Wayne) and learns what really happened on the street so long ago.

The film is a textbook **classic Western** and one of John Ford's best. Without the magnificent vistas of **Monument Valley** that are the trademark of many of Ford's films, *The Man Who Shot Liberty Valance* is a **town** Western, almost an urban Western. John Wayne takes a secondary role to Stewart. Years later the two teamed up again in Wayne's last film, *The Shootist* (1976). *See also* TOWNS.

MARION, BETH (1912–2003). Born Betty Goettsche, Beth Marion starred in numerous low-budget Westerns in the 1930s. She perhaps typified the classic virginal blonde female lead of 1930s **B Westerns** as well as anyone. Invariably, her character stands in the background of the plot, always dependent on the protection of an all-wise **cowboy hero,** coming forward to the camera only when a visual break is needed. In *Between Men* (1935), John Wellington (William Farnum), a good-hearted outlaw feels he must protect Gail Winters (Marion) from the suspicious intentions of Johnny Wellington Jr. (**Johnny Mack Brown**). Marion went on to play lead opposite such stars as **Tom Tyler,** Clifford Jones, Ken Maynard, and **Buck Jones.** She married stuntman Cliff Lyons in 1938 and withdrew from acting.

MASCOT PICTURES. Mascot Pictures was a prolific **poverty row** studio specializing in **serials** and **B Westerns** from 1926 to 1946. Nat Levine was its most prominent producer. **Gene Autry**'s *The Phantom Empire* (1935) and **Tom Mix**'s *The Miracle Rider* (1935) were produced by Mascot.

MCCOY, COLONEL TIM (1891–1978). Born Timothy John Fitzgerald McCoy, Tim McCoy was a flamboyant cowboy star who had actually lived the life he portrayed on-screen. Although he was born in Michigan, McCoy went west at a young age, ranched, and served with the U.S. Army, becoming an expert in **Native American** affairs and rising to the rank of lieutenant colonel. After finishing his service in World War I, McCoy was hired by **James Cruze** as technical consultant on *The Covered Wagon* (1923) in charge of bringing in authentic Native American crewmembers. McCoy's proficiency in Native American sign language proved as impressive as his masculine good looks, leading MGM to sign him to star in a series of **silent** Westerns to begin his long career. Usually billed as Colonel Tim McCoy, he moved easily into sound pictures with Columbia in the 1930s. The trademark **costume** of Colonel McCoy included immaculately tailored suits, an enormous ten-gallon hat with a high brim, an ornate crossover holster belt full of cartridges, and a large bandanna. In his early Westerns, he wore solid black with a white hat, but in his later Westerns he changed to a black hat, still extra large.

The costume simply reinforced his persona—that of a very large man dominating every situation for good. Standing at the entrance to the saloon, the batwing doors swinging behind him, McCoy's character would size up the situation, the camera usually showing a close-up of his trademark look: a flashing of the eyes from side to side. Friend and foe knew at once who was master of the circumstances.

Usually McCoy was associated with white horses, and his favorite was Starlight. In what was probably his most memorable screen role, McCoy played one of the **Rough Riders** in a series of cowboy films for Monogram. McCoy was the elder cowboy of the threesome, which included **Buck Jones** and Raymond Hatton. The Rough Riders series ended when McCoy was called into service again during World War II and when Buck Jones died in the Cocoanut Grove fire in 1942. Essentially, McCoy's film career ended after that. During the

1950s, he appeared frequently in **television Westerns**, but he also toured for many years with various circus companies, including the Carson Barnes Circus. In film and in the circus ring, Colonel Tim McCoy was a showman with his marksmanship, his horsemanship, and his adroitness with a whip.

MEXICANS. The earliest cinema Westerns usually developed conflict around **outlaws** and law-abiding citizens. By the mid-20th century, though, conflict more often came in response to a common enemy—usually **Indians**. Beginning in the 1960s, the common enemy in most Western plots became Mexicans. Because the **Western myth** is about unity and equality among whites, someone, somewhere must serve as the foil, savage and uncivilized. Indian bashing is no longer acceptable in American culture, but Hispanics have remained eligible for any kind of derision. Occasionally, Mexican characters of such films as *The Magnificent Seven* (1960), *Bandolero!* (1968), and *The Wild Bunch* (1969) achieve normative status. *See also* INDIANS.

MILES, BETTY (1910–1992). Betty Miles played the female lead in numerous low-budget Westerns of the 1940s, perhaps most remembered in Monogram's **Trail Blazers** series. She usually played a strong, independent woman, often with as many masculine skills as the Trail Blazers themselves, which made for good humor. An excellent rider, she did her own **stunts** on and off her horse. In *The Law Rides Again* (1943), Miles rides for the cavalry pursued by the villains, outsmarts and outrides them, and brings the cavalry to rescue **Hoot Gibson** and Ken Maynard. Miles's character was a transition from the helpless damsel in distress of the 1930s to the strong female lead beginning to appear in the 1950s. She played the pretty tomboy type in a sexy **pants role**—a beautiful, independent woman who could ride a horse, carry a gun, and protect her own ranch from the bad guys. Her riding ability was such that she often received billing with her **horse**, Sonny.

Miles's entry into film was as a stuntwoman. A Monogram Press Guide claims that while riding her horse up to a location set in 1941, Miles watched a female actor struggle with a horse through numerous retakes in a difficult action scene. Finally, Miles offered to demonstrate how to do the stunt, after which Monogram offered her a contract. Her stunts were well above the typical action for other **B Western** female actors of the time. On a Trail Blazers film, *Sonora Stagecoach* (1944), for instance, Miles makes a spectacular leap off the runaway stagecoach. Besides low-budget Western acting, Miles also doubled and stunted in full-budget films for female actors such as **Linda Darnell**. Fittingly, she followed her film career with a circus career.

THE MIRACLE RIDER (1935). **Tom Mix**, B. Reeves Eason, Armand Schaefer (directors). This 15-chapter **serial** was Tom Mix's last film and is the one upon which most of his reputation is based since it is one of the few accessible Mix films left. Like **Gene Autry**'s *The Phantom Empire* from the same year, this is a science-fiction Western. The first chapter begins with early settlement and the westward movement and the turmoils with **Indians**. Eventually the action is brought up to the present day, the 1930s, and the subject is the whites displacing Indians from a reservation. The evil Zaroff needs to run the Indians off the Texas reservation so he can mine the miracle element X-94, which will transform warfare. The serial is replete with an evil scientist in a laboratory; remote controlled, unmanned aircraft; hidden telephones; and plenty of gadgetry.

Typical of serials, every chapter ends with Tom Morgan (Mix) in some sort of inescapable dilemma, and only in the next chapter does the audience learn how he escaped or helped a supporting character escape. For example, in one chapter, Tom wrestles an oil truck (actually containing the highly explosive X-94) from the evil Indian imposter driver. While driving down the mountain road, the brakes give out and the truck goes over the cliff and explodes. Thus, the chapter ends and the audience thinks Tom was killed. But the next week, the story backs up a minute, and we see Tom jump from the truck at the last second. In another chapter, Tom enters a cave hiding the remote-powered Firebird air ship. A fight ensues. Tom falls into cockpit unconscious and Zaroff runs to the control panel, sends the Firebird up to a high altitude, and then throws it into a steep nosedive. The Firebird crashes in a ball of fire with Tom inside. End of chapter. But the next week, the film again starts a few minutes back. At the last second, Tom awakes, finds a parachute, and jumps. He gets tangled in a tree so he whistles to Tony Jr. Along comes the horse, and Tom cuts the ropes and falls into Tony's saddle. This is only one of many times in which Tony Jr. saves Tom.

The serial shows Mix's persona at its best. The cowboy is a stylish dresser and a dapper ladies' man, a Texas Ranger and friend to the Indians (all played by whites, evidently), but he also is an impish cowboy, still a kid in many ways. At one point he is tempted to steal a pie cooling outside a kitchen window. *See also* COSTUMES; INDIANS.

MITCHUM, ROBERT (1917–1997). Born in Connecticut, Robert Mitchum spent years playing heavies in **B Westerns**, including several **Hopalong Cassidy** films, before he became a certified Hollywood star in the 1950s. His mastery of an easygoing nonchalance in any situation brought him a wide variety of roles. In *River of No Return* (1954), for example, Mitchum as Matt Calder rescues Kay Weston (Marilyn Monroe), a **dance hall girl**, and her common-law partner, Harry Weston (**Rory Calhoun**), from a raging river, only to be betrayed by Harry who steals his horse. Much of the film involves Calder and Kay on the river, fleeing **Apaches** and chasing after Harry.

Mitchum and Monroe had known each other long before either of them began their careers. He was a natural choice for roles in which the line between the bad guy and the good guy was blurred. Heavy eyelids, the result of an early boxing career, and deep jaws gave an automatic appearance of toughness, while a smooth voice could make anything sound appealing. Other Mitchum Westerns include *El Dorado* (1966), *The Way West* (1967), and *Villa Rides* (1968), all **classic Westerns**. His last film, though, was the **postmodern Western** *Dead Man* (1995) in which he played one of Johnny Depp's antagonists.

MIX, TOM (1880–1940). Tom Mix, for all practical purposes, was responsible for the juvenilization of the **cowboy hero** and the development of the celebrity cowboy hero. If **William S. Hart**'s Westerns were noted for their dark realism, Tom Mix's Westerns were noted for their showmanship and glamour and for their appeal to younger audiences than had been the norm for Western cinema. Like later Western film celebrities, the on-screen persona often became confused with the off-screen persona. Mix's publicity often exaggerated his pre-film career as an authentic ranch cowboy and former lawman. He did in fact have a ranching background with the Miller Brothers 101 Ranch in Oklahoma, although most of that experience came from performing in their famous Wild West show. And he did serve for a short time as a peace officer in Dewey, Oklahoma.

Mix's connections with the 101 Ranch Wild West show eventually landed him in the movies with Selig Polyscope Company. His subsequent film career is usually divided into three phases. First is the phase of the early one- and two-reel silents made for Selig between 1909 and 1917. Most of these films were quickly produced affairs that were often more closely related to contemporary comic shorts than to other contemporary Westerns. Perhaps his best film of this period is *Chip of the Flying U* (1914), with Kathlyn Williams, based upon the B. M. Bower novel of the same title. The second phase is the late **silent era** during which Mix worked with Fox from 1917 to 1928. The Fox films were five- to eight-reelers, a number of which were non-Westerns. During this period, Mix starred in several films based on the novels of **Zane Grey**: *The Lone Star Ranger* (1923), *The Last of the Duanes* (1924), *Riders of the Purple Sage* (1925), and *The Rainbow Trail* (1925), all directed by Lynn Reynolds. While these all took great liberties with the original novels, adding plenty of classic Tom Mix **stunt** work and tricks with Tony the Wonder Horse, *Riders of the Purple Sage* reverts to the Hart model of dark Westerns, strong on tragedy but light on action. The third phase is Mix's work during the sound era from 1932 to 1935. Although he achieved great celebrity from his silent Westerns, his best work is probably in the late films of the sound era. *Destry Rides Again* (1932), based on the **Max Brand** novel, was billed as Tom Mix's return to the screen after a period working as a circus performer and is usually considered his best film. It follows the novel more closely than the later versions and shows that Mix could do more than stunt work when he had to.

The typical Tom Mix Western was seldom concerned about the West and typical tensions between the frontier and civilization common to earlier work of **Broncho Billy Anderson** and William S. Hart. The focus instead was always on Tom Mix as the performer. While the early silents especially were often shot on location with authentic Western locales, many around the Las Vegas, Nevada, area, few scenes actually celebrated the landscape. In fact, typical shots showed blank background with Mix solitary in the frame. Comic situations abounded in his films, and the action nearly always developed around opportunities for his stunt work rather than the usual violence of other early Westerns.

Mix took great pride in his athletic prowess, claiming that he always performed his own stunts. He did not, of course, but it was usually because his directors would not allow it. When the talkies came, the question for Mix, as with all actors, was whether his voice would suit the new movies, and, truthfully, his silent films are usually considered superior, but not because of his voice; the silents were more suited to his action scenes, his athletic emphasis on performing incredible stunts. The perfect Tom Mix film would have very little dialogue with or without sound technology.

Tom Mix was both actor and persona. He took great pains to develop the Tom Mix legend, which, through the reappearance of his one serial (and last film) *The Miracle Rider* (1935) and the long-running Tom Mix radio show (1933–1950), outlasted him for a decade after his death. He never hesitated in acknowledging that his persona did not reflect that of an authentic cowboy. No doubt his circus background influenced all he did on-screen. The **costume** he developed set the standard for later screen cowboys such as **Gene Autry** in that it was essentially uniform from one film to another—heavily starched and covered with intricate stitching. It was Tom Mix who first began wearing gloves regularly.

Mix's critical reputation in the United States has traditionally been low. His early silents have been compared unfavorably with those of Broncho Billy Anderson and William S. Hart. His best later films, *Riders of the Purple Sage* (1925) and *Destry Rides Again* (1932), were superseded by later, superior versions of the same stories. But his reputation in Europe was always greater than in the United States. By 1914 thousands were rushing to Paris theaters to see Tom Mix Westerns. In Italy and Great Britain as well, it was Tom Mix's Westerns that began developing a steady market for Westerns throughout the century.

Mix died a fitting death for a star of action Westerns. On October 12, 1940, his car topped a hill at a high speed near Phoenix, Arizona, and, not seeing a construction crew until it was too late, he swerved and flipped over a hill and was pinned beneath. Legend claims he was wearing a white suit, unwrinkled in the crash, along with his diamond belt buckle. The suitcase that crushed him was full of $20 gold pieces. Blake Edwards's 1988 film *Sunset* provides a greater-than-life account of Tom Mix. *See also* FRONTIER AS ESCAPE FROM THE CITY.

MODERN WESTERNS. These are Westerns set in the time period of the film's production and refer back to the **Western moment**. Films of the **classic Western** period such as *Giant* (1956) and *The Misfits* (1961) exemplify the genre well. *Brokeback Mountain* (2005) is a good example of a modern **alternative Western**.

MONUMENT VALLEY. Probably no other location in the United States is more recognizable as the setting for Westerns than Monument Valley, a vast area sprawling across Utah and Arizona on the Navajo Reservation. The valley is known for its magnificent buttes and plateaus. The first Western filmed on this location is *The Vanishing American* (1925). **John Ford** made the valley his trademark location using it in *Stagecoach* (1939), *My Darling Clementine* (1946), *Fort Apache* (1948), *She Wore a Yellow Ribbon* (1949), *Rio Grande* (1950), *Wagon Master* (1950), *The Searchers* (1956), and *Cheyenne Autumn* (1964). *See also* DETERRITORIALIZATION.

MORRICONE, ENNIO (1928–). Morricone was born in Rome and began working with Italian films early in his career. He is one of the most prolific composers for film in cinema history. He became famous in the 1960s for his work with **Sergio Leone** and **spaghetti Westerns**, especially for *A Fistful of Dollars* (1964). The music was a radical departure from typical Western cinema music of Dimitri Tiompkin or Elmer Bernstein.

One of the differences is in the way his soundtracks code the script, actually revealing elements of the plot, characters, and themes. Christopher Frayling has called this kind of work "caricatural soundtracks." In *A Fistful of Dollars*, **Clint Eastwood**'s character's actions and dialogue are complemented by high-pitched trills or single notes on a mouth harp. In *For a Few Dollars More* (1965), the same trill (and harp note) complements the Man with No Name, a lower-pitched trill signals Colonel Mortimer, and a chord on Spanish guitar indicates El Indio. As Indio lights up a joint, we hear an electronic whirr on the soundtrack—clearly indicating that this is no ordinary cigarette. In *The Good, the Bad and the Ugly* (1966), each of the characters of the title has a distinctive musical phrase, a trill, a whine—sometimes whistled, sometimes sung—all taken from the opening bars of the title theme. At times these musical phrases are the only indication of what a character is thinking: for example, a distinctive trill cluing us that Eastwood's character is not really drunk in *A Fistful of Dollars*. These musical signals can also cue the audience to laugh when moments of tension are over. Even when characters are off-screen, these musical signals can indicate their presence—the trill and whistle theme at each entrance of the Man with No Name, for example.

For his theme music, Morricone uses musical sound effects, bits and pieces from main themes to represent characters, grand orchestral passages for action sequences and panoramic **landscape** shots, majestic trumpet solos backed up by syncopated chords, and bullfight music at times. The main title themes might consist of simple electric guitar lines backed "by the addition of yells ('Quick, get back'), shrieks, gunshots, rifles being cocked, church bells, whipping sounds, trills, whines, rhythmic jew's harp, and other assorted electronic effects, to 'punctuate' the basically traditional Western score" (Frayling 1981, 167).

Morricone had scored several Westerns before meeting up with Leone. Initially, Leone was unimpressed with Morricone's work, but the collaboration for the music of the **Dollars Trilogy** proved to be one of the greatest in cinema history, producing some of the most memorable theme music ever and introducing a new kind of style and verve that changed Westerns forever.

MURPHY, AUDIE (1924–1971). Born in Texas, Audie Murphy is one of the most neglected Western stars and his work is undergoing a major revaluation. Murphy fought in World War II and returned a genuine war hero, a man who knew intense combat first hand. Audie Murphy was the most decorated soldier of the war, earning 33 medals and the Medal of Honor itself. James Cagney saw Murphy's picture on the cover of *Life* magazine and invited him to Hollywood, where he began playing bit roles in the late 1940s. In 1950 Universal signed him and began featuring the combat hero in Westerns. Audie Murphy starred in 29 Westerns of varying quality. His best films were probably *Destry* (1954); *Hell Bent for Leather* (1960); and his last film, *A Time for Dying* (1969), directed by **Budd Boetticher**. When he was killed in a plane crash in 1971, Audie Murphy was just developing into a real Western star independent of his war hero image.

MY DARLING CLEMENTINE **(1946). Henry Fonda,** Victor Mature, **Linda Darnell**, Cathy Downs, Jane Darwell, **John Ford** (director). In theory, John Ford's retelling of the **Wyatt Earp** legend and the gunfight at the **O.K. Corral** was supposed to be the most historically accurate to date. After all, Ford based his script on Stuart Lake's authorized biography of Earp, and Lake had interviewed the old lawman extensively before Earp died in 1929. Nevertheless, critics have enjoyed pointing out the film's inaccuracies through the years. Linda Darnell's character, Chihuahua, for instance, is evidently not historically accurate nor is Wyatt's affection for Clementine (Downs).

Much of the plot revolves around the **women** of the film, the hot-blooded, dark-haired **dance hall girl** Chihuahua and the virtuous, blonde Clementine, who comes from back East looking for Doc (Mature). Doc spurns her; nevertheless, Chihuahua flares out her jealousy. Wyatt, meanwhile, is attracted to Clementine. The Clantons, of course, must be dealt with, and so the film builds up to the climactic shootout between the outlaw gang and the Earps and Holliday.

Henry Fonda plays a soft-spoken, almost introverted Wyatt Earp while Mature's Doc is more Earp's rival than friend. Critics are generally divided over which **classic Western** treatment of the story is superior, John Ford's *My Darling Clementine* or John Sturges's *Gunfight at the O.K. Corral* (1957). John Ireland, a steady character actor, played in both films, first as Billy Clanton and later as Johnny Ringo. *See also* BRENNAN, WALTER; CARD PLAY AND THE COWBOY HERO; HISTORICAL AUTHENTICITY.

MYTHIC SPACE. Richard Slotkin defines mystic space as "a pseudo-historical (or pseudo-real) setting that is powerfully associated with stories and concerns rooted in the culture's myth/ideological tradition" (1992, 234). In other words, all Westerns take place in a mythic space immediately recognized by viewers as "the West," whether that

"West" is the **Great Plains**, the Rocky Mountains, or the deserts of Mexico. Significantly, the cultural image of the West for most American viewers probably comes from images on the screen in Western films rather than from either fiction narrative or geographic reality. *See also* LANDSCAPE.

MYTH OF THE WEST, MYTH OF THE FRONTIER. The significance of the frontier in American culture has often been traced back to the Puritans' "errand into the wilderness"—their attempt to convert **Native Americans** from savagery to (white) civilization. Depictions of the wilderness just ahead of the settlements as the Promised Land encouraged the idea that the frontier was something to be conquered, land to be wrested from its native inhabitants and given to, it often was claimed, God's people. Such underlying narratives eventually developed into fully articulated ideas of **Manifest Destiny**, the idea that whites were destined by God to inhabit and civilize the frontier. **"Regeneration through violence,"** became a catch phrase for what, among other things, is usually seen today as a planned genocide of native peoples.

After the United States successfully subdued Native American tribes by the 1890s, people began to revaluate what had happened. Frederick Jackson Turner's **Frontier Thesis** came to dominate historical interpretation, and Theodore Roosevelt's idea of "the winning of the West" romanticized the conquest of the frontier and the effort to keep America Anglo-Saxon. The last manifestation of this view came in the epic 1962 film, *How the West Was Won*, which, ironically, closed the curtain on any thoughts that the United States had undertaken a noble enterprise on the frontier. While the film celebrates the Western conquest, American culture of the 1960s was again revaluating the past and, as Richard Slotkin shows us, seeing the westward movement as one more example of American imperialistic greed that continued beyond the Western frontier into the invasions of Southeast Asia, South America, and the Middle East.

The myth of the West manifests itself in many ways throughout cinema Westerns. The frontier, for example, is masculine and must be subdued by raw masculine strength. However, subduing the frontier necessitates feminizing it with eastern civilization.

The untamed West represents the base savagery that lies at the heart of all humanity. Left utterly unrestrained, it manifests itself in such practices as scalping, torture, and rape. In order to tame the frontier, white masculinity must wage **savage war** against uncivilized forces. *See also* FRONTIER AS ESCAPE FROM THE CITY; INDIANS.

MYTHOLOGICAL HISTORICISM AND ALTERNATIVE WESTERNS. No matter how much a director of **alternative Westerns** may want to counter images, themes, and even **clichés** of **classic Westerns**, the cultural accoutrements of a century-long film tradition remains. Armando Pratt refers to this fact as mythological historicism. Films such as *Dances with Wolves* (1990), *The Last of the Mohicans* (1992), and *Geronimo: An American Legend* (1993) "produce not so much a new Indian as an updated version." No matter what one does, "the Indian, whom revision would present as an authentic historical person, still complies with the demand of the mythology of conquest" (Pratt cited in Cawelti 1999, 107). Despite all efforts to portray **Native Americans** authentically, in each of these films a sympathetic white character is necessary in order to validate Native pride. *See also* INDIANS.

– N –

NATIVE AMERICANS. It is no longer politically correct to refer to the indigenous peoples of the United States as "Indians," yet the term is indispensable in discussing Westerns. Throughout most of cinema history, Native Americans have been referred to by this disparaging term. Today, scholars generally use the term "Native American" when referring to actual actors or actual people, and they rarely use "Indian," only when referring to characters in films and novels. *See also* INDIANS.

NEOREALIST WESTERNS. Neorealist Westerns are a kind of **alternative Western** that began appearing after the 1970s. While paying extreme fidelity to historical reality, neorealist Westerns develop from revisionist interpretations of Western history and, thus, expose the façade of **classic Westerns** and the Western **myth** by showing previously ignored sides of the historical frontier experience. The term originated with Richard Slotkin, who identified the following subtypes: *Monte Walsh* (1970), *Wild Rovers* (1971), and *The Culpepper Cattle Company* (1972), which show the cowboy as a common working man; *The Life and Times of Judge Roy Bean* (1972), which depict the town-tamer as psychopath; and *Tell Them Willie Boy Is Here* (1969), which shows the **Native American** as ethnic outsider, not the traditional noble savage. *See also* FRONTIER AS ESCAPE FROM THE CITY; HISTORICAL AUTHENTICITY.

NEW CRITICISM. Beginning in the late 1930s, New Criticism became the dominant method of critical inquiry. It evaluates literary texts, including films, based upon a set of formal criteria involving attention to technical aspects of a work of art. The technical artistry of a work matters more than any cultural or historical context. In fact, at its extreme, New Criticism decontextualizes the work altogether. Because New Criticism so dominated academic debate until well into the 1980s, cinema Westerns, as well as popular Western novels, did not merit much respect as works of art. Since cultural contexts of a work of art are irrelevant to the "new critic," the Western was viewed as a hopelessly flawed genre. For the new critic, Westerns were trite formulaic renditions of superficial stories based primarily on **clichés**. Only after New Criticism ceased being an influence did cinema Westerns begin to develop any measure of artistic respectability at all. **Structuralism** is often viewed as the successor to New Criticism.

NEW WESTERN HISTORY. This term refers to the revisionist history of the American West associated most often with historian Patricia Limerick, who in the 1980s began questioning Frederick Jackson Turner's **Frontier Thesis** and the traditional interpretation of the frontier as being the formative feature of the American character. Turner's interpretation of the frontier was the basis of most Westerns of the classic era as well as the **silent era**. New Western history has had a profound effect on cinema Westerns since the 1990s in the creation of **alternative Westerns**. Essentially, New Western history makes four claims, as laid out by Limerick in a "nonmanifesto" in 1989:

1. The term *frontier* is nationalistic and usually racist. The westward movement was a movement of white exploitation.
2. Whether for good or ill, the westward movement occurred among a diverse group of peoples and was not confined to white males.
3. This interaction continues today. The "frontier" did not end in 1890, as Turner claimed. Much has happened since and is as important as what went before.
4. The western movement is not a story of triumph over adversity and certainly did not result in the ennoblement of the American character. Quite to the contrary: the western movement is fraught with moral ambiguity and shame.

Obviously, this view of the West is at odds with the view of the **classical Western**.

NOIR WESTERNS. Noir literally means "black cinema" and derives from the "film noirs" of post–World War II—dark, moody films, usually black and white, with strong protagonists involved in intense psychological struggle. *The Maltese Falcon* (1941) is often considered typical. Westerns of the period often partook of the noir mood. Noir Western heroes such as **Jimmy Stewart**, **Henry Fonda**, **Randolph Scott**, and **Gary Cooper** often played the strong **cowboy hero** torn between his inherent rugged individualism and the needs of oncoming civilization. His dissociation from any social group becomes the story conflict. Raoul Walsh's ***Dark Command*** (1940), William Wellman's ***The Ox-Bow Incident*** (1943), Henry King's *The Gunfighter* (1950), **Anthony Mann**'s ***Winchester '73*** (1950), and *The Naked Spur* (1953), Fred Zinnemann's ***High Noon*** (1952), and **Budd Boetticher**'s ***Seven Men from Now*** (1956) are often cited as the Western genre's contribution to noir.

One element that sets noir Westerns apart from other Westerns is the nature of the **violence** in these films. For heroes of noir Westerns such as Gary Cooper's Will Kane in *High Noon* and Jimmy Stewart's Lin McAdam in *Winchester '73*, violence is not merely a means of purging evil and anarchy as in earlier Westerns. Instead, violence becomes a means of asserting, through brute strength of character, the hero's moral determination, setting him apart from the society he has ostensibly been a part of.

Strictly speaking, noir is a mood, not a genre, and the limits of noir are difficult to place. Some would not consider any Western as noir. Some would not limit noir to black-and-white films of the postwar period but identify noir elements in any period.

NOSTALGIA. A basic subtext of the Western **myth** is nostalgia for a time in the past when life was somehow better than the present. Early Westerns consciously reminisced about the end of the frontier. But all Westerns look nostalgically to the **Western moment** in order to explore contemporary problems. The concept of nostalgia implies not just a looking back but a longing for the older times. A natural argument about Westerns, then, is that nostalgia for the days of the American frontier ultimately is the basis for everything Western, whether movies, novels, rodeos, or even Western fashion. The problem, of course, is what the nostalgia actually refers back to. *See also* FRONTIER AS ESCAPE FROM THE CITY.

– O –

OATER. *See* HORSE OPERA.

O'HARA, MAUREEN (1920–). Born Maureen FitzSimons to a prominent family in Dublin, Ireland, Maureen O'Hara was a durable female star, notable for her stunning red hair. Dubbed "the Queen of **Technicolor**," she was able to find quality film roles at every stage of her life due to her versatility and athleticism as an actor. She played Esmeralda in *The Hunchback of Notre Dame* (1939), opposite Charles Laughton, in her teens; *Miracle on 34th Street* (1947) in her twenties; *The Parent Trap* (1961) in her forties; and *Only the Lonely* (1991) in her seventies. O'Hara had a long career in Westerns and is often associated with **John Wayne**, a close friend off stage with whom she starred in five films, three of which were Westerns: *Rio Grande* (1950), *McLintock!* (1963), and *Big Jake* (1971). In *Rio Grande* she played Wayne's estranged wife who has come out West to reclaim her son, one of the colonel's new recruits sent to help fight **Apaches**. Tension is heavy between the former spouses, and O'Hara shows she is a woman capable of handling a man even on the frontier. Eventually, they discover why they used to love each other and are reconciled. Other Maureen O'Hara Westerns include *Buffalo Bill* (1944), *Comanche Territory* (1950), *The Redhead from Wyoming* (1953), *War Arrow* (1953), and *The Rare Breed* (1966). *See also* CAVALRY TRILOGY.

O.K. CORRAL. The gunfight at the O.K. Corral in Tombstone, Arizona, on October 26, 1881, has been told from every possible angle, and it would be hard to find a better example of how historical versions of an event vary widely depending on the motivation of the interpreter. The basic story is that **Wyatt Earp**, his brothers, and **Doc Holliday** met the Clancys, along with Johnny Ringo, at the corral for the most famous shootout in the history of the West. Tradition says that 30 shots were fired in 30 seconds, but only three men were killed. Inconsistencies with the historical events have meant opportunities for filmmakers. Who were the good guys? The Earps? Not necessarily. The Clantons? Perhaps. What about Johnny Ringo? Was he simply a misunderstood gunman? Among film versions of the event are *My Darling Clementine* (1946), *Gunfight at the O.K. Corral* (1957), *Wyatt Earp* (1994), and *Tombstone* (1993). *See also* HISTORICAL AUTHENTICITY.

OPEN RANGE, APPEAL OF. On-screen **towns** inevitably appear and some scenes must be shot indoors, but the most appealing shot in any Western is nearly always the panoramic sweep across the open range showing the enormous size of the **landscape** and the healthy herds of cattle roaming at will. Western characters struggle with the land, but they seldom really want to tame it. Cattle ranges are still close to nature just as the buffalo ranges were. Cattle can be raised with little damage to the open range, so Westerns celebrate cattle raising on the open range. In *Open Range* (2003), Charley (**Kevin Costner**) looks out over the enormous empty vista with Boss (**Robert Duvall**), sees someone riding at a far distance, and mutters, "It's getting crowded around here." A rider on the open range of a Western is at one with the land. The **horse** connects the rider with the land, but the solitary rider's dependence on the land is also emphasized. *See also* COST-NER, KEVIN.

ORIGINS OF THE WESTERN. Since Westerns are stories set on the American frontier, they can trace their origins back to stories of the frontier from the earliest days of the North American settlements. **Indian captivity narratives** such as that by Mary Rowlandson, *The Narrative of the Captivity and the Restoration of Mrs. Mary Rowlandson* (1682), began a trend in popular literature to portray the frontier as exotic yet savage and chaotic. James Fenimore Cooper's early 19th-century Leatherstocking Tales, set in pre-Colonial upstate New York, developed many of the formulaic features seen in later Westerns: the **chase-and-pursuit** scene, the gun fight between hero and savage, the restrained **violence**, and the regenerative power of the wilderness. Late 19th-century dime novel writers discovered a profitable niche in the market for exaggerated tales of action and violence featuring newly discovered Western heroes such as **Wild Bill Hickok** and **Wyatt Earp**. Many of the legendary stories of the West depend more on the dime novel tradition than on historical fact.

But the first novel that can accurately be called a true Western is Owen Wister's *The Virginian* (1902), which develops the laconic hero who is abiding by a carefully prescribed masculine **code** of honor and, after numerous feats of masculine prowess, faces his nemesis in a quick-draw contest that settles all. *The Virginian*, the source of numerous films, includes perhaps the most famous line in any Western—"When you call me that, smile"—delivered as the hero responds to the evil Trampas's insult with a whip of the gun. Through the 20th century up to our own time, Western popular fiction has continued to develop from the Wister tradition. Cinema Westerns beginning with *The Great Train Robbery* (1903) started their own parallel tradition, and while many films have been based on popular Western novels and cinema Westerns share many similarities in narrative, Western fiction must be considered separate from the cinema Western tradition. *See also* CODE OF THE WEST; FORMULAS, CLASSIC WESTERN; FRONTIER AS ESCAPE FROM THE CITY.

THE OUTLAW **(1943).** Jane Russell, Jack Buetel, Howard Hughes (director). The plot of this film is rather simple. **Billy the Kid** (Buetel) and Rio (Russell) attempt to outwit Pat Garrett (Thomas Mitchell), with **Doc Holliday** (Walter Huston) thrown in the mix. But what the film is known for has little to do with the plot; Jane Russell played what was, up to 1943, the most deliberately erotic role ever in a Western. After World War II, directors and producers introduced more erotic elements into Westerns for marketing purposes. This film was re-released in 1946 and in 1950 to huge box office sales. Before the war, ***Destry Rides Again*** (1939) had proven a huge success partly for **Marlene Dietrich**'s suggestive work.

Howard Hughes marketed *The Outlaw* with Russell's sex appeal, using blatant suggestiveness, and her well-endowed chest in a special bra designed by Hughes, as its sole advertising angle. Its production was widely publicized and the censors caused problems at every turn. In fact, the 2004 biographical film about Hughes, *The Aviator*, dramatizes the problems encountered by *The Outlaw*. The film came out as a fairly accurate portrayal of Billy the Kid, but the overt eroticism was a new dimension for Westerns. Throughout the film, Billy and Rio banter suggestively, and at times Billy even becomes sadistic. In retrospect we see a film in which Rio is minimized as a person and serves only as a machine for gratifying lust. One scene in particular displays this fact: Doc and Billy play cards and wonder which the winner would rather have, a horse or Rio. They decide the horse has more value. *See also* CARD PLAY AND THE COWBOY HERO; CULT-OF-THE-OUTLAW WESTERN.

OUTLAWS. Most Westerns set characters who support some form of law and order in opposition to either savages, such as **Indians** or **Mexicans**, or, more commonly, outlaws. Famous outlaws such as **Jesse James**, his brother, Frank, and the James gang; **Billy the Kid**; the Daltons; and the Clancys populate Westerns of all periods. According to typical **clichés**, outlaws wear black, while **cowboy heroes** wear white; outlaws are dirty and rough shaven; and outlaws rarely adhere to the **code of the West**. *See also* CULT-OF-THE-OUTLAW WESTERN.

THE OX-BOW INCIDENT (1943). **Henry Fonda**, Henry Morgan, **Dana Andrews**, **Anthony Quinn**, William A. Wellman (director). This **noir Western** is based on the novel by Walter Van Tilburg Clark.

Critics who usually dismiss all Westerns as unworthy often grant that if a Western could be regarded as great literature, Clark's novel might qualify. The film's trailer makes the connection to Clark's popular novel when the film's star, Henry Fonda, takes the novel from the shelf and claims a share of its status for his film. Today, *The Ox-Bow Incident* is remembered as a film from the darkest days of World War II, a period when the United States was losing the war. It was a film that captured the mood of America perfectly and because of that was rejected soundly at the box office. America needed hope at that moment, not despair. Critics have praised the film from the time of its production. If a Western movie can reach the level of significant art, this film does it.

The story depicts the futility of trying to assert one's sense of justice in the face of strong opposition. A popular rancher has been reportedly murdered and his cattle rustled. A mob organizes and pursues the murderers. At the Ox-Bow the mob finds a group of men with cattle carrying the rancher's brand, and the men do not have a bill of sale. The mob hangs them. Minutes later the mob finds that the rancher was not killed after all and that he had made a legitimate sale of his cattle to the men just hanged.

Henry Fonda plays Gil Carter, the point-of-view character. He develops plenty of inner conflict as he realizes there is no evidence to condemn the men about to be hanged. The **noir** elements at times seem overwhelming: the stark realism emphasized by sharp blacks and whites and by purely interior studio settings. The film seems utterly pessimistic. Carter is better than the others in the mob only because he votes not to hang the men. But voting, as Henry David Thoreau has said, is but a feeble effort at disapproval. Ultimately, Carter does nothing to save innocent men from hanging. Dana Andrews played Donald Martin, one of the accused, in probably his best acting performance and revealed the nature of utter hopelessness. Martin obviously knows his innocence, yet he can do nothing. Desperate to muster some measure of respectability, Martin writes a letter to his wife but insists nobody read it before he dies. They read it anyway. Even that slight gesture of humanity is denied him.

Powerful masculinity issues are explored as Major Tetley (Frank Conroy) desperately wants his son to renounce his eastern, feminizing education and be a man. When young Tetley (William Eyeth) refuses to assist in the actual hanging—out of cowardice, the major assumes—Tetley returns home and commits suicide. His own manhood has been repudiated. *The Ox-Bow Incident* was nominated for the best picture Academy Award but lost out to *Casablanca*.

– P –

PALANCE, JACK (1919–2006). Born Volodymyr Palanyuk in Pennsylvania, Jack Palance was one of the great bad guys of Westerns during his long career making a wide variety of films. His first major role was one of his best—Jack Wilson, the sadistic **gunfighter**, in *Shane* (1953). Nominated for best supporting actor for the role, Palance fit the part perfectly, dressed in solid black with huge guns jutting out from his waist, constantly fiddling with his fingers. While confronting an obviously inept townsman who was slow on the draw, Palance gets the drop, hesitates long enough to enjoy looking into the eyes of a man about to die, and then fires, dead center.

Throughout the 1950s and early 1960s, Palance regularly played villains, gunfighters, and assorted types, but when **spaghetti Westerns** came out he headed for Europe and made a string of highly popular **European Westerns** and developed a large following away from the United States. Since he began his career as a boxer, Palance was always acutely aware of his own fitness. When he accepted his Academy Award for best supporting actor in *City Slickers* (1991), the grand old man of Westerns dropped to the floor in front of the audience and began doing one-handed pushups. Jack Palance seemed just as young as when he played in *Shane*.

PANTS ROLES. Prior to the 1940s, female leads in Westerns tended to wear long riding skirts and ride sidesaddle. By the 1940s, however, cultural mores were beginning to change, and a highpoint in many films of the time came when the pretty female lead changed her skirt for sexy, tight-fitting pants and rode a horse alongside the men. Pants roles clearly emphasized independence but also gave films under the **Production Code** a means of providing sex appeal for the audience. **Barbara Stanwyck**, for example, could work her female charms while dressed in fine lace, but when she donned pants and rode her horse like a man in *Cattle Queen of Montana* (1954), she showed her charms to the audience. The images of **B Western** female stars such as **Reno Browne**, **Dale Evans**, **Evelyn Finley**, **Beth Marion**, and **Sally Payne** often depended on their pants roles. *See also* COSTUMES; WOMEN.

PAYNE, SALLY (1912–1999). Sally Payne was an unusual female lead of 1940s **B Westerns** in that she usually played strong-willed, independent **women** in **pants roles**. Rarely was she involved in romance, though she was usually more involved in the plots than most women in low-budget Westerns. In *Jesse James at Bay* (1941), Payne teams up with Gale Storm in a bit of comedy involving two reporters from back East digging for dirt on **Jesse James** (**Roy Rogers**). Other typical Payne films are **Republic**'s *Young Bill Hickok* (1940), *Robin Hood of the Pecos* (1941), and *Nevada City* (1941). In later years Payne wrote children's books.

PECKINPAH, SAM (1925–1984). At one point in *The Wild Bunch* (1969), Angel asks Pike, "Would you give guns to someone to kill your father or your mother or your brother?" Pike responds, "Ten thousand cuts an awful lot of family ties." Such an attitude set the tone for the film that did more to change not just Westerns but action films in general. Peckinpah's *The Wild Bunch* was probably the most violent Western and perhaps the most violent American film in its time. It was not so much the quantity of killing in the film but the quality of killing—the amount of blood spilled and splashed, the stylized slow-motion scenes of death. Once all restraint was gone, Hollywood films never looked back.

Peckinpah, like other directors, got his training in **television Westerns** in the 1950s, directing episodes of *Gunsmoke* and *The Rifleman* series among many others. *Ride the High Country* (1962), starring **Randolph Scott** in his last role, was Peckinpah's first cinema Western. While a solid film, it did not show much of the Peckinpah style that would surface in the next few years. He followed that with *Major Dundee* in 1965, another good Western in the **classic Western** vein. But the world had changed greatly between Peckinpah's first Western and 1969 when he released *The Wild Bunch*. **Italian Westerns** had attacked the very core classic Western values and styles.

The Vietnam War was tearing the American culture apart, and riots in the streets were commonplace. Evening news accounts of the war were showing America live images of bloody combat it had never seen before. When the film came out, it immediately captured a receptive audience. Its repudiation of all the unquestioned Western **myths** and, by extension, all the unquestioned American myths reinforced the chaos pervading the culture itself.

Peckinpah followed with other successful Westerns and non-Westerns, all continuing the assault on cultural myths. *Pat Garrett and Billy the Kid* (1973), for example, questions the famous **outlaw** legend. Kris Kristofferson, just hitting his popularity as a songwriter and singer, played **Billy the Kid**, swaggering with style in this **antimyth Western**. **James Coburn**, just coming away from his cocky performances in *Waterhole #3* (1967) and *Fistful of Dynamite, aka Duck, You Sucker* (1971), played Pat Garrett.

PLACE, ETTA (1878?–?). One of the most famous mysteries of the old West is the identity of Etta Place. We do have her picture and we have numerous early references to her in historical records, but what ultimately happened to her is unknown. Place's story in Western films, however, is usually based on one fact: if there was a need for a really gorgeous female **outlaw**, Etta Place fit the bill. Other historical **women** of the West, such as **Belle Starr** or **Calamity Jane** often lacked what Hollywood considers glamour. Place was variously an associate or a lover of Harry Longbaugh, aka, the Sundance Kid. Perhaps she was a school teacher or perhaps she was a madam of a Fort Worth brothel. Legend says that she could ride and shoot as well as either Butch Cassidy or the Sundance Kid. She evidently followed the outlaws to South America, but what happened after that remains a mystery. Katharine Ross played her role in *Butch Cassidy and the Sundance Kid* (1969). Cassidy's (Paul Newman) assessment of her may be accurate: "She was the best housekeeper in the Pampas but she was a whore at heart." *See also* HISTORICAL AUTHENTICITY.

THE PLAINSMAN (1936). Gary Cooper, **Jean Arthur**, **James Ellison**, Helen Burgess, **George Hayes**, Cecil B. DeMille (director). This high-budget epic begins with the end of the Civil War and **Abraham**

Lincoln's assassination and ends with the killing of **Wild Bill Hickok** in **Deadwood, South Dakota**. DeMille and crew worked hard to be authentic in everything except history and character as he takes the barest elements of the historical narrative and glorifies them.

According to historical accounts, Lincoln, on the afternoon before he died, profoundly pronounced, "The frontier should be secure" (a remark repeated in the film). This new "doctrine" gave permission to some of the baser sorts to head West and begin their ruthless quest for power. DeMille probably intended that this would be how we interpret the actions of the wily merchant, Lattimer (Charles Bickford)—the man who takes out crates labeled farming implements that are actually full of guns for the Indians. According to **classic Western** values, one of the vilest characters in the old West is the gunrunner who trades guns to Indians. **New Western history**, however, requires a different interpretation of this classic version of the Western **myth**. According to this new history, gunrunners are not the bad guys in the West. Instead, the postwar despoilers of the West are the baser sorts such as **Wild Bill Hickok**, Buffalo Bill, and even **Calamity Jane** (who sells her soul to be male and yet desperately wants Bill to love her).

The interpretation DeMille wanted to show the 1930s audience was probably this: The divided nation comes together after the war to finish the business of taming the West and ridding it of savagery. Brave men like Wild Bill Hickok (Cooper), Buffalo Bill Cody (Ellison), **General George Armstrong Custer** (John Miljan), and even brave **women** like Calamity Jane (Arthur), albeit always weaker than men, were needed to tame the rugged West. Men needed to separate themselves from feminizing influences, but here, Buffalo Bill has made the mistake of getting married. His new wife, Louisa (Helen Burgess), will destroy his character unless she can learn that her values are false and his are noble. Even Wild Bill must beware of giving in to his feminine side by falling in love with the masculinated (although gorgeous blonde with flawless Hollywood complexion) Calamity Jane. The minute he counts on her, she gives in to natural feminine weakness and reveals the location of an army troop in order to save his life. She redeems herself, however, by riding through withering gunfire in search of reinforcements. This is the story DeMille wanted for his audience. And, no doubt, the audience approved. Add to that the kinds of sets, outdoor scenery, **stunts**, and special effects impossible for **B Western** budgets, and we have one of the great Western spectacles of the pre–World War II era.

The Plainsman exemplifies a problem that many contemporary viewers have with older Westerns and thus shows the sharp contrast between **postmodern** values and the values of Cecil DeMille's audience. In the film, as DeMille evidently intended it to be viewed, the savage **Indians** who have captured Wild Bill confront Calamity with a choice: tell where the army troop is camped or the man she loves will be promptly killed. Which choice would serve the greater good? Wild Bill hisses, "Do not tell." She tells. The original audience surely condemned her and probably attributed her "failure" to feminine weakness. Many typical viewers today would not condemn her. They might ask whether choosing the greater good is a better choice than saving her lover. Many today might also note that Calamity does not even consider whether the greater good for the army is morally a greater good than for the Native Americans. Also, Lattimer the gun merchant, as DeMille portrays him, sneaks out West to sell guns to the Indians. Original viewers would have seen his activity as a basic evil. Yet many viewers today might question whether the historic selling of guns to Native Americans was necessarily bad. In the movie, had the white gunrunner not sold the guns, the Sioux could not have fought and destroyed Custer and his men. The film presents conflicting values, as if the values of the whites are superior to the values of the Native Americans. For many viewers today, this historical conflict of values makes a film like *The Plainsman* hopelessly dated and explains in part why audiences turn away from the older Westerns. *See also* LITTLE BIG HORN, BATTLE OF; MANIFEST DESTINY.

POSTMODERN WESTERNS. This term is often used so loosely that it is not very helpful, but there are certain Westerns released since the 1990s for which the term is appropriate. Usually, postmodernism refers to the utter rejection of the grand meta-narratives upon which modernity was based. If **alternative Westerns** assume the traditional Western **myths** of the modern period are no longer valid and instead attempt to provide an alternate view of history, postmodern Westerns from the same period no longer question the past because questioning is irrelevant. Postmodernism is fundamentally about rejecting outright any sense of myth at all. It is not that the myths are not valid; it is that there are no myths. Postmodern Westerns are stylistically different from other Westerns in that they reject any duty to portray reality. The audience knows immediately as the film begins that what it is seeing is not real, was never real, and is not to be confused with reality. In fact, reality itself is open for questioning. For the outsider, for the viewer still accustomed to watching old **John Wayne** Westerns, these films just do not make sense. They mix everything up. We have bullet holes that go clean through so that a shaft of sunlight shines through in *The Quick and the Dead* (1995). Or, in *Dead Man* (1995), we have a protagonist who is the reincarnation (evidently) of a dead English poet going on a quest through utterly surreal **landscape**. *See also* HISTORICAL AUTHENTICITY.

POST-WESTERNS. This term is often used synonymously with **antimyth Westerns** to refer to the films that came out in a short period of time from the 1960s and 1970s, including **spaghetti Westerns**. Post-Westerns were clearly influenced by the popular ideas of mid-20th-century existentialism as advocated by Jean-Paul Sartre and Albert Camus. Because they did not adequately deal with social issues such as sexism, homophobia, and racism (against **Native Americans**, **African Americans**, Hispanic Americans, and even Asian Americans), post-Westerns made a transitional philosophical statement and were then superseded by **alternative Westerns**. *See also DJANGO*; DOLLARS TRILOGY; LEONE, SERGIO.

POVERTY ROW. The really cheap **B Westerns** were produced in what was loosely called poverty row, a section of Los Angeles near Gower Street and Sunset Boulevard. Here numerous short-lived studios churned out quickly made films full of **stock footage** and company actors on subsistence contracts. Studios such as **PRC**, **Republic**, **Mascot**, **Grand National**, and Monogram were poverty row companies. *See also* STANDARD PICTURE COMMITMENT CONTRACTS; TERM PLAYER CONTRACT.

PRE-WESTERNS. Films of American frontier life set in periods earlier than the conventional **Western moment** of the post–Civil War era have sometimes been called pre-Westerns. Pre-Westerns, such as *The Last of the Mohicans* (1992) and *Drums along the Mohawk* (1939), exemplify the genre well. The term evidently originated with Philip French (1977).

PRODUCERS RELEASING CORPORATION (PRC). This company began making low-budget Westerns in 1940. Its productions were so bad that they only played in second-rate theaters. Perhaps its best series was the *Texas Rangers*, initially starring Dave O'Brien, Guy Wilkerson, and James Newill as the trio of lawmen. Later, **Tex Ritter** replaced Newill in the series. By 1947 PRC had merged into the Eagle-Lion film company.

PRODUCTION CODE. In 1930, based on recommendations of the Hays Commission, the Hollywood establishment implemented a code of moral behaviors that were acceptable on film. Movies issued prior to the Production Code naturally tend to have more sexual content than later films. Prior to the Production Code, Westerns often portrayed **women** as strong, independent, and sometimes even equal to the male hero. Viewers today are often surprised at the open sexuality portrayed in pre-code Westerns. The institution of the code and its puritanical requirements concerning male-female relationships directly resulted in female actors portraying frail, dependent, asexual heroines with little individuality.

PUNK WESTERNS. This term defines progressive Westerns—as opposed to some that look nostalgically backward—that have utterly rejected the **classic Western** myth and attempt to expose the myth's absurdities. A punk cultural perspective from the 1980s to the present has traditionally emphasized alienation from society with deliberate unconventionality in style, whether fashion, art, or music. *Dead Man* (1995), with its rock soundtrack and seemingly fatalistic worldview, typifies the genre. Jean-Claude La Marre's hip-hop Westerns, *Gang of Roses* (2003) and *Brothers in Arms* (2005), also share punk sensibilities but on a lighter scale. Sometimes these films are called post-punk Westerns, perhaps because they have come out after the 1980s punk rock era. *See also* HISTORICAL AUTHENTICITY; MYTH OF THE WEST, MYTH OF THE FRONTIER; POSTMODERN WESTERNS.

– Q –

QUANTRILL, WILLIAM CLARKE (1837–1865). Historically, Quantrill was a schoolteacher turned Southern partisan, known for developing guerilla hit-and-run raids of Union sympathizers in Kansas and Missouri. History usually portrays him as a cruel, vicious murderer and opportunist. In 1863 Quantrill's raiders sacked Lawrence, Kansas, killing over 100 people and torching the city. Like other Civil War characters, Quantrill has been interpreted both negatively and sympathetically. Among his protégés were Frank and **Jesse James**, the Dalton brothers, and Bloody Bill Anderson— all subjects of legend and numerous films. In *Kansas Raiders* (1950), Quantrill (Brian Donlevy) serves as a charismatic type of father figure to Jesse James (**Audie Murphy**). In *Dark Command* (1940), Quantrill (Walter Pidgeon) was the admired schoolteacher to the **John Wayne** and **Roy Rogers** characters, who both die in the raid. Most films about the James and Dalton gangs in some way refer to their early connections with Quantrill. An early plot element in **Clint Eastwood**'s *The Outlaw Josey Wales* (1976) has Wales joining an offshoot of Quantrill's band led by Bloody Bill Anderson (John Russell).

QUEST OR JOURNEY MOTIF. Some of the most memorable Westerns revolve around a quest or journey motif, sometimes made by the lone hero or sometimes by a band of travelers. In *The Searchers* (1956), Ethan Edwards (**John Wayne**) sets out to find a family member kidnapped by **Indians**. In *Stagecoach* (1939), a group of varied pilgrims cross the wide basin of **Monument Valley** in a stagecoach, attempting to elude warring Indians. As with traditional quests throughout literature, the quest in a Western usually involves movement from innocence to experience, naiveté to awareness. Ritualistic trials must be passed before the goal can be attained. Inevitably, the main hero undergoes major character change, as in **Anthony Mann**'s *Winchester '73* (1950).

THE QUICK AND THE DEAD (1995). Sharon Stone, **Gene Hackman**, **Leonardo DiCaprio**, **Russell Crowe**, Woody Strode, Sam Raimi (director). The town of Redemption is holding a world championship quick-draw tournament, and the best shooters from around the world have gathered. Herod (Hackman) is the mastermind behind the tournament and the town. One gunslinger who is not part of the contest is Cort (Crowe), a prisoner in chains and Herod's former partner in crime, who has now found God and become a preacher, a man of peace. One of the contestants is "The Kid" (DiCaprio), lightning fast and itching to prove himself. We learn later that he is Herod's son and has never been good enough for his father. But the center of attention is on Ellen (Stone), a mystery figure wearing her guns with confidence. Herod tries to figure out her secret, but she holds it close to the end, when we discover that she seeks revenge against Herod, who killed Ellen's father years earlier. The film provided the first major roles for DiCaprio and Crowe and it was Woody Strode's last film. He died before it was released.

Everything about this **self-reflexive Western** countered all Westerns before it. Scenes from famous Westerns of the past are parodied. When the loser gets shot, he does not just crumple and fall. He is blown upward and backward as if hit by an explosion. When Charlie Moonlight (Strode) is a bit slow on the draw, a bullet blows a hole the size of a baseball through his head. Other victims do flips in the street from their hits. As Herod falls in the last scene, a glint of sunlight shines down through the hole in the middle of his heart.

The initial reaction to *The Quick and the Dead* from fans and reviewers still adjusted to the **classic Western** tradition and even somewhat to the **antimyth** tradition was overwhelmingly negative. The film was not really a box-office success. Sam Raimi fans, however, loved it because they immediately saw the connection of the film to his Evil Dead series of horror films. *The Quick and the Dead* was quickly nicknamed "the Quick and the Evil Dead." It has since become a cult classic, though not particularly among Western fans.

Despite receiving an initial negative reaction, *The Quick and the Dead* has developed a major reputation among academic film critics as being one of the first significant **postmodern Westerns**—*postmodern* meaning the utter rejection of the grand meta-narratives upon which modernity was based, utter repudiation of the assumptions of classic Westerns of the **myth of the West**. One may well wonder whether the film is comic or serious. Can it be both? The film is often praised (or condemned) for its comic-book feel: its sharp, violent passages; its straight-line story; its simple buildup to the climax; its unusual camera angles and transitions.

This film is also considered a **feminist Western** in the same tradition as *The Ballad of Little Jo* (1993). Ellen is a **gunfighter** on a level with all the champion gunfighters of the West. The fact that she is a female is not particularly noteworthy. She does, though, have fashionable tastes, wearing styles, including sunshades, that would not be out of place in 1995 or in whatever Western period the narrative takes place. *See also* COSTUMES; GREENWALD, MAGGIE.

QUINN, ANTHONY (1915–2001). Born Antonio Rudolfo Oaxaca Quinn in Chihuahua, Mexico, Quinn first landed roles primarily as stereotypical **Mexicans** or **Indians**. His role as Juan Martinez in ***The Ox-Bow Incident*** (1943) moved beyond stereotype as the Mexican is unjustly accused of murder and cattle rustling. At first he merely responds, "No sabe," to all questions from the mob. When he is forced to speak English, Martinez speaks with stoic dignity. Brought back from an escape attempt with a bullet in his leg, he grabs a knife, grits his teeth, and digs the bullet out contemptuously. Then he goes to his hanging calmly, the way a man is expected to go, while reciting his prayers as a Catholic and a Mexican. Minutes later the rustlers find out Martinez was innocent after all.

Quinn's strongest role was in *Viva Zapata!* (1952), for which he won an Oscar for best supporting actor as Zapata's brash, semi-cultured brother, Eufemio. Two later Western roles show a maturing Quinn playing the urbane sophisticate. In ***Warlock*** (1959), Quinn played Tom Morgan, club-footed and unusually protective partner to the gunfighter turned sheriff and saloon proprietor, Blaisedell (**Henry Fonda**). Dressed with style and acting smoothly with eastern manners, Morgan seems an odd companion for a gunfighter. Quinn appears in a similar role with a comic twist in *Heller in Pink Tights* (1960), opposite Sophia Loren. Besides his Oscar for *Viva Zapata!* Quinn was nominated twice more and won one other award for best supporting actor.

– R –

RACIAL OTHERS AS THREATS TO WHITE WOMEN. A subtext in virtually all **silent** and **classic Westerns** is that the primary threat to white women is the Racial Other, who will always, given the opportunity, rape and molest in ways far worse than death. In cinema history, the characters from **D. W. Griffith**'s racist non-Western *The Birth of a Nation* (1915), as well as characters from his lesser-known early Westerns, provide the most prominent example of what the culture felt was the natural, unabated lust of **African American** males for white women. Griffith did not hesitate to portray African American Others as lurking in hiding, bug-eyed and salivating, as they observed white women with anticipation. This image continues into all areas of early cinema, including **silent** Westerns.

In later Westerns, efforts were made to mitigate such obvious black-white prejudice, but the racism was simply transferred to another Racial Other—**Native Americans**—and has remained a regular feature of Westerns up to the present. The worst horror for settlers of the frontier, according to the **myth of the West** portrayed in cinema, was for **Indian** savages to capture white women. One Western **cliché** involves the white male protector, who, during an Indian attack, saves one last bullet for his woman—just in case she is raped: the unstated, yet clearly implied subtext being that the only thing in store for a defiled woman was brutal, regularly repeated rape and enslavement. Ethan Edwards (**John Wayne**) in *The Searchers* (1956) undertakes a maniacal quest to save his kinswoman Debbie (Natalie Wood) from the savages. When he is about to rescue her from the evil Scar (**Henry Brandon**), he repudiates her as a contaminated woman. Even a more recent film, *The Missing* (2003), bases a plot element on the idea of the Racial Other's inevitable rape of white women. Such stereotyping spans the entire history of the Western despite, according to Cawelti, "considerable evidence that Indians rarely molested their female captives" (1999, 78). Historically, white women faced far greater threats of rape and molestation from white males than from Others. *See* BLANCHET, CATE.

REAGAN, RONALD (1911–2004). Born in Illinois, Ronald Reagan, the 40th president of the United States, began acting in Westerns in 1940 with *Santa Fe Trail*, in which he played **General George Armstrong Custer** opposite **Errol Flynn**. While often maligned for his pedestrian acting abilities, Reagan made a trilogy of Westerns in the 1950s that are often considered minor classics: *Law and Order*

(1953), opposite Dorothy Malone; *Cattle Queen of Montana* (1954), opposite **Barbara Stanwyck**; and *Tennessee's Partner* (1955), opposite Rhonda Fleming. In the 1960s Reagan left his film career for politics and was elected governor of California for two terms, beginning in 1966, and president for two terms, beginning in 1981. As president, Reagan cultivated his cowboy persona from his Hollywood days, regularly appearing on horseback and in Western dress in campaign photographs, and he was often criticized for governing like a cowboy. See also DE HAVILLAND, OLIVIA; FLYNN, ERROL.

REALISM. Historical authenticity refers to how closely a director attempts to replicate the historical details of the film's period. Thus, authenticity is often superficial. Realism, on the other hand, refers to how closely a director interprets life. True depth of character, arguably, is universal and timeless. Questions arise, then, as to which elements make the greater film—authenticity or realism. To go to extremes, a film like Jim Jarmusch's *Dead Man* (1995) pays little attention to historical authenticity but probes deeply into human character and the philosophical implications of **postmodern** life, while a film like *Wyatt Earp* (1994) maintains scrupulous historical authenticity but plays more like a documentary film than a dramatic exploration of the human experience.

RED RIVER (1948). **John Wayne**, **Montgomery Clift**, Joanne Dru, **Walter Brennan**, Dimitri Tiomkin (music), **Howard Hawks** (director). **John Ford** had been using John Wayne in his **Cavalry Trilogy** after World War II, so Howard Hawks decided to give Wayne a try as well in this big-budget Western that set the standard for the great **classic Westerns** of the 1950s. The film represents perfectly the values underlying classic Westerns.

The film opens in 1851 and tells the story of the building of a cattle empire along with the first cattle drive from Texas to **Abilene, Kansas**. Thomas Dunson (Wayne) leaves a wagon train, and his wife (he plans to get her later), to pursue his selfish ambitions. The next day he sees smoke and learns that savages have burned the wagon train and killed his wife. Dunson's response is puzzling. It is almost as if there is always another day. So he heads to Texas across the Red River and steals land to start a ranch, taking with him a young boy named Matt (played by Clift when the character is older) who escaped from the **Indians** at the wagon train. Agents of the land's legal owners—**Mexicans** with a land grant going back several generations— attempt to protect the property, but Dunson kills them and solves his problem. Dunson's right to claim the land from the Mexicans due to his superior power is unquestioned in the film. Years later, Dunson herds cattle to market, opening up a new trail. He runs into problems at every turn. Matt, though he has been loyal to Dunson all his life, wisely and justifiably mutinies against him, along with the other men. Howard Hawks probably assumed his audience would consider Wayne's character normative and his actions in stealing land and mistreating his men totally acceptable. Today, however, we look back on these attitudes with curiosity.

As the story continues, Matt enters a superfluous relationship with Tess (Dru), primarily so that she can bear him sons. The original audience probably considered this an appropriate motive as well. Dunson and Matt fight in the end, and Matt defeats Dunson. That should be the end, but, Dunson takes his beating and pronounces Matt a man. Again, Wayne's character is put forth as the norm, as the ultimate exemplar of masculinity. Thus, we must assume that whatever qualities Matt shows in his mutiny are subsumed in his desire to be a man, whether to please his father figure or to please his **homoerotic** other half. The original audience would have seen this as a great narrative of rugged individualism, of **Manifest Destiny**, of authority winning out, of masculinity subduing weak femininity. **Postmodern** viewers, however, see a side of the characters that the original audience would deny.

The music by Tiomkin, particularly the haunting "Missouri" in the middle, lends majesty to the film, while **Walter Brennan** adds levity through his comic **sidekick** role. The romance between Matt and Tess is hot and heavy, though complicated by her willingness to have Matt's sons.

REGENERATION THROUGH VIOLENCE. This term is usually associated with Richard Slotkin. The **myth of the West** originated from early Puritans' missions into the wilderness in order to shine the light of **civilization**. In the wilderness we rediscover our barbaric nature, which must be confronted and purged through **violence**. Violence thus regenerates civilization; it purifies and refines. It returns us, as Theodore Roosevelt asserted, to our essential Anglo-Saxon origins. Desultory and brutal as it is, necessary violence regenerates us as a civilized people. Thus, when Blaze Tracy (**William S. Hart**) in *Hell's Hinges* (1916) stares down the barrel of the last bad guy with the town being destroyed in a flaming inferno, we know that his gunplay serves a purpose of purifying utter savagery and returning us to our uncorrupted essential natures.

RENALDO, DUNCAN (1904–1980). Forever associated with the role of **the Cisco Kid**, Duncan Renaldo had an extensive film career before beginning the Cisco Kid series in 1945, even appearing, with Bob Livingston and Raymond Hatton, as one of the **Three Mesquiteers** from 1939 to 1940. Renaldo's regular stereotypical portrayal of Hispanic characters qualified him well for the Cisco Kid series, which began with *The Cisco Kid Returns* (1945) and ended with *The Girl from San Lorenzo* (1950). Thereafter, Renaldo moved the Cisco Kid from film to television in a series that ran until 1950. *See also* TELEVISION WESTERNS.

REPUBLIC STUDIOS. Herbert Yates founded Republic, one of the **poverty row** studios and distributors in 1935. Despite the low-budget quality of its films, Republic exerted a powerful influence over early 20th-century Westerns. *See* ALLEN, REX; AUTRY, GENE; B WESTERNS; *DARK COMMAND*; PAYNE, SALLY; ROGERS, ROY; THE THREE MESQUITEERS; WAYNE, JOHN.

RETRIBUTIVE JUSTICE. Retribution and revenge are essential parts of the unofficial **code of the West**. The seeking of revenge is a noble pursuit, unquestioned in **classic Westerns**: "For nearly a century the Western has celebrated the man-hunt and the man hunter. The man who with courage and skill tracks down an **outlaw** is one of our most constant heroes" (Calder 1975, 108). Thus, Josey Wales, in *The Outlaw Josey Wales* (1976), seeks retribution for the death of his family by the border territory redlegs during the Civil War. *See also* REVENGE WESTERNS.

REVENGE WESTERNS. In these Westerns, the plot is driven by revenge, perhaps the most common Western storyline of all. These

Westerns appeal to some of the basest desires of the human heart. Occasionally, as in *Winchester '73* (1950), the entire movie is built around a **chase and pursuit** of the villains. Other times, the revenge motive does not become obvious until the end. At the beginning of *Once Upon a Time in the West* (1968), for example, Harmonica (**Charles Bronson**) is simply a mystery character, appearing out of nowhere with the haunting melody of his harmonica preceding him. Yet he can competently throw a gun. We find out at the end that he seeks revenge on Frank (**Henry Fonda**), the villain who had killed Harmonica's father when he was a little boy. This revenge plot is echoed deliberately in *The Quick and the Dead* (1995) when we find out at the end that Ellen (Sharon Stone) kills Herod (**Gene Hackman**) because years earlier Herod had killed her father in the same way. The question to ask is whether the revenge motive is justified by a sense of justice or by a sense of retribution—whether the necessity of seeking personal revenge is simply assumed. A common criticism of Westerns is that revenge is simply accepted as a **code** of behavior. *See also* RETRIBUTIVE JUSTICE.

RITTER, TEX (1905–1974). Born Woodward Maurice Ritter near Murvaul, Texas, Ritter sang the Academy Award–winning theme song for *High Noon* (1952). Ritter also performed it live at the 1993 Academy of Motion Picture's presentation, where it won best song. More important than the Oscar, however, was the innovative use to which composer Dimitri Tiomkin put the song within the soundtrack of the film. Instead of using conventional music background for the lengthy nondialogue passages, Tiomkin repeated the rhythms and lyrics from the song to heighten the tension as Sheriff Kane walked the streets searching desperately for someone to help him save the town. As a result of Ritter's success with this theme song, he was called upon for more theme songs in *The Marshal's Daughter* (1953), *Wichita* (1955), and *Trooper Hook* (1957).

Prior to his success with the *High Noon* theme song, from 1936 to 1945 Tex Ritter developed a career as **singing cowboy** in a string of low-budget Westerns for **Grand National**, Monogram, Universal, and **PRC**. He differed from other singing cowboys, especially **Gene Autry**, due to his slow Texas drawl and the fact that his songs were traditional folk songs, or were written by himself in the folk style, as opposed to the smooth modern Western style favored by Autry.

As with other singing cowboy stars, though, Ritter received the most critical acclaim for a film with very little music, *The Man from Texas* (1939). And while throughout the late 1930s Ritter ranked high in *Motion Picture Herald*'s poll of top box-office draws for some of his singing cowboy movies, the films that still matter are a series of Columbia pictures in which he costarred with **Wild Bill Elliott**, films such as *King of Dodge City* (1941). In these pictures, Ritter played a variety of roles instead of merely playing the role of cowboy singer who happens to be involved in a plot.

For the last 30 years of his life, Ritter devoted himself entirely to a career as a country western singer.

ROGERS, ROY (1911–1998). Born Leonard Slye in Ohio, Roy Rogers was "the King of the Cowboys" from the 1930s until his death in the 1990s. Together with his wife, **Dale Evans** Rogers, he became a cultural symbol for a wholesome, Christian-centered old West.

After moving to California during the Great Depression, Rogers began singing with what would later become the Sons of the Pioneers. As the singing group grew in popularity and started appearing in low-budget Westerns, Rogers emerged as his own persona. At first he was billed as Dick Weston in Charles Starrett Westerns by Columbia. After appearing in several character roles, including that of a villain (though not a very bad villain) in **Gene Autry**'s *The Old Corral* (1936), Rogers received his break starring in *Under Western Stars* (1938) for **Republic** in a role intended for Autry. Rogers starred in 83 films for Republic between 1938 and 1951. From 1943 to 1954 Rogers was listed as *Motion Picture Herald*'s number one money-making Western star, the basis for his being billed "the King of the Cowboys." When Rogers began starring in films on his own, however, Republic had Gene Autry also under contract and naturally promoted the veteran over the new cowboy. Rogers's Westerns were much more cheaply made than Autry's.

Most films in the first phase of Rogers's career were set in the frontier West and were directed by Joseph Kane. Rogers's characters were often billed as Roy Rogers, even when he played roles from different historical periods. In two films, *Billy the Kid Returns* (1938) and *Jesse James at Bay* (1941), he worked the duel role gimmick, playing the **outlaws** as well as look alike characters confused with the famous outlaws. The formula of these early films has the unknown Rogers character dealing with an explosive situation while needing to prove himself worthy of trust and respect—always gained by the end of the film. His early films were not characterized by much physical violence. Rogers's youthful appearance and slender frame made him appear no match for the typical burly villains of low-budget Westerns. Rogers's usual **sidekick** beginning with the early films was **Gabby Hayes**, consistently named Gabby Whittaker in the films. Hayes's corny, homespun humor was a perfect foil for Rogers's smooth sophistication.

In 1940 Rogers departed from his usual practice and played a secondary role in what would be his finest moment of acting. *Dark Command* (1940), directed by Raoul Walsh, starred Walter Pidgeon, **John Wayne**, and Roy Rogers. The plot revolved around the notorious Confederate partisan **William Quantrill**, although Pidgeon played the role as Cantrell. It was one of Republic's few A Westerns and one film in which Rogers did not sing a note.

Films of Rogers's middle period, 1941–1943, starting with *Red River Valley* (1941), take place in contemporary settings and treat themes of the day. By now Rogers was playing himself as an already recognizable celebrity, often in law enforcement roles or in entertainment roles—as a rodeo star, a radio singer, or a recording star. Often these films feature the Sons of the Pioneers. *Ridin' Down the Canyon* (1942), *Sunset on the Desert* (1942), and *The Man from Music Mountain* (1943) are typical of this period. Beginning in 1943, Rogers's wonder **horse**, **Trigger**, a golden palomino, began receiving nearly equal billing with the cowboy star. Trigger was always billed "the Smartest Horse in the Movies."

During World War II, Rogers succeeded Gene Autry as the top **singing cowboy**, and Republic began starring him in more lavish, higher-budget Westerns with spectacular musical productions, still featuring the Sons of the Pioneers. *Man from Oklahoma* (1945) and *Bells of Rosarita* (1945) typify the period.

After the war, however, with a group of Westerns directed by William Witney, Rogers's Westerns began deemphasizing the singing cowboy role and instead began emphasizing more violence, more action, even cruelty to animals—more dirty realism than is usually associated with the earlier slick Rogers musical Westerns. Roy Rogers even shot to kill in these films. Witney Westerns such as *Heldorado* (1946) and *Apache Rose* (1947) dealt with issues of immediate importance in the postwar period: organized crime and big oil. *Spoilers of the Plains* (1951) is one of the early cold war Westerns and one of Rogers's last Republic Westerns.

In these later films, Rogers showed promise moving in the direction of more serious adult Westerns, at about the same time that John Wayne was beginning to move beyond the **B Western** circuit. Some of the best **fistfights** in B Westerns occur in these late Rogers films—hard, blood-splattering fights in mud, in water, under stampeding cattle, in burning barns; fights with clubs, fights with swinging empty rifles. However, contract disputes with Republic ended Rogers's film career early, and with it, whatever promise there had been of transitioning into more serious cinema roles. But like **William Boyd**, Rogers simply made a smooth transition to **television Westerns** with a self-produced series that ran for six years with enormous audience ratings, moving Roy and Dale Rogers's popularity far beyond what his film career had delivered.

From the 1950s to the end of their lives, Roy Rogers and Dale Evans Rogers maintained active careers in recording, personal appearances, television specials beyond their series, and writing. After his marriage to Evans in 1947, Rogers began openly professing his Christian faith in all phases of his public career. He and Evans, with their large family, began a popular museum at their Double R Bar Ranch in Southern California. In 1975, Rogers, now an American legend, appeared in his last Western, *Mackintosh and T.J.* (1975), as a wandering cowboy who sets a teenage boy on the right path in a modern-day west Texas setting.

While Rogers and Evans remained professionally active until the end of their lives, after the 1960s their legacy became mainly that of **nostalgia** for a lost innocence of the days before the Vietnam War divided America. Throughout the turbulent protest era, Rogers remained the steadfast patriot and exemplar of fading American values. He was "a softer John Wayne" (White 1998, 92). Unfortunately, the generation of children who grew up idolizing their hero moved beyond the values of Roy Rogers's Rider Rules and Roy Rogers's

Prayer. The distance between a Roy Rogers film like *My Pal Trigger* (1946) and **The Wild Bunch** (1969) reveals much about changes in American culture in the mid-20th century. Roy Rogers's Rider Rules follow:

1. Be neat and clean.
2. Be courteous and polite.
3. Always obey your parents.
4. Protect the weak and help them.
5. Be brave but never take chances.
6. Study hard and learn all you can.
7. Be kind to animals and care for them.
8. Eat all your food and never waste any.
9. Love God and go to Sunday School regularly.
10. Always respect our flag and our country.

Roy Rogers's Prayer was,

> Lord, I reckon I'm not much by myself,
> I fail to do a lot of things I ought to do.
> But, Lord, when trails are steep and passes high,
> Help me ride it straight the whole way through.
> And when, in the falling dusk, I get that final call,
> I do not care how many flowers they send,
> Above all else, the happiest trail would be
> for You to say to me, "Let's ride, my friend." Amen.

See also FORMULAS, CLASSIC WESTERN.

THE ROUGH RIDERS. This **trigger trio** consisted of **Buck Jones**, **Tim McCoy**, and Raymond Hatton. They personified "the theme of irreversible progress" (Loy 2001, 42). The Rough Riders were rangers called out of retirement for each episode, working together, often secretly, to rectify wrong. When their work was finished in each film, they would ride their separate ways back to retirement—Hatton, to Texas; McCoy, to Wyoming; and Jones, to Arizona—and bid each other "So Long, Rough Riders" as the theme song began: "The Rough Riders ride, beware/The Rough Riders ride, take care." Eight Rough Riders films were made between 1941–1942: *Arizona Bound* (1941), *The Gunman from Bodie* (1941), *Forbidden Trails* (1941), *Below the Border* (1942), *Ghost Town Law* (1942), *Down Texas Way*

(1942), *Riders of the West* (1942), and *West of the Law* (1942). *See also* TRAIL BLAZERS; TRIGGER TRIOS.

RUNNING INSERTS. In early silents, action shots were filmed with cameras on stationary platforms recording the scene as it transpired. Efforts to use mobile cameras were initially resisted as being artificial. Even **William S. Hart**'s films, while full of action, mainly relied on stationary cameras. Eventually, though, the now common technique of running a camera on a car or on tracks beside the moving subject, often a racing horse, became necessary; thus the running insert (sometimes called the running close-up) was born—a running shot in which the camera moves at a comparable speed beside the subject.

Cameraman Sol Polito pioneered this technique in Ken Maynard silents by mounting several cameras on a car running beside the racing horses. Besides keeping up with the fast-moving scene, Polito was able to create close-ups of spectacular **stunt** work, showing the subjects' facial expressions in action in such films as *The Red Raiders* (1927). Other effects pioneered in this film include running inserts of charging **Indians**, a stampede of covered wagons, and a shot of a cavalry charge, beginning at a distance and then, with the camera moving slowly backward, being overtaken by the charge for a breathtaking effect. Running inserts have become much more sophisticated since the early Westerns, but the basic principle remains the same.

RUSSELL, GAIL (1924–1961). Hollywood lore has it that two Santa Monica High School boys gave a ride to a man who turned out to be a talent scout for Paramount, and they tipped him off about the most beautiful girl in their class. The girl was 19-year-old Gail Russell, who was signed to a contract based solely on her looks. While her acting ability came from a studio coach, her hauntingly melancholy expression mixed with a sense of bubbling, innocent enthusiasm came naturally.

Russell's first Western was **John Wayne**'s *Angel and the Badman* (1947). Wayne produced the film and was rumored to be romantically involved with Russell. In the film Russell plays a young Quaker daughter of a family who out of kindness nurse a stranger (Wayne) back to health. While the stranger is in a fevered, unconscious condition, Penelope Worth (Russell) falls in love with him. As it turns out, the stranger is a notorious outlaw. In a plot reminiscent of a **William S. Hart** film, Russell's angelic character displays a confident innocence that wins the hardened heart of the badman.

Russell's other Western was **Budd Boetticher**'s *Seven Men from Now* (1956), opposite **Randolph Scott**. In this film, past failures haunt an aging ex-sheriff (Scott) as he helps a young couple, Annie (Russell) and John (Walter Reed), negotiate the treacherous wilderness in their covered wagon. One of the outlaws the sheriff is hunting (Lee Marvin) sarcastically accuses him of carrying on an affair with the wife. Russell brings to her role a sexual innocence that exacerbates the tension of Scott's situation. The story behind the scenes, though, was that this film was Russell's last chance to prove herself after being dismissed by her studio for alcoholism. She clearly sought to excel in this role out of a sense of desperation, and while this film is a minor masterpiece, Gail Russell could not re-create her life. News reports of the day say that on August 26, 1961, Russell, age 36, was found dead in her apartment from an alcoholic stupor.

– S –

SANTA FE TRAIL SERIES. In the 1940s Warner Brothers released a series of eight two-reel, 20-minute shorts starring Robert Shayne. These films are sometimes referred to as Warner Brothers featurettes. Several were remakes of well-known feature films using **stock footage** from the original films. For example, *Oklahoma Outlaws* (1943) played off *The Oklahoma Kid* (1939) with Shayne playing the role James Cagney had played in the original film. *Frontier Days* (1945), a **Technicolor** short, used stock footage from *Dodge City* (1939) and had Shayne in the role **Errol Flynn** played in the original. The Santa Fe Trail series exemplifies probably the lowest point in **B Western** history. These were not just low-budget Westerns; they were cheap rip-offs of top-notch films.

SAVAGE WAR. This term was popularized by Richard Slotkin. The traditional Western cowboys-versus-**Indians myth** that is the basis of a large percentage of Westerns stems from a basic fear of **Native Americans** that white settlers have held since the earliest colonial days. Savage battles did in fact take place historically, though the Native Americans were far less often the aggressors than were the white U.S. Cavalry and other white Indian hunters. In cinema Westerns, however, these brutal encounters have been used to reflect cultural fears from outside aggressors.

While 20th- and 21st-century American audiences no longer had to fear battles with Native Americans, the reenactment of Indian battles allowed filmmakers to reflect contemporary fears of such things as Nazism, communism, and other invading outside forces. When the whites fought the Indians on-screen, they always won and they always overcame evil through savage war. Savage war has been necessary in order to purify white America of traces of nonwhite culture. Westerns thus have always appealed to this basic cultural fear and have appeased it. After the **classic Western** era, filmmakers turned from Native Americans to **Mexicans** for waging savage war. See also APACHES; CHASE AND PURSUIT; CAVALRY TRILOGY; WESTERNS, CULTURAL VALUE AND SIGNIFICANCE OF.

SCOTT, FRED (1902–1991). Billed as "the Silvery-Voiced Buckaroo," Scott was one of the **singing cowboys** in the operatic tradition rather than in the country music tradition. He performed in his first film, *Romance Rides the Range* (1936), right after appearing in a San Francisco Opera Company production of *Salome*. His comic **sidekick** was Al St. John playing his Fuzzy character. Spectrum Pictures films with Scott and others were inevitably filmed on the cheap and proved to be rather shoddy affairs.

SCOTT, RANDOLPH (1898–1987). Randolph Scott was the standard by which to judge Western cowboy stars and the perfect image of the American cowboy. Tall and lean, Scott had a tough, square-jawed face, lined and weathered but handsome. Rumor has it that he smiled and laughed in one of his films, but evidently the footage is lost. Scott had a serious look about him in all that he did. A fortuitous encounter with future Hollywood mogul Howard Hughes landed Scott bit parts in films during the 1920s. In 1939 he played a secondary role in *Jesse*

James with **Henry Fonda**, and by the 1940s he began a long career as a leading Western star, playing in such early films as *Western Union* (1941), *Belle Starr* (1941), and *Abilene Town* (1946). By the 1950s Randolph Scott had become one of the most recognizable names in Westerns, easily working his way through a steady if undistinguished career.

In 1956, though, Scott began making a series of films with **Budd Boetticher** that changed his reputation from that of a competent actor to that of a serious actor in serious films. *Seven Men from Now* (1956) is one of the best films of the 1950s. Scott plays ex-sheriff Ben Stride, a man who has just lost his wife due to personal negligence. He sets out on the trail of her killers, knowing that he had some personal responsibility in her death. But he has no personal language with which to express his feelings, even to himself. Only through action can he express his sublimated frustrations—action in the process of gunning down the killers, but also hindered action in an illicit romantic attraction for the young wife (**Gail Russell**) of a couple he finds out on the trail in need of help. Scott followed this film with *The Tall T* (1957), *Decision at Sundown* (1957), *Ride Lonesome* (1959), and *Comanche Station* (1960), all with Boetticher. Randolph Scott's last film, *Ride the High Country* (1962), was the first significant film of another major director, whose work would dominate the 1960s, **Sam Peckinpah**.

When the shift in Westerns began with the popular **spaghetti Westerns** in the 1960s, Scott resisted going to Europe to work in European Westerns as so many American actors did, and settled into a comfortable and long retirement. He will be remembered for his persona of a man of psychological depth who nevertheless could throw a gun, albeit reluctantly.

THE SEARCHERS (1956). John Wayne, Jeffrey Hunter, Natalie Wood, Vera Miles, **Henry Brandon**, **Ward Bond**, **John Ford** (director). In 1956, communism was the fear at the front of most Americans' minds, not just a fear of invasion or destruction through intercontinental ballistic missiles, but also the fear of those who were indoctrinated, or "brainwashed," by communists. In such a cultural environment, *The Searchers* appeared and immediately touched a nerve with American culture. Here was a film that took the myths that had made America great and used them to explore contemporary concerns.

The film revolves around a classic **revenge** plot. Ethan Edwards's (Wayne) two nieces have been captured by Comanches. Edwards sets out in **chase and pursuit**. With him is Martin (Hunter), half Indian and half white. Staying at home is Laurie, Martin's intended. The chase lasts years. One of the nieces' bodies is found mutilated and, we assume, sexually violated. It soon becomes evident that the evil Comanche chief, Scar (Brandon), has taken Debbie (Wood) for his own wife. Martin keeps postponing his wedding with Laurie, but in a scene of comic relief, he accidentally marries an **Indian** maiden. She sacrifices herself at one point to save Ethan and Martin. When they finally find Debbie, years have passed and she now is a young woman. Ethan has dedicated his life to pursuing the Indians who kidnapped her and killing as many of them as he can. When at last he finds Debbie, he has become so much an Indian hater that he cannot bear the thought of her being an Indian's wife. In a fit of revulsion, he rushes at her with intent to kill; in his mind, she would be better off dead than red. Martin saves her and in a final fight to the death, he kills Scar.

The Searchers illustrates a number of basic assumptions, basic conventions, of **classic Westerns**—and particularly of John Ford's Westerns—that would be strongly questioned less than 10 years after the film's release. The Indians attack, burn the cabin, and brutally kill all except the little girls, Lucy and Debbie, clearly establishing who the good people are and who the savages are. Martin Pawley determines to follow Ethan Edwards, yet Edwards feels nothing but contempt for Pawley because he is half Indian and, therefore, only half white (Jeffrey Hunter, who played Martin, was a very white Hollywood actor). The cavalry brutally slaughters an Indian village. The film attempts a slight bit of remorse, but very little. Later, a bumbling cavalry assists the rescue. As so often happens, the weak woman, the love interest, Laurie Jorgenson (Miles) begs Martin not to go, asking him to stay time and again. He always goes. For five years he is gone, so she agrees to marry the obviously inferior Charlie (**Ken Curtis**). Martin returns on their wedding day. She is distraught but understands why he did what he did and accepts him back. The 1950s audience must have considered Laurie's actions and attitudes commendable. The other woman in the film, often neglected, is Look (Beulah Archuletta), Martin's Indian wife. She is clearly a prized Indian maiden, but Martin does not realize he is marrying her. Ethan does, but he sits back and observes with amusement. Look becomes one of the few admirable characters in the film as she seeks to be a dutiful wife, following the two men as they try to shake her loose. Eventually, she sacrifices her life for her husband, but he never seems to appreciate her at all.

The issues emerge, though, when we consider Ethan. For some reason Edwards feels contempt not only for Martin's race but also for his lack of masculinity (at one point the younger man even cries). For some reason Ethan feels that Martin must prove his manhood; he must develop some version of masculinity that Ethan feels (and the audience accepts) he himself already possesses. Interestingly, at the end of the film Martin's compromised masculinity triumphs—he is the one who kills Scar. Ethan's chase and pursuit after the Indians who captured the girls is understandable, but eventually his mission changes from a rescue mission to a mission of revenge. When Ethan finds the captured Debbie and sees that she has become a savage, he starts to kill her. Later he even says she is already dead since she is now Comanche. Yes, Martin saves her, but how many in a 1956 audience would have thought that Ethan had a point? Ethan is so manly that he is superior even to the Texas Rangers, even to the effeminate Cavalry, to the settlers, to Martin—to everyone but Scar, the embodiment of evil (played by a white actor). The film leaves open the question: Who is worse—Ethan or Scar? Does either ever change? In the end, Ethan scalps Scar after he kills him.

The Searchers, then, explores the rampant racism that was finally receiving serious attention. Emmett Till had just been brutally beaten in 1955, and the nation had witnessed the subsequent patently corrupted murder trial. The same year Rosa Parks started the Montgomery bus boycott. A director with a social conscience such as Ford, who wished to treat America's racist character, could not have dealt with the issue directly in the tense atmosphere of the day. In a way similar to how he used the **Cavalry Trilogy**, Ford distanced the issue in the historical past and placed it in the context of the foundational Western **myth**.

Many critics today consider *The Searchers* to be John Ford's best film and possibly the best acting of John Wayne's career. The premise is significant—the classic Indian **captivity narrative**. The film should be compared to *The Missing* (2003) for a 21st century version of a similar situation.

SELF-REFLEXIVE WESTERNS. Quite often, Westerns of the late 20th century, perhaps due to a nostalgic feeling that the genre was losing force, became reflexive, became commentaries on the genre itself. **Clint Eastwood**'s later Westerns such as *Unforgiven* (1992), *The Outlaw Josey Wales* (1976), and *Pale Rider* (1985) are commentaries on the genre itself as much as anything else. Another such film is ***The Quick and the Dead*** (1995).

SERIALS. Serials were popular forms of entertainment in the pre-television era, providing a consistent and reliable audience for theaters. They began even in the **silent era**, primarily as novelty films. *The Hazards of Helen* (1914–1917), with 119 episodes of one reel each, is sometimes seen as the first serial with Western elements, although it does not run a continuous, unbroken storyline. Serials especially came to prominence in the 1930s and 1940s and were often directed at youth audiences. A prototype for all serials might be **Gene Autry**'s first film, *The Phantom Empire* (1935), an early science-fiction Western of 12 episodes. Autry discovers the underground kingdom of Murania and gets involved in fantastical sequences involving robots, death rays, and radio broadcasts—all the while trying to get back to the ranch to air his weekly radio show, which is in danger of being taken off the air. Each episode ends with the obvious death or near death of Autry or the two youngsters who share his adventures. However, the first few minutes of the subsequent episode would backtrack long enough to show how the **singing cowboy** was able to escape at the last possible second. Many serials were in later years edited for release in one feature. Thus *The Phantom Empire* became the de-serialized *Men with Steel Faces* in 1940, reducing the running time from 245 minutes to 70 minutes.

SEVEN MEN FROM NOW **(1956). Randolph Scott**, Lee Marvin, **Gail Russell**, **Donald Barry**, and **Budd Boetticher** (director). Ben

Stride (Scott) is an ex-sheriff, rejected at the last election. His wife is then forced to work at Wells Fargo. The Wells Fargo office is robbed, his wife is killed, and now, in order to reassert his masculinity, he is in pursuit of the seven killers who have probably scattered. When the film begins, Stride has already killed two. Four minutes into the film, he kills another two. Then he comes across a young pioneer couple with their covered wagon stuck in mud, and he helps them out.

Shortly, two thugs (Marvin and Barry) join them. Marvin played a wonderful villain (Bill Masters), flamboyant (he wears his pistols butt forward and a brightly colored bandanna) and attractive in his meanness. Barry played his grunt. Masters is upfront in his intentions. He plans to follow the sheriff and see him kill the robbers. Then he will get the gold from him. (It turns out that the gold is in the covered wagon all along.) Sheriff Stride and the young wife (Russell) begin to fall for each other, and Masters sees right through them. In the covered wagon during a rainstorm, he tells a long story of a man just like Stride falling in love with a pretty wife like Annie. But the sheriff is virtuous despite the temptation. Eventually Stride finds the robbers in Flora Vista. The gang sends out two of them to kill the sheriff, but Stride kills them both, getting badly wounded in the leg in the process. Stride discovers the gold and intends to offer it to the robbers, but since he cannot come to them, he places the gold out in the open. The robbers try to get it, and in a fantastic shootout, Stride kills them all. But Masters has been waiting. Now he comes forward, and we have a classic quick-draw shootout. Marvin loses. Stride heads for town. Earlier, the young husband had shown his masculinity in a daring move to contact the sheriff during the face-off, and he is killed. Thus, at the end Annie and Stride are free. We assume they will now marry.

Three incredible acting jobs make this movie: Randolph Scott, the stoic Westerner who cannot express himself except through action, tormented for losing his wife, tormented by love for another man's wife; Lee Marvin, loud, boastful, virally handsome, and colorful yet bad through and through (he shoots his partner in cold blood when he is no longer needed); and Gail Russell, gorgeous with her bright smile and beautiful blue eyes, yet not at all a glamour girl.

Budd Boetticher's *Seven Men from Now* is a powerful film that, while working within the **classic Western formula**, explores all the passions fully. Nothing is unambiguously black and white. No actions by anybody are fully validated except the pursuit of masculinity. *See also* FORMULAS, CLASSIC WESTERN.

SHANE (1953). Alan Ladd, Jean Arthur, Van Heflin, **Brandon De Wilde, Jack Palance, Ben Johnson**, George Stevens (director). Here is another candidate for perhaps the greatest **classic Western** ever filmed. The film is based on a highly acclaimed novel by Jack Schaefer, and George Stevens used one of the great Western novelists, A. B. Guthrie Jr., on the script. It has breathtaking cinematography by Loyal Griggs and haunting music by Victor Young. *Shane* is a near perfect portrayal of the classic **myth of the West**.

Shane (Ladd) rides inconspicuously through the cinematically gorgeous early spring **landscape** of snowcapped mountains in the background and runoff streams from the melted snow in the foreground. The grass is lush and verdant. The sky above is perfectly calendar blue. It was filmed in Jackson Hole, Wyoming, and the snow-capped Grand Tetons are in nearly every scene. We soon find out that the homesteaders with whom we are expected to sympathize are weakened and demoralized by the greedy land baron. Ladd is an angel-like savior figure, coming from nowhere, saving the day, returning from whence he came.

The film works the Western myth and all the **clichés** (it also originates many of the clichés). For example, the two gunfighters wear black and white hats. Jack Palance played the devil-like gunslinger Wilson perfectly, wearing black. In one scene, Stonewall (Elisha Cook Jr.), the loudmouth homesteader, responds to Wilson's taunts in the mud-splattered street. He draws on the professional gunfighter, but Wilson is fast. His gun is out and pointing at Stonewall before the clumsy man even has his gun out of the holster. But Wilson does not shoot. He pauses as Stonewall looks down the barrel knowing he is about to die. Wilson savors the moment. Then he fires and knocks the man down and dead in an instant. Stevens worked all gunplay realistically, even using special sound effects in theaters to sound like real gunfire.

We understand that Jack Wilson in his black suit is thoroughly evil. But what about Shane? Nobody knows who he is except that he is also a gunfighter, a gunfighter haunted by his demons and a gunfighter who, during his stay with the Starretts, has a glimpse of what a good life might be. Is Shane in his white hat simply Jack Wilson a few years later? If so, what does the film say about the possibility even for a Jack Wilson?

Shane offers a classic confrontation between the land barons of the **open range** and the homesteading farmers. The film allows the chief villain, Ryker (Emile Meyer), to express his view of how he came to the valley first, how he subdued it, how he worked hard for years to legally settle it. Both sides in this movie have a point. But Ryker hires a professional killer to protect his interests, and the audience loathes him. The farmers, by chance, have Shane, a professional (albeit reluctant) killer, on their side, and their killer happens to be better. The audience generally sides with the homesteaders, but the film allows us to question whether that was the correct choice; thus the film's complexity.

Interestingly, in Westerns as a whole, both sides are represented equally. The **Hopalong Cassidy** movies, set on the Bar 20 Ranch, take the ranchers' side (although Cassidy never burns out homesteaders' houses as Ryker does). Essentially this film takes the side of the good-hearted but weak homesteaders trying valiantly and against the odds to carve out farms and ranches for themselves in the valley. Shane forces the ranchers to accommodate them. But consider the inevitable result. The farmers will fence off the land, divide up the land, attract more settlers, build real **towns**, and essentially bring an end to the Western era—and thus despoil the edenic West. Shane, like all **cowboy heroes**, works to end the life in which he has prospered.

Shane has been attacked as being too idealistic. But the film is told from the point of view of Joey (De Wilde), who truly idolizes Shane, and of Marian (Arthur), whose eyes constantly ask, "What if?" When Joey goes running after Shane at the end, calling out, "Shane, come back," we realize that it is a coming-of-age film for the boy. He has grown up with something that will no longer exist when he is older but that has taught him a lifelong lesson about his own approaching manhood. Interestingly, without Joey, Shane would have been killed. Shane goes to town at one point without guns. Joey asks him to bring back a soda pop. As a result when Shane goes into the saloon to ask for soda pop, he is forced (reluctantly) to show his manhood in a **fist-fight**. Later, when Shane returns with his guns to face Wilson at the saloon, he proves his deadly skill to all, except for one last opponent who would have easily killed him had not Joey shouted, "Shane!" The film was nominated for six Academy Awards and won one. *See also* FARMING.

SIDEKICKS. Of all stock characters in **B Westerns**, the sidekick is perhaps the most common. The sidekick rides beside the **cowboy hero** and provides companionship and, often, comic distraction from the main action. Often the sidekick has one or two character traits that are exploited for comic effect. For example, in *Tumbleweeds* (1925), Carver (**William S. Hart**) rides with Kentucky Rose (Lucien Littlefield), who regularly stumbles into one bit of trouble or another as Carver attempts to make it on time for the Oklahoma Land Rush. Several actors developed sidekick personas with multiple cowboy stars. **Smiley Burnette**, usually playing Frog, the gravelly throated singer, rode with **Gene Autry** and **Roy Rogers**. **Gabby Hayes**, the rascally but loveable curmudgeon, rode with Roy Rogers and **William Boyd**. Other top sidekicks were Al St. John, Fuzzy Knight, Andy Clyde, and Martin Garralaga (Pancho in **The Cisco Kid** films).

Sidekicks played an important role in balancing the quality of the acting. Typically, when a studio introduced a new cowboy star in a series, it would surround him with an experienced sidekick and an experienced villain. For example, Roy Rogers was signed by **Republic** primarily for his singing ability, apparently having little inherent sex appeal and a small physical frame. The studio then made sure to have a strong sidekick with him, Burnette first, then Raymond Hatton, and ultimately Hayes. Rogers went without a sidekick in his final films. More sophisticated sidekicks were used in full-budget Westerns. **Walter Brennan**'s role in *Red River* (1948) was certainly that of sidekick. Even in later **alternative Westerns** we see sidekicks. Clint Eastwood's sidekick in *Unforgiven* (1992) was Morgan Freeman. *See also* ETHNIC MALE COMPANIONS; HOMOEROTICISM.

SILENT ERA CINEMA. The beginnings of cinema Westerns is an exciting story considering that there was still a lot of untamed frontier in the western United States when filmmakers started making Westerns back East. It all began in 1903 when the first Western, and the first narrative film, was made—***The Great Train Robbery.*** Perhaps because of the success of Western novels such as Owen Wister's bestseller ***The Virginian*** (1902), film Westerns quickly proliferated. Legendary figures from the historic old West such as **Al Jennings**, a real **outlaw**, and Ben Tilgman and **Wyatt Earp**, real lawmen, became part of the film industry. Those earliest Westerns were mostly one-reel shorts such as ***The Battle of Elderbrush Gulch*** (1913). Later, more sophisticated full-length features were produced by early directors like **James Cruze** and **Thomas Ince**. *The Pony Express* (1925) and ***The Covered Wagon*** (1923), both directed by Cruze, were some of the first big-budget, epic Westerns. Early silent actors such as **Broncho Billy Anderson**, **William S. Hart**, and **Tom Mix** became some of the first real movie stars from Hollywood. By the late 1920s the silent era was fading away; starting in about 1927, both a silent version and sound version were made of each film. *The Light of Western Stars*, released in 1930, was the last silent Western.

Westerns thrived during the silent era. They were full of action and intense but simple plotting. Not much had to be said in a Western. So when talkies became a realistic change of medium, there was considerable concern that Westerns might not make the transition. And indeed the earliest Western talkies were little more than silent Westerns with a smattering of essential dialogue. Fortunately, the **singing cowboy** came along and music saved Westerns in the early sound era. One of the earliest experiments with sound in film was with a Western. Thomas Edison developed a synchronization process whereby sound, played separately, was synchronized with film. He had tried it with some one-reel shorts, but in 1918 Metro Pictures issued *The Claim* in which Edith Storey sang "Annie Laurie." Unfortunately, theaters found the system too complicated so they usually just ran a silent version of the film.

Just as later periods of cinema Westerns have their own characteristics based on the cultural assumptions of their periods, so silent Westerns were made within definite cultural contexts reflected in the films themselves. Traditional American values were being attacked as the early silent Westerns moved into, if not maturity, at least adolescence. Early filmmakers saw their role as affirming these values. Thus, they developed Westerns that examined new ideas about male-female relationships and about the transformative powers of nature.

The "new morality" of post–World War I began to develop out of ideas stemming from Freudian, Darwinian naturalist, socialist, and feminist concerns.

In Western fiction of the period, **Zane Grey**, B. M. Bower, Clarence Mulford, and **Max Brand** explored all aspects of the new morality and humanity's relationship with nature. Particularly for Grey, the West served as a rejuvenating natural force for character development as opposed to corrupt civilizing influences of the East. Heroic relationships between men and women served to make meaning out of an otherwise meaningless universe. Violence thus served a regenerative purpose in purifying harmful corruptions derived from eastern influences. For other Western writers such as Mulford and Brand, nature served no particularly noble purpose and thus **violence** in their Westerns rarely serves any regenerative purpose. Thus the influence proved negligible until the sound era of the 1930s. William S. Hart's films owe a great deal to Zane Grey's sentimental vision of the moral power of nature, especially nature in the West. Perhaps a greater cultural influence on films of the later silent era was the early novels of Ernest Hemingway and F. Scott Fitzgerald, which explored the possibility of tragedy in an amoral universe. Westerns, though, easily passed from tragedy quickly to melodrama.

In reasserting traditional American values at a time when others were questioning them, silent Western filmmakers developed a primitive vision in which heroic action serves to preserve traditional gender roles. There are many parallels, then, between William S. Hart's characters and such Zane Grey characters as Lassiter in the 1912 novel *Riders of the Purple Sage*. *See also* REGENERATION THROUGH VIOLENCE; STUNTS; *THE VANISHING AMERICAN*.

SILVERHEELS, JAY (1912–1980). Born on the Six Nations Indian Reserve in Canada, Jay Silverheels, from the Mohawk tribe, is probably best known for his long-running role as Tonto, the Lone Ranger's **Native American sidekick** in the long-running **television** series as well as in three films: *The Legend of the Lone Ranger* (1952), *The Lone Ranger Rides Again* (1955), and *The Lone Ranger* (1956). His **horse** was named Scout. But Silverheels had a long career in Western films beginning in 1940, mostly with uncredited Native American roles. Perhaps his best role was with **Glenn Ford** in *Santee* (1973).

SINGING COWBOY. Hollywood's singing cowboy of the 1930s and 1940s did not originate in genuine cowboy folk balladry from ranch work in frontier times as is often assumed. The music draws its roots from itinerant, flamboyant medicine show musicians traveling through the South in pre-radio days and from early mountain, or hillbilly, folk music, which became popularized in early blues of Southern white singers such as Jimmie Rogers. Cowboys on the plains did not, for instance, yodel to their cows at night to settle them down. The singing cowboy yodel directly relates to novelty acts at medicine shows and the like. The image of the singing cowboy—white, clean shaven, costumed, and handsome—allowed Southern-style country music, associated with racist attitudes, to move into the national consciousness without open Southern associations.

SOCIETY, THREE LEVELS OF. In the traditional Western, a necessary tension between the wilderness and the **town** underlies the basic narrative. The wilderness surrounding the town contains the savages, whether **Native American** or **outlaw**, in a state of unrestrained lawlessness; this is the first level of society. These characters move across the **landscape** at will on fast-riding horses. Inside the town, the second level of society, are residents restrained by law and custom. These are the shopkeepers, the church people, people with families, and all women. They are static and dependent on others for protection. Rarely do these characters wear guns or ride horses. When they leave the town, they leave in buggies or carriages and are vulnerable to whatever dangers lurk in the wilderness. Thus, there is a basic tension between townspeople and savages. The third level of society is represented in Westerns by the **cowboy hero**, who is the only character able to move easily between town and wilderness. He possesses civil manners and respectability in common with townspeople, yet he is also at home outside of town with his horse, his guns, and his skills for survival. Naturally, then, the basic plot revolves around him.

SPAGHETTI WESTERNS. By the 1960s cinema Westerns were becoming so popular worldwide, especially in Europe, that the supply was having difficulty meeting the demand. **Cinecittà Studios**, among others, had been specializing in cheaply made, quickly produced action movies often based on mythological stories such as the Hercules legends. It was not difficult for the studios to experiment in Westerns to try and meet the demand. The market, then, was ready when **Sergio Leone** produced *Per un pugno di dollari* (*A Fistful of Dollars*) in 1964. The film changed Westerns forever despite the initial negative response. Almost immediately, scornful American critics labeled these Italian-made, filmed-in-Spain movies "spaghetti Westerns" as a term of derision. In many ways, negative critical response was justified. The films looked cheap with grainy, washed-out color, the result of using **Techniscope** instead of **Technicolor**. Speech was obviously dubbed in, and American audiences, who did not see Leone's films until 1967, were not used to overdubbing, especially for Westerns.

Sergio Leone's original **Dollars Trilogy**, starring **Clint Eastwood**, was released in the United States in 1967: *Per un pugno di dollari* (*A Fistful of Dollars*); *Per qualche dollaro in più* (*For a Few Dollars More*); *and Buono, il brutto, il cattivo, Il* (*The Good, the Bad and the Ugly*). But Italian studios had already been busy developing Westerns, and soon, series such as the **Django** series, the Stranger series, and the **Trinity series** began appearing. Like Clint Eastwood, several American Western stars such as **Lee Van Cleef**, **Jack Elam**, and Eli Wallach entered the European market and boosted careers that might have been nearly finished. Several Italians also developed significant fan followings with their Westerns: **Terence Hill** (Mario Girotti) and **Franco Nero** (Francesco Sparanero), for example.

These films certainly have their idiosyncrasies. The narrative setting is usually the borderlands between the United States and Mexico, mainly because the terrain resembles the Spanish and Italian terrain where the films were usually made. **Historical authenticity** is suggested by excessive grime and dirt, lots of crooked teeth, crude eating habits, even normative characters. Because of language issues and dubbing, speech is second to action. Reportedly, Sergio Leone's original cast of *Per un pugno di dollari* (*A Fistful of Dollars*) spoke such a variety of first languages that, since all would be dubbed anyway, he simply had all lines spoken in the cast members' native languages so that there was no version of the film without language dubbing.

U.S. production companies naturally began emulating the Italian Westerns. Clint Eastwood's fourth spaghetti Western, *Hang 'em High*

(1968), was filmed on location in New Mexico in Technicolor and had an American director, Ted Post. The ultimate convergence of Italian and U.S. Westerns was Leone's 1968 *Once Upon a Time in the West* (*C'era una volta il West*), filmed in the United States (in Utah) and in Italy. Nearly every cast member brought a different kind of legitimacy to this spaghetti Western: **Claudia Cardinale** was an established Italian actor who had appeared in **Richard Brooks**'s *The Professionals* (1966), in retrospect a forerunner of the Italian Westerns; **Charles Bronson** was an established American star of action movies; and **Henry Fonda**, a veteran of some of the greatest **classic Westerns** ever. Further, Fonda played a role far removed from that of his classic Western, the role of a vicious, disturbed killer **gunfighter**. By the mid-1970s, spaghetti Westerns as a definable Italian product had played out, but their influence continues to be considerable.

Except for a few classic Westerns yet to come with **John Wayne** and others, every Western since the 1960s has been influenced by Italian spaghetti Westerns. These films indulged in great quantities of **violence** out of the sheer joy of doing so, and they delighted in developing as many different and new forms of violence as possible. Nothing in these films resembled the **regeneration through violence** expressed in Westerns heretofore. When the Man with No Name rides away from San Miguel in *Per un pugno di dollari* (*A Fistful of Dollars*), he leaves utter destruction behind him, having destroyed both the Rojos and the Baxters. We can only wonder whether he has brought any redemption, any cleansing, any purgation to the town. Violence in Westerns henceforth had new meaning.

The protagonists of spaghetti Westerns can hardly be compared to classic **cowboy heroes**. They are rarely cowboys and seldom heroes. Often the only thing that makes one character a protagonist and another the antagonist is that the film's point of view favors the one character over the other. Neither seems to have a particular moral center to which we can attribute normalcy.

Italian Westerns rarely have a place for the kind of **women** who people traditional American Westerns. There are no schoolmarms, no young Quaker girls, no romantic heroines. Instead these Westerns focus on the marginalized—prostitutes, peasants, widows. Hereafter women in Westerns were much different than the classic heroines of the past. Sergio Leone said, "Even in the greatest Westerns, the woman is imposed on the action, as a star, and is generally destined to be 'had' by the male lead. But she does not exist as a *woman*. If you cut her out of the film, in a version which you can imagine, the film becomes much better. In the desert, the essential problem was to survive. Women were an obstacle to survival! Usually the woman not only holds up the story, but she has no real character, no reality. She is a symbol. She is there without any reason to be there, simply because one must have a woman, and because the hero must prove, in some way or another, that he has 'sex-appeal'" (Frayling 1981, 129).

Early on it became evident that these Westerns represented a major new trend in cinema and that their influence would not be merely faddish. Superficially they might be cheaply made but that was never really a concern. They were attacked for two primary reasons. First, they were not real "Westerns." They had no cultural roots in the historic West. They made no pretense at being authentic or realistic. They did not have the grand vision of the West that a **John Ford** film could convey. Second, they repudiated the moral universe in which all Westerns share. Essentially, these Westerns rejected the classic **myth of the West**.

All these observations were accurate, but that was just the point. These Westerns rejected the myth of the West, they rejected notions of the frontier being formative both of individual character and of national character. Thus, they have been termed **antimyth Westerns**. In many ways, they actually resembled the best features of **B Westerns** rather than classic Westerns. Today many critics would say that these films extracted the essential universal ingredients of the Western genre and dispensed with those ingredients that limited the Western to a purely American film genre, and thus they universalized Westerns forevermore.

STAGECOACH **(1939). Claire Trevor, John Wayne, John Carradine, Tim Holt, Tom Tyler,** Louise Platt, Thomas Mitchell, **John Ford** (director). By the late 1930s Westerns had fallen out of favor with major studios and there was talk once again that the Western genre was dead. The **poverty row** studios were still producing plenty of cheap material, but the Western seemed relegated to the past. John Ford's *Stagecoach,* along with several other good A Westerns produced in 1939, seemed to change the trend and showed how the best of the **B Westerns** could be made into quality Westerns. Ford took a rather ordinary short story by pulp writer Ernest Haycox; constructed a set in **Monument Valley**, Utah; brought together an ensemble cast, many of whom acted regularly in B Westerns; and produced what many have considered the most perfect Western of all time. Certainly, it is one of the most important.

The plot works around a standard formula of several characters, all with individual problems, getting on the stage for one last trip to Lordsburg before it gets too dangerous to travel due to an **Apache** uprising. Along the way they pick up a fugitive from prison, the Ringo Kid (Wayne), who is to be returned to jail, but who also hopes to shoot it out with Luke Plummer (Tyler) when he gets to Lordsburg. The characters are all stereotyped, and standard values of perceived morality are overturned. The town's most distinguished citizen, the banker, is on the run with a bag of embezzled cash. The prostitute (Trevor) becomes the savior of the righteous new bride (Platt). The drunken doctor (Mitchell) sobers up and delivers a baby in an emergency. The sheriff respects the **outlaw** and allows the outlaw and the prostitute to escape and head to Mexico at the film's end.

Although John Ford had a long career behind him already, *Stagecoach* was the real beginning of what would be perhaps the most successful director's career in the history of cinema Westerns. In the same way, John Wayne had a long list of film credits behind him, but this film moved him to the top ranks of Hollywood stardom. Thomas Mitchell won an Academy Award for supporting actor, and altogether, *Stagecoach* was nominated for seven Academy Awards, winning four of them. *See also* FORMULAS, CLASSIC WESTERN.

STANDARD PICTURE COMMITMENT CONTRACTS. Most actors in the 1930s and 1940s for budget studios such as **Republic** worked the standard commitment; in other words, they were paid per day or per week for work on specific films, as opposed to **term players** who worked under yearly salaries.

STANWYCK, BARBARA (1907–1990). Born Ruby Stevens in New York, Barbara Stanwyck played a variety of strong, independent female roles in Westerns and non-Westerns from the 1930s through the early 1960s and then developed a second career in **television Westerns**. She rarely played weak-willed **women** or women who could not handle a horse as well as anyone else in the picture. From the start she played strong women in such films as *Annie Oakley* (1935) and *Union Pacific* (1939). She played **pants roles** to perfection. Her best work in Westerns, however, came in the 1950s. ***Cattle Queen of Montana*** (1954) is often seen as her best Western and she played opposite **Ronald Reagan**, who very much played a secondary role to Stanwyck. She did her own **stunts** for the film and so impressed the Blackfeet tribal members hired as extras that they made her a blood sister and gave her the Indian name of Princess Many Victories. She followed the film with *The Violent Men* (1955), opposite **Glenn Ford**; *The Maverick Queen* (1956) and *Forty Guns* (1957), both opposite Barry Sullivan; and *Trooper Hook* (1957), opposite Joel McCrea.

STARR, BELLE (1848–1889). Probably the most famous woman **outlaw** of them all, Belle Starr rode with the Younger and the **Jesse James** gangs, mothered Cole Younger's child, and carried herself perfectly well with the men. At least that is the way most cinema Westerns portray her. She operated out of **Indian Territory** and had a hideout in what today is called Robbers Cave in Oklahoma. Gene Tierney played the bandit queen in *Belle Starr* (1941), opposite **Randolph Scott**. The real Belle Starr died in action in 1889. *See also* JAMES, JESSE.

STATUS QUO, AFFIRMATION OF. Cinema Westerns are commercial consumer productions, and as such, they must find a popular market. Westerns of the classic era, before the multiplication of media choices at the turn of the 20th century, necessarily appealed to a broad audience, which demanded satisfactory resolutions of conflicts and a resounding affirmation of its own cultural values. **Classic Westerns**, then, did not challenge the audience's values. **Howard Hawks**'s *Red River* (1948), for instance, reinforces post–World War II cultural values of white hegemony over all that can be conquered and possessed. While classic Westerns could and did explore individual psychological motivations of characters, as in **Anthony Mann**'s Westerns, they did not, as a rule, explore new interpretations of American history. **Alternative Westerns** of the 1990s, however, influenced by the **New Western history** of such revisionist historians as Patricia Limerick, began rejecting the values of the classic Western's audience and began a process, still in progress, of reinterpreting the **myth of the West**. Some critics attribute a decline in popularity of cinema Westerns at the turn of the new century to this shift away from affirming the status quo of the broad range of cinema audiences.

STEWART, JAMES "JIMMY" (1908–1997). Born in Indiana, Pennsylvania, Jimmy Stewart probably remains the all time most beloved actor in Western cinema. Over a long career he made 17 Westerns, beginning with *Destry Rides Again* (1939) and ending with *The Shootist* (1976), a film in which he costarred with **John Wayne**. During his lifetime, Stewart was often compared with Wayne, but unlike Wayne, whose critical reputation has never been very high due to the outspoken political conservatism and nationalism of his last years, Stewart has maintained his popularity and appreciation for his artistic achievement is increasing. Stewart and his characters, instead of being considered the embodiment of some of the worst elements of the American character, seemed to share the frustrations as well as the dreams of ordinary filmgoers.

After a career on the New York stage, during which he became close friends with fellow struggling actor **Henry Fonda**, Stewart signed his first Hollywood contract with Metro-Goldwyn-Meyer in 1935. Through the years he starred in a wide variety of films besides Westerns, including *Mr. Smith Goes to Washington* (1939) and *It's a Wonderful Life* (1946). His first Western proved to be one of the best ever made, *Destry Rides Again* (1939), with **Marlene Dietrich** in the lead. But it was Stewart's association with director **Anthony Mann** that led to his best efforts. The **noir Western** film *Winchester '73* (1950), as well as *Bend of the River* (1952), *The Naked Spur* (1953), and *The Far Country* (1954), earned a measure of critical acclaim few other Westerns have ever achieved.

Other great Stewart Westerns include **John Ford**'s *The Man Who Shot Liberty Valance* (1962) in which Stewart plays an eastern lawyer who lives his life believing he was the one who shot the famed gunfighter many years ago only to find out that another (John Wayne) had fired simultaneously from the shadows yet had allowed the lawyer to enjoy the fame. The film serves as an excellent vehicle for comparing the acting styles of Stewart and costar Wayne. For Stewart's long career on-screen, the American Film Institute awarded him the Lifetime Achievement Award in 1980. Stewart was also nominated for five Academy Awards and won one.

Jimmy Stewart was one of the great American personalities for much of the 20th century. He lived a life of action beyond the sound stage, serving a full career in the U.S. Army and, later, Air Force, flying 25 missions over enemy territory in World War II and eventually rising to the rank of brigadier general in 1959.

STOCK FOOTAGE. Western filmmakers have often taken film footage from archival stock to insert into new films, thereby saving themselves from shooting expensive cattle stampedes, massive Indian battles, and panoramic location shots. **B Westerns**, especially, were prone to extensive use of stock footage. **Grand National** and **Republic** Westerns of the 1930s and 1940s were often built around available footage with new action filmed on a three-day schedule. **Tex Ritter**'s films produced by Edward Finney were filled out almost entirely around stock footage. For example, Finney copied the complete **Indian** attack sequences from **Thomas Ince**'s *The Deserter* (1916) and inserted them into *Roll Wagons Roll* (1940). But even higher-budget Westerns replay old Indian battles. The dramatic fight to the death at the ford of a river between Indians and cavalry in *The Great Man's Lady* (1942) was reused in the later Fox films *Pony Soldier* (1952) and *Siege at Red River* (1954). Mel Brooks's 1974 Western spoof, ***Blazing Saddles***, which makes fun of every possible Western **cliché**, illustrates well the sometimes clumsy art of integrating stock footage into low-budget Westerns, inserting huge panoramic scenes of such standards as wagon trains that obviously came from older films.

Spectacular **stunts**, particularly of **Yakima Canutt**, often found life in multiple films. One unsophisticated method of using inserted stock footage involves having the hero, who has worn a certain dark **costume** in the entire film, suddenly change to a white shirt just before the big chase scene. The change is necessary because the stunt rider in the stock footage wore white. Warner Brothers took footage of trick riding from Ken Maynard's silent films and inserted it in early **John Wayne** films because of Wayne's lesser riding skills. "The historical resonance of a 'B' film could be (and was) cheaply enlarged by splicing in footage from a silent or early sound epic—often with only the most perfunctory efforts at matching the lighting, costuming, or speed of the original. Thus the visualized **landscape** of the 'B' Western was, to a considerable extent, made out of pieces of other movies rather than out of scenes newly observed or constructed to create a particular historical setting" (Slotkin 1992, 272).

STOREY, JUNE (1918–1991). Born in Canada, June Storey was one of **Gene Autry**'s female leads from 1938 to 1939. While she played a variety of roles, Storey's most characteristic role was that of the spoiled rich girl. In both *Rancho Grande* (1940) and *Ride, Tenderfoot Ride* (1940), the eastern girl comes West to claim an inheritance and makes foolish mistakes based on her pride and haughty nature. Autry must educate her in the ways of the West as well as develop in her a measure of humility. She held a **term player contract**, which she chose not to renew.

STRUCTURALISM. Structuralism is a critical theory that became dominant for a short time in the 1970s and 1980s. Because it was partly a reaction to **New Criticism**, it reevaluated forms of literature and art previously considered non-art, such as Westerns. By the 1980s, makers of cinema Westerns were reevaluating their own genre, and thus structuralist critics were able to decontextualize the films from their associations with low culture and bad taste and to examine the multiple structures of narrative in relation to archetypes, myths, and **symbolism**. The problem with structuralism as with New Criticism was that it ignored cultural contexts and thus had no way of dealing with such pressing issues as **women** and **Native Americans** in Westerns, or with early century American imperialism and colonialism in Westerns. While structuralist critics such as Will Wright in *Six Guns and Society* (1974) and John G. Cawelti in his original *Six-Gun Mystique* (1984) gave Westerns critical respectability, it remained for the cultural critics of the 1990s, such as Richard Slotkin and Jane Tompkins, to open the way for postmodern critical acceptance of cinema Westerns.

STUNTS. Spectacular stunt work is, of course, a staple for any Western or action film today. But early Western directors were slow to develop methods of using extra, stunt actors to perform death-defying tricks on-screen. When the hapless victims are thrown from the coal tender at the end of *The Great Train Robbery* (1903), it is obvious that dummies are being used for the fall. The earliest **silent era** Westerns rarely show much more than feigned fist fighting for action, although **William S. Hart** rode Fritz through a plate glass window, without trick photography, in *Truthful Tulliver* (1917). Early studios such as **Biograph** and **Essanay** were slow to develop a "star system," and as a result, directors felt no need to protect actors from dangerous scenes. With the development of the star system, the need for extras arose. By the late silent era, Westerns were becoming famous for the spectacle of their action scenes. At first, to film horses falling, directors experimented with a technique called the "Running W," in which a series of wires were stretched across the path so that the horses, unawares, would trip. The riders, of course, were prepared and jumped on cue. Naturally, complaints about animal cruelty eventually ended the use of such devices.

Yakima Canutt is usually considered the first great stunt actor and a pioneer in developing original stunts. His favorite stunt was to ride after a speeding stagecoach, jump off at the rear, pull himself up over the top, engage in a drawn-out fight while the stage careens out of control, and end with both actors falling on the horses and underneath the rolling coach. Through the years various cowboy stars such as **Tom Mix**, **Johnny Mack Brown**, and Ken Maynard developed reputations for doing their own stunts. Favorites included falling off a horse on an incline, jumping off trains atop horses, and knock-down saloon fights. *See also* AUTRY, GENE; BRENNAN, WALTER; BROWNE, RENO; CORRIGAN, RAY "CRASH"; EUROPEAN WESTERNS; FINLEY, EVELYN; GUN BELTS; HORSE (COWBOY HERO'S HORSE); JOHNSON, BEN; JONES, BUCK; MARION, BETH; MILES, BETTY; ROGERS, ROY; RUNNING INSERTS; STANWYCK, BARBARA; STOCK FOOTAGE; TRINITY SERIES; VIOLENCE.

SUR-WESTERN. This term comes from **French criticism** for what in **classic Westerns** is usually termed the Western **myth**, except it makes *myth* synonymous with the film itself, not as a separate construct. André Bazin in "Discours sur la méthode du Western" (1955) referred particularly to early **noir Westerns** of **Anthony Mann**, Edward Dmytryk, and Robert Aldrich, which stressed "the *romanisation* of frontier themes, using a very happy expression in our opinion. It is exactly the '*Sur-Western*' of today that is the basis for a truly remarkable series of experiments . . . in order to achieve in due time, and with sensitivity, cultural research, and a genuine enthusiasm, a new approach" (Feinin and Everson 1962, 19–20).

SYMBOLISM. The geographical West has always been a defining characteristic of the United States' national identity. The vastness of the western space naturally lends itself to huge panoramic opening scenes in Western films. But the West has always been symbolic as much as it has been visual. The earliest cinema Westerns looked back at a West that still existed but was fading fast. Westerns of the **classic era,** up until World War II, tended to view the western frontier in terms of the future, in terms of what might yet be ahead for America. After World War II, however, the West became less a symbol for a place than a symbol for a way of life, a life of rugged individualism. **Ronald Reagan**, a respectable Western actor in his own right (*Cattle Queen of Montana* [1954]), parlayed his cowboy image into a political career that led ultimately to the presidency of the United States. The image he cultivated was that of a tough, independent westerner who handled his problems without help from the paternal eastern government. The film image of the westerner thus became an image for political change and governance. *See also* FRONTIER AS ESCAPE FROM THE CITY.

– T –

TECHNICOLOR. When we think of color movies, we inevitably think of Technicolor, the most famous name associated with the color process of filmmaking. The original Technicolor process, which reached its peak usage in the 1950s, was a revolutionary development in film. Its color quality was considered exact reality, but, ironically, it was so realistic that it was thought unrealistic, and directors and viewers tended to see black-and-white cinematography as more real, more serious. Technicolor was used for high-budget show spectacles and **costume** dramas—including Westerns. While today the term is often used loosely for any color process, the trade-marked label actually refers to the multitude of color innovations developed by Technicolor Moving Entertainment Company. *See also* TECHNISCOPE.

TECHNISCOPE. Techniscope was a low-budget color process widely favored by European studios during the **spaghetti Western** era while American studios preferred **Technicolor**. The process, equivalent to pulp processes in publishing, gave the film a cartoon-like appearance that complemented the subject matter of the films. *See also* CINECITTÀ STUDIOS, ROME; *DJANGO*.

TELEVISION WESTERNS. For much of the parallel history of television and feature films, television has been looked down upon as an inferior cinematic medium; it has been the case since television's beginning. Television Westerns evolved not from big-budget cinema Westerns of the 1930s and 1940s but from **B Westerns**.

During the 1930s and 1940s, low-budget studios on **poverty row** issued dozens of hastily produced B Westerns, often in series with the same characters. After World War II ended and the United States' economy was at an all time high, radio network executives began seriously exploring the commercial prospects of television, the new technology whose development had been put on hold due to the war. Their first programming efforts consisted of recycling recently made B Westerns, so Westerns were the genre television began with. The first nationwide made-for-television series appeared on NBC in 1949—the *Hopalong Cassidy Show* developed by a media savvy **William Boyd**, who had had the foresight years before to purchase the television rights to his character and his films when studio executives did not particularly care. Boyd moved from making hour-long films to making weekly 30-minute episodes. **Roy Rogers** and **Gene Autry** soon followed with their own shows. Even **Gabby Hayes** had a show for a while.

For the first few years, network executives considered Westerns strictly for the youth demographic, both boys and girls. Early shows such as *Annie Oakley* (1954–1956) and *Buffalo Bill Jr.* (1955–1956) always had children in their casts. For the fall season of 1955, however, the networks began exploring "adult" Westerns. *Gunsmoke* (1955–1975) began its long run on CBS and *Cheyenne* (1955–1963) was scheduled by ABC. *Gunsmoke*, though, proved to be phenomenally influential. The cast consisted strictly of adults working out adult problems in adult ways: Marshal Dillon (**James Arness**), for example, could walk into a saloon and order a beer. (**Hopalong Cassidy** usually avoided saloons, but his **sidekicks** occasionally ordered milk at the bar.)

From 1956 through the end of the decade, the rush was on, and Westerns dominated television: *Wagon Train* (1957–1965), with **Ward Bond**; *Have Gun—Will Travel* (1957–1963), with **Richard Boone**; *The Rifleman* (1958–1963), with Chuck Connors; and *Wanted: Dead or Alive* (1958–1961), with Steve McQueen, were some of the most popular shows. They had far more popularity than any of the old B Westerns.

The glut had a significant impact on American culture. As the cold war intensified and as the John F. Kennedy administration took office, Westerns began to be criticized for their mindless **violence** and easy morality. Much had changed with the genre during the decade. When Chairman of the Federal Communication Commission (FCC) Newton Minow famously declared television a "vast wasteland," he was primarily referring to the preponderance of Westerns on the air.

Thus, during the 1960s a new kind of television Western emerged. *Gunsmoke* continued, but even that venerable show changed with the times. Instead of violent Westerns like *Wanted: Dead or Alive*, new family-friendly Westerns emerged, notably *Bonanza* in 1959. The show emphasized family themes with a father and his adult sons. Gunplay was rare. Good humor was common. *Bonanza* was the first television show filmed in color. Its episodes aired in the early evening so that retailers could turn their new color television sets on for the show, thus promoting their product. Other shows followed the trend: *The Big Valley* (1965–1969) and *The High Chaparral* (1967–1971). *Rawhide*, a show about cattle drives, had a successful run from 1959–1966. **Clint Eastwood**, a secondary actor on the show, continued making episodes even after finishing his filming in Italy and Spain on the **Dollars Trilogy**.

As the 1960s progressed and as a new cynicism pervaded American culture, Westerns again changed. Comic Westerns such as *Maverick* (1957–1962) and *The Wild Wild West* (1965–1969) set the tone, although *Gunsmoke* and *Bonanza* continued. When the Western spoofs such as *F Troop* (1965–1967) began showing, it was obvious that the end was near for television Westerns. By 1970 the Western was nearly gone from television. Between 1970 and 1988, only 28 Westerns were developed for network television. The baby boomer generation was growing up, the Vietnam War and major cultural changes were dividing the country, and, for most viewers, Westerns no longer seemed relevant.

Through the years to come, a few series such as *Dr. Quinn, Medicine Woman* (1993–1998) or *Kung Fu* (1972–1975) had popular runs, but they were not traditional Westerns by any means. *Little House on the Prairie* (1974–1983) probably typified where Westerns were headed by the 1980s.

But Westerns did return to television in the 1990s, and after the turn of the new century, miniseries such as Larry McMurtry's *Lonesome Dove* (1989) brought the Western back. Made-for-television movies were regularly Westerns. In 2004 the most popular television Western ever began its run, *Deadwood*, a truly adult Western with graphic sex and colorful language in abundance. Those who said back in the 1980s that Westerns were dead were simply mistaken.

Television Westerns have shared a parallel history with cinema Westerns. While 30-minute Western series dominated television in the 1950s, cinema Westerns were also flourishing, at least in quantity. When television Westerns slumped in the 1980s, so did cinema Westerns. In the beginning, older Western stars such as Roy Rogers and Gene Autry finished their careers in television, but television has also produced many major cinema Western actors: Clint Eastwood, Steve McQueen, **James Garner**, and others.

TERM PLAYER CONTRACT. Actors in the 1940s who had term player contracts with such **poverty row** studios as **Republic** worked on a yearly salary. In exchange for security and a regular paycheck, the studio could use an actor as it pleased. *See also* B WESTERNS; STANDARD PICTURE COMMITMENT CONTRACTS; STOREY, JUNE.

THE THREE MESQUITEERS. Perhaps the most famous **Trigger Trio** of the **B Western** era, the Three Mesquiteers series was produced by **Republic** from 1935 to 1950, interchanging actors throughout. The concept for the series gives a Western twist to Alexander Dumas's *Three Musketeers*. The idea was based on characters in a series of Western novels by William Colt MacDonald, published beginning in 1933.

Ray Corrigan, Bob Livingston, and Max Terhune were the original Mesquiteers. Others were inserted into the roles interchangeably: Raymond Hatton, Bob Steele, **Tom Tyler**, **Duncan Renaldo**, and even **John Wayne** in *New Frontier* (1939). The same recurring characters made up the Mesquiteers: Rusty or Lullaby Joslin, an old hunter type providing comic relief; Tucson Smith (originally played by Ray Corrigan), the more normal of the three who is in the middle age-wise; and Stony Brooke (originally Bob Livingston, also John Wayne), always a hot-tempered, romantic cowboy.

The 3M Ranch is under the joint ownership of the Three Mesquiteers, but various business interests and general ranch work, such as trail drives, brings them adventures of every sort. Over time they evolve from being roaming cowboys doing good wherever they go to being part-time government agents. Plots of the films involved searching for air-transport hijackers; rustlers using refrigerated trucks; a foreign spy ring that is about to obtain "monium," a top secret metal that will change everything. Through it all, the Mesquiteers ride horses and even call upon the U.S. Cavalry when they need help.

Interestingly, different episodes would be set in different historical periods with no explanation. The early films were set in the general period of the historic West, during the period of the **open range**. *The Three Mesquiteers* (1936), though, has the three returning from World War I, yet they find themselves aiding a covered-wagon train. Later films were set during the Civil War, the 1940s, and, again, the historic West. "In this expanded 'Western' space," Richard Slotkin says, "past and present are superimposed on each other—or, more precisely, confront each other—and through their conflict produce a moral drama" (1992, 275).

3:10 TO YUMA **(1957). Glenn Ford**, Van Heflin, **Delmer Davies** (director). Ben Wade (Ford) and his gang ride into town to report that the stagecoach has been robbed and the driver killed. The marshal rounds up a reluctant posse and takes chase even though they are all pretty sure they left the real robbers back in town. Wade splits up his men and sends them across the border, while he remains in the quiet town making love to a **dance hall girl** he once knew in **Dodge City**. Potter (Henry Jones), the town drunk, rides out to the posse to alert them that Wade is still in town. The posse returns with Dan Evans (Heflin), a quiet rancher who had earlier been humiliated by the **outlaws** in front of his two young sons. Once the posse gets the drop on Wade in the saloon, the only two townsmen the marshal can get to take the outlaw to the nearest rail town, so he can catch the train to court, are Evans and Potter. Evans goes for the money; Potter goes to redeem his self-dignity.

Holed up in a hotel room waiting for the 3:10 train to **Yuma**, Wade begins working on Evans's mind, trying to convince him to let him go or to make a mental mistake that will prove fatal. Herein lies the film's importance: There is little action except at the beginning and the end. Most of the film takes place in the hotel room as the men constantly look at the watch hanging by the bedstead, ticking the minutes until the train arrives. Wade charms both Evans and the audience with his dryly smug bravado. The rancher nearly succumbs until his own wife appears, and he knows he must do what is right in the face of overwhelming odds. Everyone deserts Evans—everyone except Potter, who at the end dies protecting Evans from Wade's gang as they descend on the hotel. Ultimately, in a spectacular shootout through the streets on the way to the depot, Evans gets Wade to the train. Just as one of Wade's men is in position kill Evans, Wade calls out and Evans shoots the gang member. Wade saves the rancher's life and voluntarily climbs on the train to prison. He has met the man he wishes he could have been.

A 2007 remake of *3:10 to Yuma*, directed by James Mangold and starring Christian Bale as Evans and **Russell Crowe** as Wade, takes the original Elmore Leonard short story and develops themes that would not have worked in 1957, such as a brief sexual encounter between Wade and the dance hall girl (Vinessa Shaw). Evans's wife (Gretchen Mol) also disappears from the story once Wade is captured and on his way.

***TOMBSTONE* (1993).** Kurt Russell, Val Kilmer, **Sam Elliott**, George P. Cosmatos (director). This is one of the 1990s versions of the **Wy-**

att Earp legend bent on portraying the lawman as utterly unsympathetic, mean, and vicious. Earp (Russell) shows no love, no compassion for his wife, who is addicted to laudanum, and rejects her for a **dance hall girl**. But, of course, that is the point; there was no heroism involved in the legend. In this **alternative Western** even the gunfight at the **O.K. Corral** is decentered from the narrative. Many fans thought Val Kilmer as **Doc Holliday** made the movie. *See also GUNFIGHT AT THE O.K. CORRAL.*

THE TOLL GATE **(1920). William S. Hart**, Anna Q. Nilsson, Lambert Hillyer (director). William S. Hart was at the height of his career when he filmed this classic **silent** Western. Deering (Hart) is the leader of a band of desperados, but he knows it is time to change his way of life. First, he must do one last job, a train robbery. But he and his men are set up by the unfaithful Jordan (Joseph Singleton), and all are killed except Deering, who is captured. The soldiers who capture him recognize him as someone who saved them in an **Indian** attack in the past, so they let him escape. Impoverished and afoot, Deering wanders into a nearby town only to find out that Jordan now runs the town. Matters quickly deteriorate for Deering: He is framed for a crime and seeks revenge himself. The saloon burns as Deering and Jordan fight. Then Deering flees, followed by a posse. His horse goes lame. Afoot again, he comes upon a farm house. Suddenly a little boy falls into the water and Deering, knowing it is the end if he stops, nevertheless saves the boy. The beautiful blonde Anna Q. Nilsson, playing the mother, saves Deering and gives him some of her long-disappeared husband's dry clothes (who turns out to be Jordan). The posse captures Deering, but the sheriff offers to pardon him for killing Jordan. Obviously in love with the mother and idolized by the child, Deering can now marry and settle down. But that would not be right. Instead he leaves with the sheriff to serve his prison sentence. He will come back, but first he must pay "the toll" for his crimes. Thus, the film ends without a happy ending, which was typical for Hart. *See also HELL'S HINGES.*

TOONES, FRED (1906–1962). Fred Toones was an **African American** actor in **B Westerns** of the pre-civil rights era. Due to the racist culture of the time, he was cast exclusively as the **comic Negro** in menial, service-type roles, always deferring to white authority. Toones was often billed as "Snowflake." He appeared as a cook in *Gold Mine in the Sky* (1938) and *Bells of San Angelo* (1947). Sometimes, as in *Hawaiian Buckaroo* (1938), he was required to reinforce the stereotype of the shiftless, lazy black person, constantly being scolded for loafing. In *Raiders of the West* (1942), a Texas Rangers film, Snowflake refuses to enter a house that he thinks is haunted by ghosts. Laughed at by the Rangers, he explains, "Spooks may not bother white folks, but they got a special attraction for us colored folks." In *The Lonely Trail* (1936), Snowflake, playing the role of an uneasy servant, is serving drinks when he is told to drop everything and answer the door. Childlike, he does just that: he drops the tray of glasses and answers the door. One of the great ironies of African American actors such as Toones is that after the **civil rights** era, many of the scenes in which they appeared were deleted from films, for good reason. Yet, at the same time, these practices effectively erased these actors' roles, which were performed in the only way open to African Americans at the time.

TOWNS. An avid watcher of Westerns can easily spot the same back lot studio set Western town being used in film after film because towns in Westerns stereotypically do not vary greatly. While certain historic towns such as **Abilene** and **Dodge City, Kansas**, develop a significance in themselves in cinema Westerns, towns in general serve a purpose and often are the thematic focus. Towns are the link to **civilization**. In towns are stagecoach lines and train depots, the means for traveling to civilized cities back East, or to civilized Western cities such as San Francisco. In towns are telegraph offices and post offices for communicating with civilization. The law, both sheriffs' offices and judges' courts, is situated in Western towns if anywhere at all. Merchants in towns may have the fashionable clothing from back East.

But towns are also the link to the frontier, the last stopping place on the train line before the untamed wilderness. Bill Blake (Johnny Depp) in *Dead Man* (1995) can go no further on the train. He gets off and the adventure begins. Lawlessness often prevails in the absence of a sheriff or a strong justice system. Saloons usually symbolize the essential link between civilization and frontier anarchy. In films like *Will Penny* (1968), towns often sprout out of nowhere on the western plains, isolated and often serving no obvious use beyond providing a saloon and trouble for a drifting cowboy. More often than not, a town in Westerns is dying, having lost its mine or its reason for economic existence.

If towns in Westerns look the same from one film to another—with their main street through town, false fronts on stores and other buildings, hitching posts, a few ornamental ethnic characters squatting next to buildings or meandering along idle streets—that is because appearance is more important than reality. Townspeople desperately want their towns to imitate eastern towns, and so we might see churches and schools, but by the side of these re-spectable institutions, we invariably see the large saloons and lav-ish bawdy houses. This surface paradox often manifests itself in the character of the townspeople, who, likely as not, are hypocrit-ical and weak. Churchwomen might run women of ill repute out of town as in **Stagecoach** (1939). Townspeople might be too weak to overcome lawless forces as in **High Noon** (1952) or **High Plains Drifter** (1973).

The **cowboy hero**'s relationship with the town is usually problem-atic. While he may be able to carry himself respectably among towns-folk, it is always clear that he is not one of them. He comes to town from the wilderness, and thus he must reconcile himself with the town—most often through **violence**, either by saving the town or by purifying it. The classic quick-draw contest between the cowboy hero and the film's villain, almost always occurs in town, not outside. *See also* FRONTIER AS ESCAPE FROM THE CITY.

THE TRAIL BLAZERS. After Monogram's popular **Trigger Trio** se-ries, **The Rough Riders**, ended due to the death of **Buck Jones** and **Tim McCoy**'s entry into the military during World War II, the com-pany brought **Hoot Gibson** and Ken Maynard out of retirement and partnered them with Bob Steele as the Trail Blazers. Some of their films include *The Law Rides Again* (1943) and *Westward Bound* (1944), both featuring **Betty Miles** as the female lead, who proves she can hold her own with the Trail Blazers. Maynard and Gibson were past their prime and overweight, so Steele was the one who got the romantic parts. The Trail Blazer films were *Wild Horse Stampede* (1943), *The Law Rides Again* (1943), *Blazing Guns* (1943), *Death Valley Rangers* (1943), *Westward Bound* (1944), and *Arizona Whirlwind* (1944).

TREVOR, CLAIRE (1910–2000). Born Claire Wemlinger in New York City, Claire Trevor began her career on the stage and made her film debut in 1933. With her blonde hair and small stature, Trevor was often cast as a hardened, experienced yet tempting case; she could seduce any male on the set with her smoky, come-on voice. Her real break came with ***Stagecoach*** (1939), where she played the prostitute Dallas. The upstanding ladies of the town escort Dallas to the last stagecoach out of town, where she accompanies a drunken physician and a whiskey drummer, a professional gambler, and a reputable banker (who has actually just embezzled from his own bank). One more passenger gets on—the officer's wife, Lucy, very pregnant and going to meet her husband. Every passenger is desperate to get out of town, even if the **Apaches** are on the warpath. Outside of town, the stage meets the Ringo Kid (**John Wayne**), who has escaped from prison. Much of the film centers on the tension between the respectable passengers and the disrespectable ones. Dallas is immediately an outcast on the stagecoach, just as she was in town, but the Ringo Kid stands up for her. Eventually it is the prostitute and the drunken doctor who must deliver Lucy's baby as matters deteriorate with the Apaches. Trevor's character in one sense centers the plot between the competing interests of all the other characters. She followed *Stagecoach* with another Western, ***Dark Command*** (1940), where once again she played John Wayne's love interest. Then came *Texas* (1941), where **Glenn Ford** and **William Holden** fought over her. Later Westerns include *Best of the Badmen* (1951) and, opposite **Randolph Scott**, *The Stranger Wore a Gun* (1953). Through the years Trevor was nominated three times for best supporting actress and won the award once.

TRIGGER (1932–1965). "The Smartest Horse in the Movies." Born Golden Cloud in San Diego, California, Trigger's big break in Hollywood came at age three when he appeared in *The Adventures of Robin Hood* (1938) ridden by **Olivia de Havilland**. However it was with **Roy Rogers** that the golden palomino is forever associated. His first film with Rogers was *Under Western Stars* (1938). He was named Trigger after **sidekick Smiley Burnette** called him quick on the trigger. Trigger never let Rogers down. Through 80 films and a long career in **television Westerns**, he never once fell. Trigger was early on billed as "the Smartest Horse in the Movies" and starred in his own right in *My Pal Trigger* (1946) and *Trigger Jr.* (1950). After Trigger's death, Rogers had him mounted and placed on display at his museum in Victorville, California.

TRIGGER TRIOS. Besides **singing cowboy** films of the 1930s and 1940s, another common **B Western** type was the Trigger Trio film. Several studios developed various series based on the exploits of a trio of heroes with equal billing. Probably the most famous Trigger Trio was **Republic**'s **Three Mesquiteers**. Monogram developed the **Rough Riders**, the Range Busters, and the **Trail Blazers**. PRC produced the **Frontier Marshals** series from 1942 to 1947, with Lee Powell, **William Boyd**, and Art Davis, and the Texas Ranger series from 1942 to 1944 with Dave O'Brien, James Newill, and Guy Wilkerson. *See also* THE THREE MESQUITEERS.

TRINITY SERIES. After **Sergio Leone**'s Westerns, the most popular **spaghetti Westerns** were those of the Trinity series, directed by Enzo Barboni and starring **Terence Hill** and Bud Spencer. These **antimyth Westerns** were comic send-ups of everything the **classic Western** represented. The protagonist, Trinity, unlike the traditional **cowboy hero** and unlike **Clint Eastwood**'s Man with No Name, is a carefree soul whose primary aim in life is to get by with as little work as possible. In one film, he naps while traveling in a travois being pulled by his riderless horse. The gimmick in all his movies was to see how he could top the previous one for traveling without really riding. "He drives his horse like a Lamborghini" (Frayling 1981, 96). With the help of a little camera speed, Trinity has a inhumanly fast draw, which he displays constantly. His brother, Bambino (Spencer), the heavy-set part of the team, tries desperately to be left alone to carry out his own, usually illegal, affairs. But before long, both are involved in saloon brawls worthy of the cartoons, with amazing **stunt** falls in every which direction.

True to spaghetti Western tradition, the stars, Hill and Spencer, are Italians with Anglicized names. Spencer is Carlo Pedersoli (1929–) from Naples, and Hill is Mario Girotti (1939–) from Venice. The two have made 19 films together and both continue making films in Europe and the United States. Hill also brought **Lucky Luke**, the French cowboy from the comics, to the screen. Spencer is now involved in Italian politics.

TYLER, TOM (1903–1954). Born Vincent Markowski in New York, Tom Tyler had a long career as a cowboy star in low-budget Westerns from the **silent era** into the 1930s. Always good-looking in a cowboy **costume**, he usually worked the bottom rung of the Western film industry with **poverty row** studio productions. But late in his career he did land serious character roles. As the oily gunman Luke Plummer in *Stagecoach* (1939), Tyler played foil to **John Wayne**'s Ringo Kid. The shootout at the saloon was perhaps Tyler's greatest moment in the movies. While his Western career disintegrated in the 1930s to playing Captain Marvel **serials**, he did manage to end with significant roles in *The Younger Brothers*, *I Shot Jesse James*, and *She Wore a Yellow Ribbon*, all in 1949. Tom Tyler's last days were spent in **television Westerns**.

TYPE CHARACTERS. The Western genre operates much like stage comedies in that it depends heavily on type characters—people in the film that can be quickly sized up according to the role they play. Often these types become **clichés**. Some common type characters often seen in Westerns, good and bad, include

- undertakers who are tall, skinny, and wear dark suits, often with tails and top hat;
- blacksmiths who dispense cracker barrel philosophy to their customers;
- store keepers who are mild men with a wife and family;
- doctors who are genial though perhaps dependent on the bottle;
- judges who are heavyset and pompous;
- lawyers and the newspaper editors who are sometimes part of a corrupt power regime or who might be straight and decent;

- respectable **women**, with their children, who are in the background somewhere;
- clergymen who are almost always Protestant preachers, usually effeminate and ineffective;
- bartenders who are invisible;
- saloon owners who often exert economic power in a community; and
- schoolmarms who are quietly beautiful when they let their hair down and take off their glasses.

– U –

UNFORGIVEN **(1992). Clint Eastwood, Gene Hackman,** Morgan Freeman, **Richard Harris,** Clint Eastwood (director). Nominated for nine Academy Awards and winner of four—including best picture, best director, and best supporting actor (Hackman)—*Unforgiven* has often been touted as the Western that brought Westerns back. The 1990s, which also saw the release of *Dances with Wolves* (1990), was a great decade for Westerns and one that changed the genre significantly. While some reviewers saw Bill Munny (Eastwood) as simply a much older Man with No Name from Eastwood's **spaghetti Western** days, this film departs considerably from those **antimyth Westerns.** Munny is not an antihero. Nor is he a **Shane**-like ex-gunfighter who badly wants to put the past behind him.

The complication is that this character is a genuine family man. The legacy of his wife forces him, not reluctantly, to settle into farming, and only desperation sends him on a very reluctant **quest** with his guns. There is much good humor in the film as the beaten-down **farmer**, Munny, sets off with his **sidekick** (Morgan Freeman), and a nearly blind kid gunfighter, The Schofield Kid (Jaimz Woolvett), to exact justice for the brutal disfigurement of a prostitute. *Unforgiven* does not merely question the great Western **myth**, it ignores it and develops its narrative not on a premise that this story is special or mythical, but on the premise that this story is one of many that happened in the long ago. The West as a concept, as a special moment does not matter in this **alternative Western.**

– V –

VAN CLEEF, LEE (1929–1989). From the earliest days in his film career it was obvious that Lee Van Cleef would always be bad. His first role, though a nonspeaking part, is still memorable—that of one of Frank Miller's thugs in *High Noon* (1952). Even here, the glare of sheer evil is evident in Van Cleef's character's menacing eyes. Throughout the 1950s he played the secondary heavy in Westerns, good and bad. Among the best are *Gunfight at the O.K. Corral* (1957), *The Tin Star* (1957), *Ride Lonesome* (1959), and *The Man Who Shot Liberty Valance* (1962).

Like other American character actors, though, Van Cleef found a new career in Europe during the 1960s with Italian Westerns. His first role was in **Sergio Leone**'s 1965 film *For a Few Dollars More* (*Per qualche dollaro in più*) in which he played Colonel Mortimer opposite **Clint Eastwood**. He followed the next year as Angel Eyes in *The Good, the Bad and the Ugly* (*Buono, il brutto, il cattivo, Il*). From there he played in numerous **spaghetti Westerns**, rising to major stardom in Europe and to a lesser degree back in the United States. Van Cleef devotees, though, usually see the 1969 *Sabata* (*Ehi amico . . . c'è Sabata, hai chiuso!*) as his best. Long after he left the scene, Lee Van Cleef has been seen as the quintessential antihero. The French **Lucky Luke** comics have a recurring character based on Van Cleef's character in the Western spoof *Shanghai Noon* (2000).

THE VANISHING AMERICAN (1925). Richard Dix, Lois Wilson, George B. Seitz (director). This **silent** film was an early big-budget epic that demonstrates the panoramic sweep available in early cinema. It was the first Western filmed in **Monument Valley**, Utah. **Zane Grey**'s novel by the same title is the film's basis, and since Grey was at the height of his popularity, he gets significant billing. Besides the simple grandeur of the cinematography, the film's real significance is in its sympathetic portrayal of **Native Americans**. The sympathy comes from Grey, not from the **classic Western** tradition that was already developing in the films of **D. W. Griffith**, **Thomas Ince**, **James Cruze**, and even the very early work of **John Ford**.

The narrative begins with a pre-story, which tells the history of Native Americans from the valley in which the story is set—from the time of the prehistoric basket weavers to the pueblos to the coming of the Spanish and the introduction of horses. Then it shows 19th-century experiences with Kit Carson and brings the story up to the present, the post–World War I period. The theme underlying all these historic episodes is the relocation of oppressed people, one wave after another, off the land and out of the valley. Then the main narrative begins. It involves an interracial romance, purely platonic, never expressed, between Nophaie (Dix) and the Indian Bureau's schoolteacher, Marion (Wilson) at the Indian school. Nophaie is the vanishing American. He dies saving the whites of the town from disgruntled **Indian** veterans returning from the war to find that their way of life is destroyed. Nophaie tries to talk sense into his enraged comrades, but he is eventually killed by his own people. His death, however, is the cause of the Indians reconciliation with the whites. The added bonus is that at the end, Marion can marry the very white Army captain (Malcolm McGregor) and thus foresee a respectable life ahead.

It is easy for us today to see the problems in the film's vision for Native America. It makes no apology, for example, in transforming the Indian way of life into white American culture at the end. Indians are fated to vanish. Indian schools are presented without apology and Americanism is extolled. Nearly every scene shows lazy Indians in the background, and the villainous Indian Agent Booker (**Noah Beery**) is worse than the well-meaning whites because he deliberately exploits Indians for personal gain. All the others shed a tear for the vanishing tribe, but, unwittingly, they are as much a part of the problem themselves.

VERA CRUZ (1954). **Gary Cooper**, Burt Lancaster, Sara Montiel, **Ernest Borgnine**, **Charles Bronson**, **Jack Elam**, **Henry Brandon**, Robert Aldrich (director). In light of the **spaghetti Westerns** of the 1960s and 1970s that often take place in Mexico, and in light of **Sam Peckinpah**'s *The Wild Bunch* (1969), *Vera Cruz* has become quite a curiosity piece. Ernest Borgnine, Charles Bronson, and Jack Elam play character roles here that are similar to their much more prominent roles a decade later.

What would happen if we took the classic **cowboy hero** from one of the hundreds of pre–Vietnam era movies (say, any of the Western characters Gary Cooper plays elsewhere) and place him in the ruthless no-law-but-that-of-power environment of Mexico (or a similar non-U.S.setting) just after the Civil War, perhaps during the reign of Maximilian I? What might happen is what does happen in this film. Gary Cooper and Burt Lancaster played ruthless mercenaries willing to fight for whichever side of the revolution—Juaristas or Maximilian's regime—is willing to pay the highest price. Neither side matters. Neither Benjamin Trane (Cooper) nor Joe Erin (Lancaster) has a shred of moral integrity. The one normative character is probably Nina (Montiel). Vera Cruz is the equivalent of a 1950s spaghetti Western. One problem complicating this common interpretation is that Robert Aldrich probably intended his original audience to feel that Trane (a former Confederate officer) is supposed to be admirable. After all, he has fled south of the border because his side lost the war. It is difficult, of course, for 21st-century viewers to accept that interpretation.

VIOLENCE. As with many other elements of **silent** film, early Western stars depended more on style for displaying violence than on elaborate effects. When **Broncho Billy Anderson** and **William S. Hart** shot someone, the effect was real. The audience would gasp, but not because of bloody wounds. It would gasp because the silent stars could convey the horror of the moment through gestures, movements, and facial expressions. An argument has often been made that for film audiences in the first decades of the 20th century, blood and gore did not horrify or make one squeamish. After all, the United States was still predominantly a rural culture, so audience members handled blood all the time when they prepared chickens for dinner, when they slaughtered hogs in the winter, when they hunted for food. So early film violence tended to be clean but effective.

After sound and color arrived, bloody wounds were still rarely emphasized, and most violence was subordinated to trick riding, roping, and elaborate **stunts**. Early silent Westerns' violence was often much more shocking than the violence of the 1930s and 1940s. The 1950s, however, saw a different kind of violence in Westerns. While there had always been plenty of gunfire in older **John Ford** films, there was not much significant violence. But with **Anthony Mann** and **Budd Boetticher**, things changed. These directors portrayed violent acts by isolating them in the moment, by giving their films a certain sparseness whereby the violent acts, whether gunfire or **fistfights**, were underlined, so to speak. Boetticher's *Ride Lonesome* (1959) and *Comanche Station* (1960) illustrate this well. In both films, **Randolph Scott**'s character is hard, not a soft spot in him except his sense of what is right and what is wrong. When he shoots, there is a certain gritting of the teeth and setting of the jaw that indicates this moment is right. Killing in a Boetticher movie is a philosophical consideration. Often it is casual, spontaneous. For Mann, violence is strained. It is difficult. But it is basic to human character. These trends established a context for new kinds of violence the rest of the century. In **spaghetti Westerns**, violence is bloody but fun. **Trinity** kills with style and with the least amount of effort he can manage. **Django** whips out enormous machine gun–like contraptions and lets loose— all to great laughs from the audience. In **Sam Peckinpah**'s *The Wild Bunch* (1969) violence is life, and it is bloody. This film changed not just Westerns but all of film history with its unrestrained violence. After *The Wild Bunch*, graphic detailed violence became standard for all Westerns.

For much of the 20th century, Westerns were nearly always considered the most violent of the film genres. That is no longer the case, but the issues of violence relating to Westerns are informative for all film studies. One of the main concerns about violence in Westerns concerns the question of which is more shocking: the quantity of violence in a given film or the kind of violence portrayed. The violence in *The Wild Bunch* is sustained, detailed, and pervasive. One of the common concerns about the film is that the more sustained visual emphasis on the blood and the impact of the bullet, the less attention is paid to the impulse behind the killing. The killing in such films, for all its quantity, may be less horrifying than the killing **Lee Van Cleef** does, pure evil in his eyes as he squeezes the trigger. There is just as much violence in many of Shakespeare's plays as in any Western, but there is a significant difference: "In the Western violence is characteristically the hero's means of resolving the conflict generated by his adversary; in Shakespeare it is the means by which the hero destroys himself or is destroyed. . ." (Cawelti 1999, 12).

Violence and Masculinity. The **cowboy hero** is distinguished immediately as a man with a gun. Westerns inevitably center on gunplay and the resulting violence. **Alternative Westerns** and **postmodern**

Westerns regularly treat themes of the erosion of masculine potency in a turn-of-the-century culture that seems to devalue traditional masculine roles. Late 20th-century and early 21st-century Westerns, such as *Young Guns* (1988) and ***American Outlaws*** (2001), allow us to examine contemporary masculinity issues through the Western **myth** of man (not woman) against wilderness and savagery, fighting to establish civilization against tremendous odds. The man with the gun is able to confront threats to manhood decisively in a fantasy of times gone by. The gun becomes the ultimate phallic symbol, proving the power once again of male potency.

Significance of Western Violence to Our Own Time. "Violence is as American as apple pie," so goes the popular adage. The United States has always been a violent society, one that resolves conflict with guns. Some cultural critics trace such deeply ingrained attitudes to the fundamental myth of its culture, the myth of the West, and its emphasis on violence: "Not only does America, and the West in particular, have a violent heritage, it admires the heritage" (Calder 1975, 135). So, when it comes to the study of cinema Westerns, the question is: What can we learn about violence in our culture from Westerns? Perhaps because war in the 20th and 21st centuries has been seen as a prelude to annihilation, violence in fiction and cinema has been treated with increasing ambiguity. Certainly, such is the case with cinema Westerns. The cowboy hero and his gun help define the genre. "Perhaps one source of [his] appeal is the way in which he resolves this ambiguity by giving a sense of moral significance and order to violence" (Cawelti 1999, 41).

"If you want to call me that, smile," the Virginian (**Gary Cooper**) drawls as he diffidently stares down the cowardly Trampas in ***The Virginian*** (1929), a film based on Owen Wister's 1902 novel by the same title. The cowboy hero knows how to use a gun, and he uses it with deadly effectiveness, but only as a last resort. His masculinity requires him to act his role as a man of honor, but honor demands restraint and self-discipline. The Virginian, as with all classic cowboy heroes, displays supreme self-control and shows no inner conflict, no doubts about the honorable course of action. The hero's restraint suggests the difference between his violence and the **outlaw**'s violence. Restraint allows the hero to sublimate his aggressive nature and to indulge in controlled, legitimated violence. His control contrasts with the outlaw's lack of control. His restraint provides significance, and his participation in the ritualistic shootout creates aesthetic order out of chaos. He kills, but he kills cleanly and fairly. He kills with a six shooter at close range.

These ritualistic patterns mattered in the cold war 1950s and 1960s as the Western commented on international tensions. At the end of the 20th century, after the cold war, violence in Westerns became less restrained, less ritualistic, and less endued with moral significance. Purgation of moral impurities no longer dominated Westerns after Sam Peckinpah's *The Wild Bunch* (1969) and the **Sergio Leone** spaghetti Westerns. Instead, violence tended to reflect the jaded meaninglessness of end-of-the-century amorality. Skulls pop and ooze as they are stepped on (***Dead Man*** [1995]) and bullets blast holes into bodies so wide that sunlight shines through (***The Quick and the Dead*** [1995]). What does it matter? directors seem to be asking. *See also* FISTFIGHTS; HOMOEROTICISM; REGENERATION THROUGH VIOLENCE; *THE VIRGINIAN*.

THE VIRGINIAN. Owen Wister's novel, published in 1902, is usually considered the prototype for the enormous number of film Westerns and popular Western novels that came after. An instant best seller, the novel captured the American audience's imagination with its laconic **cowboy hero**; its romance between the Virginian and Molly the schoolmarm, who comes out West; its end-of-novel showdown between the Virginian and the evil Trampas. Four film versions of *The Virginian* have been made as well as a television series and a made-for-television movie. All versions include perhaps the most famous line of any Western. When Trampas, over a drink, calls the Virginian "a son of a bitch," the Virginian whips out his guns and says, "When you call me that, smile!" *See also* COOPER, GARY; FORMULAS, CLASSIC WESTERN; FRENCH CRITICISM; HART, WILLIAM S.; HORSE (COWBOY HERO'S HORSE); ORIGINS OF THE WESTERN; SILENT ERA CINEMA; VIOLENCE.

– W –

WARLOCK **(1959). Henry Fonda**, **Richard Widmark**, **Anthony Quinn**, Dorothy Malone, Dolores Michaels, and Edward Dmytryk (director). Edward Dmytryk's film, based on the highly regarded novel by Oakley Hall, is one of the most psychologically developed Westerns of the late classic period. The **town** of Warlock is beset by an outlaw gang, so it seeks out the renowned **hired gun** Clay Blaisedell (Fonda). When the gunman arrives he brings with him Tom Morgan (Quinn), a well-dressed sophisticate who is sensitive about his clubfoot. Morgan serves as Blaisedell's handler. He is officious in his care for the gunman, and some critics note a **homoerotic** theme in their relationship. The gunman is ever busy with his colt revolvers. Once Blaisedell cleanses the town of its **outlaw** problem, he stays around. One of the outlaws, Johnny Gannon (Widmark), repudiates the gang and stays to take the town's badge as lawman. But the plot is much more complex than merely having Gannon and Blaisedell face off in a showdown. Instead, Blaisedell and Morgan have a falling out, which culminates in the showdown. Two women enter the scene, and the plot really becomes complicated.

WAYNE, JOHN (1907–1979). Born Marion Robert Morrison in Winterset, Iowa, John Wayne, nicknamed "the Duke," is for many the name most associated with movie cowboys. A star University of Southern California football player, he turned a summer job as general laborer on the Fox Studios lot (given to him by **Tom Mix**) into a long career spanning from 1926 to 1976. Early on he made friends with director **John Ford**, who became his mentor, and began playing bit parts in Ford's movies. His first starring role was in Raoul Walsh's *The Big Trail* (1930), which, however, did little to promote his career. Throughout the 1930s he starred in dozens of low-budget movies, mostly Westerns. He even starred in some as Sandy the **singing cowboy**, though his songs were evidently dubbed. The high point of his **B Western** career was probably his appearances in the quality low-budget **Three Mesquiteer** series.

Few of the B Western cowboy stars ever made a career transition to A Westerns, but in 1939, John Ford gave Wayne the role of the Ringo Kid in *Stagecoach*. This film has occasionally been considered Wayne's best, and it probably was the best Western he was in, whether or not it was his best acting. The Ringo Kid's sudden appearance on the road to Lordsburg—standing in the middle of the stage's path, holding his saddle and gear, thumbing a ride—became an iconic image of John Wayne. He played opposite **Claire Trevor**, who, along with **Maureen O'Hara**, became one of the few female stars associated with Wayne during his career. Thereafter, he worked both higher-budget Westerns as well as lower-budget films for **Republic**. But on the success of *Stagecoach*, Republic placed him in its most ambitious Western ever, *Dark Command* (1940), in which Wayne costarred with **Roy Rogers**. Again, Wayne excelled in the ensemble cast.

World War II, though, made John Wayne a true American movie star. While he continued to play in a few Westerns, his pro-American, patriotic war films developed his persona as a hard-edged, uncompromising warrior, unafraid to take any chance, legal or not, ethical or not, so long as it ensured American victory. The combat films made both during the war and in the years immediately following were action packed and, as Richard Slotkin has pointed out, were essentially Westerns in plot, characterization, and mood. With the war over and the United States flush in the midst of a booming economy, audiences were ready to celebrate its victory by revisiting the myths of the past, and John Wayne filled a vital cultural role with the Western roles he assumed in the late 1940s and early 1950s.

Angel and the Badman (1947) moved Wayne's career solidly back to Westerns. It was the first film he produced with Batjac, his own production company that was involved in most of his future films. Quirt Evans (Wayne) is the badman, a recovering **outlaw** of the persona closely associated with Wayne. The agent of the badman's recovery is a Quaker family—utterly pacifist, utterly nonviolent—and the young daughter (**Gail Russell**) in particular takes care of Evans. Here Wayne, in his own film, presents the triumph of masculinity in a complex dilemma facing the outlaw: not only whether to return to his past or to accept a Quaker nonviolent life out of love, but how to survive in a world incompatible with nonviolence and yet respect and save those ideals.

Howard Hawks's *Red River* (1948) began to move Wayne into more mature roles. Tom Dunson (Wayne) was the father-older brother figure for Matt Garth (**Montgomery Clift**). Their rivalry for masculine superiority results in one of the great **fistfights** in the history of Westerns. The fight begins with mutual rage but ends with an almost **homoerotic** embrace in total exhaustion as Tom acknowledges that Matt is now worthy of his manhood. John Ford called on

Wayne once again, this time to transfer his role as combat officer in war films to cavalry officer in the West in *Fort Apache* (1948), the first of Ford's **Cavalry Trilogy**, followed in 1949 with *She Wore a Yellow Ribbon* and in 1950 with *Rio Grande*.

The usual attack on John Wayne's acting ability is that he developed one persona and never changed, his own private personality eventually merging with his film personality so that when John Wayne acted, he always played John Wayne. There is much truth in this assertion. While the young Ringo Kid in *Stagecoach* was a refreshing new character for Westerns, the Ringo Kid had grown up by the 1950s and was becoming little more than a **cliché**. One reason **antimyth Westerns** dominated in the 1960s is because of Wayne's domination of the genre in the 1950s.

But with John Ford's ***The Searchers*** (1956), Wayne would extend his acting as far as he ever would extend it. He played Ethan Edwards, who comes home to Texas from the Civil War. This character is the classic Wayne persona, but that persona changes beyond anything seen in other Wayne films. The Comanches attack the homestead and kidnap Edwards's two young nieces, so he sets out in pursuit. The **quest** lasts years. One of the girls is found dead, naked, brutally violated. Edwards becomes obsessed. He pursues the evil Chief Scar (**Henry Brandon**), knowing he has taken Debbie (Natalie Wood) as his own. At the end of the quest, when he finally finds Debbie, thoroughly Indian now, Edwards's racist rage has consumed and destroyed his character. He looks on his niece with sheer hatred at what she has become and starts to kill her because she is no longer white. Martin (Jeffrey Hunter) struggles to stop Ethan's hand, barely succeeding. Then Martin is the one who kills Scar, not Ethan.

John Wayne really did become another character in *The Searchers*. In other films—even ***The Man Who Shot Liberty Valance*** (1962)— John Wayne always played John Wayne. In *True Grit* (1969) and *The Shootist* (1976), John Wayne has simply grown old. In *The Searchers*, however, though he walks onto the screen as John Wayne, his character turns into an obsessed, maniacal **Indian** hunter intent on saving a white woman, a character not seen in any of his other films.

As with *Stagecoach* and *Dark Command*, some of Wayne's best later films are ensemble films. *Rio Bravo* (1959) is one of his lighter films, perhaps the closest to comedy he ever came. He played the town sheriff holding a prisoner who has lots of family and friends try-ing to break him free. The only help Wayne's character has is his old deputy named Stumpy (**Walter Brennan**), the town drunk (Dean Martin), and a teenaged **gunfighter** (Ricky Nelson) itching for action. Complications multiply with one misstep after another.

Wayne usually let John Ford or others do the directing of his films, but he had long been passionate about developing a film based on the Texas battle of the Alamo in 1836. *The Alamo* (1960), a big-budget affair filmed near San Antonio, Texas, proved to be a doctrinaire film that audiences even then saw (rightfully so) as heavy on American-ism at the expense of history. Wayne himself played Texas hero David Crockett, who at one point proclaims, "Republic. I like the sound of the word. It means people can live free, talk free, go or come, buy or sell, be drunk or sober, however they choose. Some words give you a feeling. Republic is one of those words that makes me tight in the throat—the same tightness a man gets when his baby takes his first step or his first baby shaves and makes his first sound as a man. Some words can give you a feeling that makes your heart warm. Republic is one of those words." Because Wayne associated himself so much with the movie and its message of America first, his reputation in the American mind began to change from being a top box-office Western star to being an exemplar of American conserva-tive patriotism. While *The Alamo* was not a box-office failure, its crit-ical reception was a severe blow to Wayne.

As in the past, when Wayne needed to renew his appeal, he re-turned to John Ford, this time with *The Man Who Shot Liberty Valance*, another ensemble film with **Jimmy Stewart**, Vera Miles, and Lee Marvin. Stewart is the real star as an eastern lawyer who in-sults Liberty Valance (Marvin) and is called out onto the street. He can barely shoot, but by sheer luck he guns down the killer. He be-comes famous and builds a political career. Only years later does he find out that Wayne's character had been in the shadows that night and had protected him, killing Valance. Consistent with his character, John Wayne remained in the shadows of this excellent film.

Early Wayne films followed the common low-budget-Western practice of keeping the star's name for the character's name. Thus, in his early B films he nearly always played a character named John, or occasionally Tom, Wayne. Wayne's case illustrates a common feature of the star persona in that while his performance character, as well as his real life character, was nearly always referential to frontier days or to Western times, in reality, his character was referential only to films of the West, only to depictions of history, not to authentic time or place. This merging of star persona with the actor's real person was responsible for both the greatness of John Wayne and the decline in his critical reputation after his death.

While some of Wayne's best films came out of the 1960s, his image as an all-American hero took a beating during this period. Westerns themselves were undergoing profound change as they began questioning the values that Wayne found most dear. He had not changed, but his culture and his favored movie genre was changing. A decade earlier, when Senator Joseph McCarthy searched for communists in Hollywood, many stories of heroism emerged as members of the film community resisted McCarthy and his minions, often at great personal cost. Wayne, however, worked with the Motion Picture Alliance for the Preservation of American Ideals in helping purge Hollywood of communism. He had publicly complained that *High Noon* (1952) was un-American. So when American culture became divided over the war in Vietnam, Wayne felt a similar urge to advocate patriotism and American values. The quintessential Western hero tried once again to parlay his reputation as a soldier into a combat film on the Vietnam War, *The Green Berets* (1968). But Wayne was too old by now, older than any real person could possibly be in combat in the real war. His performance proved embarrassing and a blow to his reputation from which he could never recover, and because the war had become so unpopular by the time the film was released, the American public could not accept its premise and thus could no longer accept John Wayne.

During this same time, his health was failing as he entered a 15-year battle with cancer. His public service commercials fighting cancer showed the all-American hero as frail and failing quickly. A natural sentimental **nostalgia** gave Wayne's career one last boost with his only Academy Award for his role in *True Grit*, a film about an aging **bounty hunter** searching **Indian Territory** for the murderer of a young girl's father.

John Wayne's last movie was a deliberate farewell to the public. *The Shootist* (1976) depicts the story of an aging gunfighter who discovers he is dying of cancer. The cast included friends who had acted with Wayne through the years: **Jimmy Stewart**, **Lauren Bacall**, and **John Carradine**. Wayne died of cancer three years later. For many, his death in 1979 signified the end of the **classic Western** era. No other actor, save perhaps **Clint Eastwood**, continued the long line of Western actors identified primarily as symbols of the Western **cowboy hero**. Fortunately, the association of Wayne's death with the demise of the Western has proven unfounded.

   John Wayne became more than just an actor of Western movies. He is a perfect example of how a star persona can be transferred from screen to life. His Congressional Medal honored him for representing the ideals of American military heroism, though Wayne never actually served in the military. For many, he came to represent the great ideals of the "American" character. Unfortunately, by the end of his life, he had, for many more people, come to represent unquestioning patriotism and all that was corrupt about the American character. Unfortunately, his political reputation too often clouds our judgment of his role in establishing the classic Western film as a major film genre and a major cultural force in the 20th century.

WESTERN MOMENT. The historical period of the old West is nearly always seen in cinema Westerns as occurring after the Civil War and before the turn of the 20th century—the Western moment. Even when a film is set in later times, such as ***Butch Cassidy and the Sundance Kid*** (1969), which tells of events occurring roughly from 1900–1908, it inevitably reminds one of the Western moment.

WESTERNS, ARTISTIC VALUE. For most of the history of cinema, Westerns have been considered the lowest of low culture. For many older critics, even the few great films of **John Ford** fall far below the mark of what one might consider high art. These critics dismiss Westerns by pointing to the excessive use of **clichés**, to the reliance on plot **formulas**, to the emphasis on action and plot over character as typical features of Westerns. In the last several decades, however, cultural critics, literary critics, and even film critics have begun to study cinema Westerns seriously. There have been plenty of bad Western films made through the years; one has only to mention *The Terror of Tiny Town* (1938), a film with an all midget cast, to make that point. But there have been many Westerns that, except for the fact that they are Westerns, qualify as significant art, making significant observations on the human condition.

Two areas where the Western genre contributes uniquely to significant art are in the ways it treats **violence** and the ways it treats humanity's relation to the land. No other film genre can isolate individual violence, one human against another human, in the way Westerns can. Combat films can treat mass violence. Gangster films, while violent, are more concerned with other issues. But, in one sense, Westerns are all about violence. Not many Western films mentioned in this dictionary are without gunfire at some point. Also, Westerns relate to the land, to **landscape**, in ways no other film genre does. The land becomes integral to the narrative. Character is determined, whether for good or bad, by the actual land in which one exists within the film. *See also* FORMULAS, CLASSIC WESTERN.

WESTERNS, CULTURAL VALUE AND SIGNIFICANCE OF. While many Hollywood Westerns are little more than whimsical stories of legitimated violence, serious Westerns attempt to examine social issues in ways that no other medium can. An underlying assumption of all serious study of Westerns is that a Western film is never about the historic old West. It is always about the cultural present, the present of the film's production and marketing. The **myth of the West**, with its historical moment, and its geographic space, allows writers and directors freedom to distance controversial issues in such a way as to make them acceptable themes to audiences who would resist direct representation. Westerns of the **classic** period, thus, could deal with American race issues through films dealing with conventional **Native American** conflicts in the past. Issues relating to war and combat were often dealt with in the cavalry Westerns of the World War II era and the **Mexican** Westerns of the Vietnam War era. Recent Westerns have dealt with feminist issues and homosexuality issues. Beyond that, Robert Warshow has argued, one of the primary claims that Westerns have "high seriousness" results from its "serious orientation to the problem of violence which can be found almost nowhere else in our culture" (cited in Cawelti 1999, 56). The best Westerns have always treated the ambiguity of legitimate, **regenerative violence** relative to the illegitimate **violence** of savagery. *See also* REGENERATION THROUGH VIOLENCE; SAVAGE WAR.

WHITE FLASH. White Flash was **Tex Ritter**'s **horse** throughout the 1930s and 1940s. During the years that Ritter worked with **Grand National** and Monogram, he used different studio horses all dubbed "White Flash," but in 1941 Ritter decided to find a permanent White Flash. Eventually he bought White Flash from Jerome Eddy, an Arizona horseman. Glenn Randall trained the horse, and Ritter used it for his remaining films and personal appearances. White Flash's career ended in 1952 with Ritter's tour of Europe.

WIDMARK, RICHARD (1914–2008). Born in Minnesota and raised in Illinois, Richard Widmark broke into film at his peak, winning an Academy Award nomination for his first film, *Kiss of Death* (1947). While he was never again nominated, he nevertheless developed a long, distinguished career, first in war movies and films noir. But Widmark also played in many great Westerns. He usually played the quick-witted, fast-talking cynic, in contrast to the stereotypical silent **cowboy heroes** such as **Gary Cooper**, with whom Widmark was paired in one of his first Westerns, *Garden of Evil* (1954). Hooker (Cooper) and Fiske (Widmark) are on their way to the gold fields when their ship is forced to put up at a Mexican port for repairs. A desperate Leah Fuller (Susan Hayward) hires them to go deep into Mexico to rescue her husband, who is trapped at a gold mine. Hooker keeps his stiff, silent demeanor while Fiske, a gambler, keeps up a steady pace of cynical one-liners and rapid-fire card tricks.

Widmark was one of **Delmer Davies'** favorite actors, using him in *The Last Wagon* (1956), opposite Felicia Farr; *Warlock* (1959); and *Alvarez Kelly* (1966). In Warlock, the sharp-tongued Johnny Gannon (Widmark) is paired with the stonily silent Blaisedell (**Henry Fonda**). **John Ford** cast Widmark as his lead in *Cheyenne Autumn* (1964), and **John Wayne** cast him as Jim Bowie in *The Alamo* (1960). *The Way West* (1967) and *Death of a Gunfighter* (1969) were Widmark's last Westerns. *See also* CARD PLAY AND

THE COWBOY HERO; CLASSIC WESTERNS; GAMBLER, PROFESSIONAL.

THE WILD BUNCH (1969). **William Holden**, **Ernest Borgnine**, Robert Ryan, **Sam Peckinpah** (director). The bloodiest Western ever made; with this film Westerns changed forever—these are the usual talking points for *The Wild Bunch*. Perhaps the most memorable scene is the first. A group of United States Army soldiers, dressed in World War I–era uniforms, rides slowly into a prosperous Texas border town. A Salvation Army parade is in progress. Children are playing everywhere. We find out that the soldiers are actually about to rob a bank, but they are riding into a trap. Gunmen are at the top of every building. The shooting starts, and the Salvation Army band is caught in the middle. Tubas and bass drums fly everywhere. Children are trampled. Gatlin guns tear through everything. In graphic slow motion, we see bullets hitting flesh and blood spurting out. We see bodies torn to shreds slowly and in clear vision **Technicolor**. That is just the first 10 minutes of *The Wild Bunch*. The narrative is based on the exploits of a historically real **outlaw** gang at the turn of the 20th century. *Butch Cassidy and the Sundance Kid* (1969), produced the same year, is a feel-good movie version about a different element of the Wild Bunch.

Nobody in this film represents the values of **classical Westerns**. The gang is ruthless and evil, being chased into Mexico by quasi-government agents who are every bit as ruthless and evil as the Wild Bunch. There is no moral center in this film because Peckinpah questions whether a moral center even exists anymore. The film resonated perfectly with a generation that was questioning and rejecting every value it had ever been taught. One of the cultural artifacts of that generation's past had been the classic Westerns and the **B Westerns** of their childhoods, which now seemed to have been based on superficial and false assumptions about human nature and about social value. *See also* ANTIMYTH WESTERNS; VIOLENCE.

WILDERNESS-TURNED-GARDEN THEME. The grand appeal of the West was its untamed **frontier**, and Westerns celebrate its desolate **landscape**. But the undercurrent of all Westerns is the steady encroachment of **civilization** and ultimately the cultivation of the desert for useful purposes. Typical of this theme is *The Man Who Shot Liberty Valance* (1962), where the eastern lawyer, derided early in the film, ultimately goes to Congress and brings irrigation to the area, thus civilizing it and turning the desert into a garden. Also typical is *Cimarron* (1960), where we watch the process of the no man's land of **Indian Territory** become the early 20th-century oil empire of Oklahoma.

WILSON, WHIP (1911–1964). Born Roland Charles Meyers, Whip Wilson began being promoted after World War II as a successor to **Buck Jones** by Monogram. He starred in 22 **B Westerns** rounding up bad men with his trusty whip. As part of his competition with **PRC** star Lash La Rue, he used a whip as his gimmick. His first film was *Crashing Thru* (1949) and his last was *Wyoming Roundup* (1952). Monogram attempted to make Wilson's character a cross between Buck Jones and Lash La Rue. His **horse** was variously named Silver Bullet, Bullet, and Rocket. Andy Clyde and Fuzzy Knight played **sidekick** at different times while **Reno Browne** was the female lead most often associated with Wilson.

WINCHESTER '73 (1950). **Jimmy Stewart**, **Shelley Winters**, Dan Duryea, Stephen McNally, **Anthony Mann** (director). This **noir Western** is the first in the series of Westerns that Stewart made for Anthony Mann. The others are *Bend of the River* (1952), *The Naked Spur* (1953), *The Far Country* (1954), and *The Man from Laramie* (1955). *Winchester '73* is the only one in black and white.

Winchester '73 is one of the great **revenge Westerns** of the **classic era**, but the motive for revenge is deemphasized. Lin McAdam (Stewart) is more concerned with proving his superiority over his brother, Dutch Henry (McNally), than seeking revenge, even though Dutch had killed their father. Dutch is just bad; he wears the black hat. Nobody knows why he turned to bank robbery and outlawry early in life. We are expected to see McAdam as morally superior, although we are never told why; he wears the white hat. One of the best scenes is when Lin whips Waco Johnnie (Duryea) at the saloon bar. The rage in Stewart's face reveals pure hatred. Duryea's character is perfect—too perfect. We have to love him in all his crude badness. Of course, Lola (Winters) is intensely attracted to him. Her fiancée,

Charles Drake (Steve Miller), plays the stereotypical coward. At one point, in sheer white-panic fear, he flees from the **Indians** leaving Lola at their mercy, which is unforgivable according to the masculine **code**. But he returns immediately and begins the process of redemption—which occurs when he attempts at last to save Lola in a gunfight (futile from the start) with Waco Johnnie. Rock Hudson plays an Indian chief, but his character is silly; nobody would think Young Bull is Native American. Tony Curtis also plays a bit part. The unifying plot device is the special gun, the Winchester '73, only a 1,000 of which were made. The film follows the progress of the gun from one hand to another.

WINTERS, SHELLEY (1920–2006). Born Shirley Schrift in St. Louis, Missouri, Shelley Winters was nominated for four Academy Awards and won the best supporting actress award twice. While most of her great films were non-Westerns, she did play the sexy **dance hall girl** Lola Manners in **Winchester '73** (1950). Her flirtations with Waco Johnnie (Dan Duryea) probably take most viewers aback as they associate Winters with her later roles as a frumpy matron. She also starred in the Western *Untamed Frontier* (1952).

WOMEN. Westerns traditionally have been stories of men struggling against the forces of the frontier. Women's roles in these stories have usually been secondary at best. Symbolically, however, women have played a major role. While the frontier is a world of men, the **town** is dominated by women. Women thus exert a feminizing influence on the frontier. The westward movement, then, can be seen as a process of feminization. Women, moreover, represent repressed sexual desires. Men lose their masculinity if they actually settle down and marry. Thus, any attachment to women must be purely sexual and nonconsensual if frontier men are to maintain their inherent maleness. Therefore, the **cowboy hero**'s relations with women always involve the hero repressing his latent sexual urges. When a man cannot repress his desires, he becomes the savage. Women, then, are frail and must be protected at all costs. They are subject to sexual violation by savages. Thus, in films such as *The Searchers* (1956) and *The Missing* (2003), rescuing the women captured by savages becomes an obsessively desperate mission.

The cowboy hero is often torn between his attraction to savagery and his attraction to civilization. This can be symbolized with a dichotomy of the blonde and the brunette—the blonde offering the hero a pure and utterly respectable relationship and the brunette offering a tantalizingly forbidden relationship. Will Kane in *High Noon* (1952), for example, must choose between Amy Fowler, the blonde Quaker, and Helen Ramirez, the ambitious, dark-haired saloon girl. The one represents civilized respectability while the other represents a move toward savagery.

Different eras have emphasized different stereotypes of the heroines who rode opposite the cowboy heroes. The **silent era** of **William S. Hart** featured hapless maidens such as that played by Anna Q. Nilsson in *The Toll Gate* (1920). **B Westerns** of the 1940s, on the other hand, often featured heroines such as **Dale Evans**, who wore jeans and could ride a horse as well as anyone else on the set. Other stereotypes have been the long-haired, wild-riding hellions; girls dressed as boys; chocolate-box heroines; decorative heroines; and spunky heroines. Perhaps the most common stereotype is the dark-haired girl and the fair-haired girl vying for the same cowboy hero. Whatever the stereotype, the fact is that cinema Westerns have been guilty throughout their history of relegating women to roles as Others. *See also ANGEL AND THE BADMAN*; ARTHUR, JEAN; BACALL, LAUREN; *BANDOLERO!*; BARDOT, BRIGITTE; BLANCHETT, CATE; BROWNE, RENO; CAPTIVITY NARRATIVES; CARDINALE, CLAUDIA; *CATTLE QUEEN OF MONTANA*; CIVILIZATION VERSUS WILDERNESS; CRAWFORD, JOAN; DANCE HALL GIRLS; DANDRIDGE, RUBY; DARBY, KIM; DARNELL, LINDA; DAVIS, GAIL; DE HAVILLAND, OLIVIA; DICKINSON, ANGIE; DIETRICH, MARLENE; *DUEL IN THE SUN*; EVANS, DALE; EVANS, MURIEL; FEMINIST WESTERNS; FINLEY, EVELYN; *GANG OF ROSES*; GREENWALD, MAGGIE; HART, MARY; HOLT, JENNIFER; JANUARY, LOIS; *JOHNNY GUITAR*; JURADO, KATY; KELLY, GRACE; MALE GAZE; MARION, BETH; MILES, BETTY; O'HARA, MAUREEN; *THE OUTLAW*; PANTS ROLE; PAYNE, SALLY; RUSSELL, GAIL; PRODUCTION CODE; SILENT ERA CINEMA; SPAGHETTI WESTERNS; STANWYCK, BARBARA; STOCK FOOTAGE; STOREY, JUNE; *THE QUICK AND THE DEAD*; *THE TOLL GATE*; TOWNS; TREVOR, CLAIRE; WINTERS, SHELLEY.

– Y –

YUMA, ARIZONA. Westerns frequently refer to Yuma. Bad guys come on-screen, and we find they just came from Yuma. Yuma is in the hottest part of the Arizona desert and its state prison is a hell hole from which nothing good can come and from which no one ever escapes. **Delmer Davies'** *3:10 to Yuma* (1957) is based upon this common knowledge about Yuma, Arizona.

Bibliography

CONTENTS

INTRODUCTION

A basic assumption of understanding art, whether visual, literary, or film, is that art cannot exist without criticism, for criticism is the natural response to art. As the previous pages show indirectly, cinema Westerns have always been popular with movie audiences, in some decades more than others, and from the beginnings of Hollywood much has been written about Westerns. But what was written was always for fan consumption and little more; Westerns did not receive the same kind of critical treatment from reviewers as "serious" films. Two reasons are usually offered for this lack of serious academic critical scrutiny. First, the art of film itself was late in being received seriously by critics and scholars. Universities did not begin offering film programs widely until after the 1960s. Prior to that, academic journals and presses rarely considered film criticism on the same level as literary and dramatic criticism. If even the best works of the cinema masters received little attention, it is no wonder that Westerns received even less attention.

Second, the primary critical approach through most of the 20th century was "New Criticism," sometimes called formalism. New Criticism based its judgment of what made a work of literature great strictly on the text itself, independent of any historical or social considerations. The complexity of the individual parts fitting perfectly together was what mattered for most critics prior to the 1970s and 1980s. Such basic assumptions about the nature of art worked well with the great literary texts of English, American, and French literature, as well as for certain kinds of serious, aesthetic films, primarily European. But critics grounded in formalist assumptions of art would naturally reject outright any kind of popular literature or film as having serious value.

It was not until New Criticism lost its influence that critics could even begin to consider popular art and take popular culture seriously. The first significant study of Westerns as an art form, was Will Wright's *Six Guns and Society: A Structural Study of the Western*, published in 1975. Wright examined the patterns of Western plots in order to discover the universal patterns of narrative. From then on, serious studies of Westerns became common in academic journals, presses, and conferences. Others followed after Wright, examining every conceivable aspect of the genre.

Today, serious studies of Westerns are part of literary studies, film studies, communication studies, and cultural studies at most major universities in the United States and to a significant degree in Great Britain and some other countries. One need no longer apologize for developing a research project on John Ford's films, outlaw films, women in Westerns, or Native Americans in Westerns. Even studies of B Westerns, the films of Dale Evans, or Hopalong Cassidy are now commonplace in serious academic circles.

For someone just beginning the serious study of Westerns, the first place to go should be John G. Cawelti's *The Six-Gun Mystique Sequel* (1999). Cawelti has done much of the preliminary work any student of Westerns would ordinarily need to do. He has outlined in detail virtually all the major theoretical approaches, and he has reviewed all the major studies of Westerns up to the late 1990s. *The Six-Gun Mystique Sequel* is a basic handbook for research into Westerns.

Another major study to consider is Richard Slotkin's massive *Gunfighter Nation: The Myth of the Frontier in Twentieth-Century America* (1992). Slotkin takes a cultural approach to the basic myths of the West as expressed throughout various media, especially popular fiction and film. He provides detailed analyses of nearly all the significant Western films.

After Cawelti and Slotkin, there are numerous studies that form the basis of Western scholarship today, some of the best written by women. Jenni Calder's *There Must Be a Lone Ranger: The American West in Film and Reality* (1975) tackles the most common questions asked about Westerns and their relation to reality. Jane Tompkins in *West of Everything: The Inner Life of Westerns* (1992) examines, among other things, the major films and novels in their relation to women. Lee Clark Mitchell's *Westerns: Making the Man in Fiction* (1996), on the other hand, discusses Westerns in relation to their constructions of masculinity.

The history of cinema Westerns has received much attention as well. Studies of the different historical periods, kinds of Westerns, studios, and film production are common. A recent groundbreaking study of silent Westerns is Nanna Verhoeff's *The West in Early Cinema: After the Beginning* (2005). With reference to hundreds of obscure silent films, Verhoeff changed the way we previously considered this period. In two volumes—*Westerns and American Culture: 1930–1955* (2001) and *Westerns in a Changing America: 1955-2000* (2004)—R. Philip Loy surveys the thematic and historic trends in Westerns from the complex B Western era to the end of the 20th century. Other works listed in the bibliography that follows have shown relations between Westerns and war, particularly the cold war, and changes in media, among other things.

John Ford and Sam Peckinpah have received the most critical attention among filmmakers and actors, and their films are regularly analyzed in detail in journals and scholarly monographs. But there are also significant studies of nearly every Western director and actor and critical analyses of the noteworthy Western films.

In the following bibliography, I have attempted to show not only the most significant scholarship on Westerns but also the range of topics commonly discussed. Most of the entries are readily available at most university libraries or through some form of interlibrary loan. Also included is a small sampling of biographies, autobiographies, and other publications intended for non-scholarly audiences but which should prove valuable. A few general websites are listed, though nearly all significant films, directors, and actors have numerous searchable websites devoted to them. I hope that this list will serve both those developing research projects in Westerns as well as those who simply want to learn more about this fascinating field.

CRITICAL AND THEORETICAL APPROACHES TO WESTERNS

Aquila, Richard, ed. *Wanted Dead or Alive: The American West in Popular Culture*. Urbana: University of Illinois Press, 1996.

Bazin, Andre. *What Is Cinema?* 2 vols. Ed. and trans. Hugh Gray. Berkeley: University of California Press, 1971.

Buscombe, Edward, and Roberta E. Pearson, eds. *Back in the Saddle Again: New Essays on the Western*. London: British Film Institute, 1998.

Calder, Jenni. *There Must Be a Lone Ranger: The American West in Film and Reality*. New York: Taplinger, 1975.

Cameron, Ian, and Douglas Pye, eds. *The Book of Westerns*. New York: Continuum, 1996.

Cawelti, John G. *The Six-Gun Mystique Sequel*. Bowling Green, Ohio: Bowling Green State University Press, 1999.

Corkin, Stanley. *Cowboys as Cold Warriors: The Western and U.S. History*. Philadelphia, Pa.: Temple University Press, 2004.

Coyne, Michael. *The Crowded Prairie: American National Identity in the Hollywood Western*. London: Tauris, 1997.

Davis, Robert Murray. *Playing Cowboys and Indians: Low Culture and High Art in the Western*. Norman: University of Oklahoma Press, 1992.

Doyle, Michael. *American West on Film: The Agrarian Frontier*. Dubuque, Iowa: Kendall-Hunt, 1996.

Elkin, Frederick. "The Psychological Appeal of the Hollywood Western." *Journal of Educational Psychology* 24 (1950): 72–86.

Emert, Scott D. *Loaded Fictions: Social Critique in 20th Century Westerns*. Moscow: University of Idaho Press, 1996.

Engel, Leonard, ed. *The Big Empty: Essays on Western Landscape as Narrative*. Albuquerque: University of New Mexico Press, 1994.

French, Peter A. *Cowboy Metaphysics: Ethics and Death in Westerns*. Lanham, Md.: Rowman & Littlefield, 1997.

French, Philip. *Westerns: Aspects of a Movie Genre*. 2nd ed. New York: Oxford University Press, 1977.

Hamilton, Cynthia. *Westerns and Hard-Boiled Detective Fiction in America: From* High Noon *to* Midnight. Iowa City: University of Iowa Press, 1982.

Kitses, Jim, and Greg Rickman, eds. *The Western Reader*. 2nd ed. New York: Proscenium, 1999.

Lenihan, John H. *Showdown: Confronting Modern America in Western Film*. Urbana: University of Illinois Press, 1980.

Mitchell, Lee Clark. *Westerns: Making the Man in Fiction*. Chicago: University of Chicago Press, 1996.

Nachbar, Jack, ed. *Focus on the Western*. Englewood Cliffs, N.J.: Prentice, 1974.

O'Leary, Brian. "Camera Movements in Hollywood's Westering Genre: A Functional Semiotic Approach" *Criticism* 45 (2003): 197–222.

Pilkington, William, and Don Graham, eds. *Western Movies*. Albuquerque: University of New Mexico Press, 1979.

Prats, Armando. *Invisible Natives: Myth and Identity in the American Western*. Ithaca, N.Y.: Cornell University Press, 2002.

Rollins, Peter C., and John E. O'Connor, eds. *Hollywood's West: The American Frontier in Film, Television, and History*. Lexington: University Press of Kentucky, 2005.

Slotkin, Richard. *Gunfighter Nation: The Myth of the Frontier in Twentieth-Century America*. New York: Harper, 1992.

Solomon, Stanley J. *Beyond Formula: American Film Genres*. New York: Harcourt, 1976.

Tompkins, Jane. *West of Everything: The Inner Life of Westerns*. New York: Oxford University Press, 1992.

Tuska, Jon. *The American West in Film: Critical Approaches to the Western*. Westport, Conn.: Greenwood Press, 1985.

Walle, Alf H. *The Cowboy Hero and Its Audience: Popular Culture as Market Derived Art*. Bowling Green, Ohio: Bowling Green University Press, 2000.

Worland, Rick, and Edward Countryman. "The New Western American Historiography and the Emergence of the New American Western." In *Back in the Saddle Again: New Essays on the Western*, Eds. Edward Buscombe and Roberta E. Pearson. London: British Film Institute, 1998: 182–196.

Wright, Will. *Six Guns and Society: A Structural Study of the Western*. Berkeley: University of California Press, 1975.

———. *The Wild West: The Mythical Cowboy and Social Theory*. London: Sage, 2001.

Wright, Will, and Steven Kaplan, eds. *The Image of the American West*. Pueblo: University of Colorado Press, 1997.

HISTORICAL STUDIES OF WESTERNS

Adams, Les, and Buck Rainey. *Shoot-em Ups: The Complete Guide to Westerns of the Sound Era*. Metuchen, N.J.: Scarecrow Press, 1985.

Byman, Jeremy. *Showdown at* High Noon*: Witch Hunts, Critics, and the End of the Western*. The Scarecrow Filmmakers Series, No. 11. Lanham, Md.: Scarecrow Press, 2004.

Costello, Matthew J. "Rewriting *High Noon*: Transformations in American Popular Political Culture during the Cold War, 1852–1968." In *Hollywood's West: The American Frontier in Film, Television, and History*. Eds. Peter C. Rollins and John E. O'Connor. Lexington: University Press of Kentucky, 2005: 175–197.

Dixon, Wheeler W., ed. *Producers Releasing Corporation: A Comprehensive Filmography and History*. Jefferson, N.C.: McFarland, 1986.

Green, Douglas B. "The Singing Cowboy: An American Dream." *Journal of Country Music* 7(1978): 4–61.

———. *Singing in the Saddle: The History of the Singing Cowboy.* Nashville: Vanderbilt University Press, 2002.

Hafling, Barrie. *Westerns and the Trail of Tradition: A Year-by-Year History, 1929–1962.* Jefferson, N.C.: McFarland, 2001.

Hitt, Jim. *The American West from Fiction (1823–1976) into Film (1909–1986).* Jefferson, N.C.: McFarland, 1990.

Hoffman, Henryk. *Western Film Highlights: The Best of the West, 1914–2001.* Jefferson, N.C.: McFarland, 2003.

Holland, Ted. *B Western Actor's Encyclopedia: Facts, Photos and Filmographies for More Than 250 Familiar Faces.* Jefferson, N.C.: McFarland, 1997.

Hurst, Richard Maurice. *Republic Studio: Between Poverty Row and the Majors.* Metuchen, N.J.: Scarecrow Press, 1979.

Jewell, Richard B., and Verna Harbin. *The RKO Story.* London: Octopus, 1983.

Kalton, C. Lahue. *Winners of the West: The Sagebrush Heroes of the Silent Screen.* New York: Citadel, 1959.

Keller, Alexandra. "Historical Discourse and American Identity in Westerns since the Reagan Era." In *Hollywood's West: The American Frontier in Film, Television, and History.* Eds. Peter C. Rollins and John E. O'Connor. Lexington: University Press of Kentucky, 2005: 239–260.

Lentz, Harris M., III. *Western and Frontier Film and Television Credits, 1903–1995.* 2 vols. Jefferson, N.C.: McFarland, 1996.

Lewis, C. Jack. *White Horse, Black Hat: A Quarter Century on Hollywood's Poverty Row.* The Scarecrow Filmmakers Series, No. 96. Lanham, Md.: Scarecrow Press, 2002.

Loy, R. Philip. *Westerns and American Culture: 1930–1955.* Jefferson, N.C.: McFarland, 2001.

———. *Westerns in a Changing America: 1955–2000.* Jefferson, N.C.: McFarland, 2004.

McDonald, Archie P., ed. *Shooting Stars: Heroes and Heroines of Western Film.* Bloomington: Indiana University Press, 1987.

Newman, Kim. *Wild West Movies: Or How the West Was Found, Won, Lost, Lied About, Filmed, and Forgotten.* London: Bloomsbury, 1991.

Parish, James Robert, and Michael R. Pitts. *The Great Western Pictures.* Metuchen, N.J.: Scarecrow Press, 1976.

———. *The Great Western Pictures II.* Metuchen, N.J.: Scarecrow Press, 1988.

Pierson, David. "Turner Network Television's Made-for-TV Western Films: Engaging Audiences through Genre and Themes." In *Hollywood's West: The American Frontier in Film, Television, and History*. Eds. Peter C. Rollins and John E. O'Connor. Lexington: University Press of Kentucky, 2005: 281–299.

Rainey, Buck. *The Reel Cowboy: Essays on the Myth in Movies and Literature*. Jefferson, N.C.: McFarland, 1996.

Schatz, Thomas. *Hollywood Genres: Formulas, Filmmaking, and the Studio System*. New York: Random House, 1981.

Simmon, Scott. *The Invention of the Western Film: A Cultural History of the Genre's First Half-Century*. Cambridge: Cambridge University Press, 2004.

Smith, Andrew Brodie. *Shooting Cowboys and Indians: Silent Western Films, American Culture, and the Birth of Hollywood*. Boulder: University of Colorado Press, 2003.

Smyth, J. E. "The New Western History in 1931: RKO and the Challenge of *Cimarron*." In *Hollywood's West: The American Frontier in Film, Television, and History*. Eds. Peter C. Rollins and John E. O'Connor. Lexington: University Press of Kentucky, 2005: 37–64.

Stanfield, Peter. *Hollywood Westerns and the 1930s: The Last Trail*. Exeter: University of Exeter Press, 2001.

———. *Horse Opera: The Strange History of the Singing Cowboy*. Urbana: University of Illinois Press, 2002.

Tatum, Stephen. *Inventing Billy the Kid: Visions of the Outlaw in America, 1881–1981*. Albuquerque: University of New Mexico Press, 1982.

———. "The Western Film Critic as Shootist." *Journal of Popular Film and Television* 11 (1983): 114–121.

Thomas, Tony. *The West That Never Was: Hollywood's Vision of the Cowboys and Gunfighters*. Secaucus, N.J.: Citadel, 1989.

Turner, Matthew R. "Cowboys and Comedy: The Simultaneous Deconstruction and Reinforcement of Generic Conventions in the Western Parody." In *Hollywood's West: The American Frontier in Film, Television, and History*. Eds. Peter C. Rollins and John E. O'Connor. Lexington: University Press of Kentucky, 2005: 218–238.

Tuska, Jon. *The Filming of the West*. Garden City, N.Y.: Doubleday, 1976.

———. *The Vanishing Legion: A History of Mascot Pictures, 1927–1935*. Jefferson, N.C.: McFarland, 1982.

Variety *Film Reviews*. 23 vols. New Providence, N.J.: R. R. Bowker, 1994.

Verhoeff, Nanna. *The West in Early Cinema: After the Beginning*. Film and Culture in Transition Series. Amsterdam: Amsterdam University Press, 2005.

Walker, Janet, ed. *Westerns: Film through History*. New York: Routledge, 2001.

White, Raymond E. "Hollywood Cowboys Go to War: The B Western Movie during World War II." *Under Western Skies* 25 (1983): 23–66.

THEMATIC STUDIES

Bataille, Gretchen, and Charles L. P. Silet, eds. *The Pretend Indians: Images of Native Americans in the Movies*. Ames: Iowa State University Press, 1980.

Canfield, J. Douglas. *Mavericks on the Border: The Early Southwest in Historical Fiction and Film*. Lexington: University Press of Kentucky, 2001.

Churchill, Ward. *Fantasies of the Master Race: Literature, Cinema, and the Colonization of American Indians*. 2nd ed. San Francisco: City Lights, 1998.

Friar, Ralph E., and Natasha A. Friar, eds. *The Only Good Indian: The Hollywood Gospel*. New York: Drama Book Specialists, 1972.

Greb, Jacqueline K. "Will the Real Indians Stand Up?" In *Back in the Saddle: Essays on Western Film and Television Actors*. Ed. Gary A. Yoggy. Jefferson, N.C.: McFarland, 1998: 129–144.

Haskell, Molly. *From Reverence to Rape: The Treatment of Women in the Movies*. 2nd ed. Chicago: University of Chicago Press, 1987.

Hilger, Michael. *The American Indian in Film*. Metuchen, N.J.: Scarecrow Press, 1986.

———. *From Savage to Nobleman: Images of Native Americans in Film*. Lanham, Md.: Scarecrow Press, 1995.

Homans, Peter. "Puritanism Revisited: An Analysis of the Contemporary Screen-Image Western." *Studies in Public Communication* 3 (1961): 73–84.

Hutton, Paul Andrew. "Correct in Every Detail: General Custer in Hollywood." In *The Custer Reader*. Ed. Paul Andrew Hutton. Lincoln: University of Nebraska Press, 1992.

Kilpatrick, Jacquelyn. *Celluloid Indians: Native Americans and Film*. Lincoln: University of Nebraska Press, 1999.

Lackman, Ron. *Women of the Western Frontier in Fact, Fiction, and Film*. Jefferson, N.C.: McFarland, 1997.

Neale, Steve. "Vanishing Americans: Racial and Ethnic Issues in the Interpretation and Context of Post-war 'ProIndian' Westerns." In *Back in the Saddle Again: New Essays on the Western*. Eds. Edward Buscombe and Roberta E. Pearson. London: British Film Institute, 1998: 8–28.

Pettit, Arthur C. *Images of the Mexican American in Fiction and Film*. College Station: Texas A&M University Press, 1980.

Rollins, Peter C., and John E. O'Connor, eds. *Hollywood's Indian: The Portrayal of the Native American in Film*. Lexington: University Press of Kentucky, 1998.

Sadoux, Jean-Jacques. *Racism in the Western Film from D. W. Griffith to John Ford: Indians and Blacks*. New York: Revisionist, 1980.

Schackel, Sandra. "Women in Western Films: The Civilizer, the Saloon Singer, and the Modern Sister." In *Shooting Stars: Heroes and Heroines of Western Film*. Ed. Archie P. McDonald. Bloomington, Indiana University Press, 1987: 196–217.

CRITICAL ANALYSES OF INDIVIDUAL DIRECTORS AND ACTORS

Anderson, Lindsay. *About John Ford*. London: Plexus, 1981.

Anobile, Richard J., ed. *John Ford's* Stagecoach, *Starring John Wayne*. New York: Avon, 1975.

Basinger, Jeanine. *Anthony Mann*. Boston: Twayne, 1979.

Baxter, John. *The Cinema of John Ford*. New York: Barnes, 1971.

Beard, William. *Persistence of Double Vision: Essays on Clint Eastwood*. Alberta: University of Alberta Press, 2000.

Bingham, Dennis. *Acting Male: Masculinities in the Films of James Stewart, Jack Nicholson, and Clint Eastwood*. New Brunswick, N.J.: Rutgers University Press, 1994.

Bliss, Michael, ed. *Justified Lives: Morality and Narrative in the Films of Sam Peckinpah*. Carbondale: Southern Illinois University Press, 1993.

———. *Doing It Right: The Best Criticism on Sam Peckinpah's* The Wild Bunch. Carbondale: Southern Illinois University Press, 1994.

Bogdonovich, Peter. *John Ford*. Berkeley: University of California Press, 1967. Reprint, 1978.

Breivold, Scott. *Howard Hawks: Interviews*. Conversations with Filmmakers Series. Jackson: University Press of Mississippi, 2006.

Burke, Frank. "Divining Peckinpah: Religious Paradigm and Ideology in *Convoy* and *The Ballad of Cable Hogue*." In *Sam Peckinpah's West: New Perspectives*. Ed. Leonard Engel. Salt Lake City: University of Utah Press, 2003.

Butler, Terence. *Crucified Heroes: The Films of Sam Peckinpah*. London: Gordon Fraser, 1979.

Canham, Kingsley. *The Hollywood Professionals: Michael Curtiz, Raoul Walsh, Henry Hathaway*. New York: Barnes, 1973.

Collins, Jim. "Faces without Names." In *Back in the Saddle: Essays on Western Film and Television Actors*. Ed. Gary A. Yoggy. Jefferson, N.C.: McFarland, 1998: 145–160.

Cumbow, Robert C. *Once Upon a Time: The Films of Sergio Leone*. Lanham, Md.: Scarecrow Press, 1987.

Darby, William. *John Ford's Westerns: A Thematic Analysis with a Filmography*. Jefferson, N.C.: McFarland, 1996.

Davis, Ronald L. *John Ford: Hollywood's Old Master*. Norman: University of Oklahoma Press, 1995.

———. *William S. Hart: Projecting the American West*. Norman: University of Oklahoma Press, 2003.

Dickens, Homer. *The Films of Gary Cooper*. Secaucus, N.J.: Citadel, 1970.

Dukore, Bernard Frank. *Sam Peckinpah's Feature Films*. Urbana: University of Illinois Press, 1999.

Ellis, Kirk. "On the Warpath: John Ford and the Indians." *Journal of Film and Popular Culture* 8 (1980): 34–41.

Engel, Leonard, ed. *Sam Peckinpah's West: New Perspectives*. Salt Lake City: University of Utah Press, 2003.

Fenwick, J. H., and Jonathan Green-Armytage. "Now You See It: Landscape and Anthony Mann." *Sight and Sound: International Film Quarterly* 34 (1965): 186–189.

Frayling, Christopher. *Clint Eastwood*. London: Virgin, 1992.

———. *Sergio Leone: Something to Do with Death*. New York: Faber, 2000.

Fulwood, Neil. *The Films of Sam Peckinpah*. London: Batsford, 2002.

Gallagher, Tag. *John Ford: The Man and His Films*. Berkeley: University of California Press, 1986.

Gifford, Barry. *Brando Rides Alone: A Reconsideration of the Film* One-Eyed Jacks. Berkeley, Calif.: North Atlantic, 2003.

Gossett, Sue. *Audie Murphy: Now Showing*. Albany, N.Y.: Empire, 2002.

Gourlie, John. "Peckinpah's Epic Vision: *The Wild Bunch* and *The Ballad of Cable Hogue*." In *Sam Peckinpah's West: New Perspectives*. Ed. Leonard Engel. Salt Lake City: University of Utah Press, 2003.

Gourlie, John M., and Leonard Engel. "A Terrible Beauty Is Born: Peckinpah's Vision of the West." In *Sam Peckinpah's West: New Perspectives*. Ed. Leonard Engel. Salt Lake City: University of Utah Press, 2003.

Graham, Don. *No Name on the Bullet: A Biography of Audie Murphy*. New York: Viking, 1990.

Hertzberg, Ludvig. *Jim Jarmusch: Interviews*. Conversations with Filmmakers Series. Jackson: Southern Illinois University Press, 2001.

Hillier, Jim, and Peter Wollen, eds. *Howard Hawks: American Artist*. London: British Film Institute, 1997.

Hulse, Ed. *Zane Grey and the Movies*. Burbank, Calif.: Riverwood, 1994.

Humphries, Reynold. "The Function of Mexicans in Peckinpah's Films." *JUMP CUT: A Review of Contemporary Cinema* 18 (1978): 17–20.

Kagan, Norman. *American Skeptic: Robert Altman's Genre-Commentary Films*. Ann Arbor, Mich.: Pierion, 1982.

Kerbel, Michael. *Henry Fonda.* New York: Pyramid, 1975.

Kiehn, David. *Broncho Billy and the Essanay Film Company.* Berkeley, Calif.: Farwell Books, 2003.

Kitses, Jim. *Horizons West: Anthony Mann, Budd Boetticher, Sam Peckinpah: Studies of Authorship within the Western.* Bloomington: Indiana University Press. 1969.

———. *Horizons West: Directing the Western from John Ford to Clint Eastwood.* London: British Film Institute, 2004.

Knapp, Laurence F. *Directed by Clint Eastwood: Eighteen Films Analyzed.* Jefferson, N.C.: McFarland, 1996.

Koszarski, Diane Kaiser. *The Complete Films of William S. Hart, a Pictorial Record.* New York: Dover, 1980.

Kramer, Gary. "Tex Ritter: America's Most Beloved Cowboy." In *Back in the Saddle: Essays on Western Film and Television Actors.* Ed. Gary A. Yoggy. Jefferson, N.C.: McFarland, 1998.

Loy, R. Philip. "The Cisco Kid: Evolution of a Film Character." *Films of the Golden Age* 19 (1999–2000): 76–84.

Mast, Gerald. *Howard Hawks, Storyteller.* New York: Oxford University Press, 1982.

McBride, Joseph. *Hawks on Hawks.* Berkeley: University of California Press, 1982.

———. *Searching for John Ford.* New York: St. Martin's, 2001.

McKinney, Doug. *Sam Peckinpah.* Boston: Twayne, 1979.

Merrill, Robert. "Sam Peckinpah and the Western Film Tradition." In *Sam Peckinpah's West: New Perspectives.* Ed. Leonard Engel. Salt Lake City: University of Utah Press, 2003.

Mesce, Bill. *Peckinpah's Women: A Reappraisal of the Portrayal of Women in the Period Westerns of Sam Peckinpah.* Lanham, Md.: Scarecrow Press, 2001.

Miller, Cynthia J. "Tradition, Parody, and Adaptation: Jed Buell's Unconventional West." In *Hollywood's West: The American Frontier in Film, Television, and History.* Eds. Peter C. Rollins and John E. O'Connor. Lexington: University Press of Kentucky, 2005: 65–80.

Murray, Gabrielle. *This Wounded Cinema, This Wounded Life: Violence and Utopia in the Films of Sam Peckinpah.* Westport, Conn.: Praeger, 2004.

Nott, Robert. *Last of the Cowboy Heroes: The Westerns of Randolph Scott, Joel McCrea, and Audie Murphy.* Jefferson, N.C.: McFarland, 2000.

Parrill, William. *Heroes' Twilight: The Films of Sam Peckinpah.* Minneapolis, Minn.: Alpha Editions, 1983.

Pechter, William S. "John Ford: A Persistence of Vision." In *Great Film Directors: A Critical Anthology.* Eds. Leo Braudy and Morris Dickstein. New York: Oxford University Press, 1978.

Place, J. A. *The Western Films of John Ford.* Secaucus, N.J.: Citadel, 1974.

Plecki, Gerard. *Robert Altman.* Boston: Twayne, 1985.

Prats, Armando. "Auguries of Redemption: Peckinpah's Mythological Critique of American History." In *Sam Peckinpah's Westerns: New Perspectives.* Ed. Leonard Engel. Salt Lake City: University of Utah Press, 2003.

Prince, Stephen. "The Aesthetics of Slow-Motion Violence in the Films of Sam Peckinpah." In *Screening Violence.* Rutgers Depth of Field Series. Ed. Stephen Prince. New Brunswick, N.J.: Rutgers University Press, 2000.

——. "Genre and Violence in the Work of Kurosawa and Peckinpah." In *Action and Adventure Cinema.* Ed. Yvonne Tasker. London; New York: Routledge, 2004.

——. *Savage Cinema: Sam Peckinpah and the Rise of Ultraviolent Movies.* Austin: University of Texas Press, 1998.

Pye, Douglas. "The Collapse of Fantasy: Masculinity in the Westerns of Anthony Mann." In *The Book of Westerns.* Eds. Ian Cameron and Douglas Pye. New York: Continuum, 1996: 167–173.

Richard, Jeffrey. "John Ford and the American National Myth." In *Social and Political Identities in Western History.* Eds. Keith Stringer, Alexander Grant, and Claus Bjorn. Copenhagen: Akademisk Vorlog, 1994.

Roth, Lane. *Film Semiotics, Metz and Leone's Trilogy.* New York: Garland, 1983.

Sarris, Andrew. *The John Ford Movie Mystery.* Bloomington: Indiana University Press, 1975.

Seydor, Paul, *Peckinpah: The Western Films: A Reconsideration.* Urbana: University of Illinois Press, 1997.

Sinclair, Andrew. "The Man on Horseback: The Seven Faces of John Wayne." *Sight and Sound: International Film Quarterly* 48 (1979): 232–235.

Stovall, Peter. *John Ford.* Boston: Twayne, 1986.

Studlar, Gaylyn, and Matthew Bernstein, eds. *John Ford Made Westerns: Filming the Legend in the Sound Era.* Bloomington: Indiana University Press, 2001.

Thomas, Tony. *The Films of Errol Flynn.* Secaucus, N.J.: Citadel, 1969.

——. *The Films of Kirk Douglas.* Secaucus, N.J.: Citadel, 1972.

Tibbetts, John C. "Clint Eastwood and the Machinery of Violence." *Literature Film Quarterly* 21 (1993): 158–169.

Wellington, Mike. "Auteur and Genre: The Westerns of Delmer Davies." *Cinema* 4 (1969): 6–9.

Willis, Donald C. *The Films of Howard Hawks.* Metuchen, N.J.: Scarecrow Press, 1975.

Wood, Robin. *Howard Hawks.* London: British Film Institute, 1983.

Zmijewsky, Boris, and Lee Pfeiffer. *Films of Clint Eastwood.* Revised and updated. New York: Citadel, 1990.

CRITICAL ANALYSES OF INDIVIDUAL
FILMS AND TYPES OF FILMS

Bach, Steven. *Final Cut: Dreams and Disasters in the Making of* Heaven's Gate. New York: Morrow, 1985.

Bignell, Jonathan. "Method Westerns: *The Left Handed Gun* and *One-Eyed Jacks*" In *The Book of Westerns*. Eds. Ian Cameron and Douglas Pye. New York: Continuum, 1996: 111–112.

Blake, Michael F. *Code of Honor: The Making of Three Great American Westerns*. New York: Taylor, 2003.

Busch, Niven. *Duel in the Sun*. London: W. H. Allen, 1947.

Buscombe, Edward. *The Searchers*. London: British Film Institute, 2000.

———. *Stagecoach*. London: British Film Institute, 1992.

Countryman, Edward, and Evonne von Huessen-Countryman. *Shane*. London: British Film Institute, 1999.

Coursen, David F. "John Ford's Wilderness: *The Man Who Shot Liberty Valance*." *Sight and Sound: International Film Quarterly* 47 (1978): 237–241.

Drummond, Philip. *High Noon*. London: British Film Institute, 1997.

Eckstein, Arthur, and Peter Lehman, eds. The Searchers: *Essays and Reflections on John Ford's Classic Western*. Detroit: Wayne State University Press, 2004.

Eleftheriotis, Dimitris. "Spaghetti Western, Genre Criticism and National Cinema: Re-defining the Frame of Reference." In *Action and Adventure Cinema*. Ed. Yvonne Tasker. London, New York: Routledge, 2004.

Engel, Leonard. "Freedom, Entrapment, and 'Playing the String Out to the End': Enclosure in Sam Peckinpah's *The Wild Bunch*." In *The Big Empty: Essays on Western Landscape as Narrative*. Ed. Leonard Engel. Albuquerque: University of New Mexico Press, 1994.

———. "'Who Are You?' 'That's a Good Question': Shifting Identities in Sam Peckinpah's *Pat Garrett and Billy the Kid*." In *Sam Peckinpah's West: New Perspectives*. Ed. Leonard Engel. Salt Lake City: University of Utah Press, 2003.

Frayling, Christopher. *Spaghetti Westerns: Cowboys and Europeans from Karl May to Sergio Leone*. London: Routledge, 1981.

Fridlund, Bert. *The Spaghetti Western: A Thematic Analysis*. Jefferson, N.C.: McFarland, 2006.

Gallafent, Edward. "Four Tombstones 1946–1994." In *The Book of Westerns*. Eds. Ian Cameron and Douglas Pye. New York: Continuum, 1996: 302–311.

Gifford, Barry. *Brando Rides Alone: A Reconsideration of the Film* One-Eyed Jacks. Berkeley, Calif.: North Atlantic, 2003.

Gourlie, John. "Peckinpah's Epic Vision: *The Wild Bunch* and *The Ballad of Cable Hogue.*" In *Sam Peckinpah's West: New Perspectives.* Ed. Leonard Engel. Salt Lake City: University of Utah Press, 2003.

Grant, Barry Keith, ed. *John Ford's* Stagecoach. Cambridge: Cambridge University Press, 2003.

Grist, Leighton. "*Unforgiven.*" In *The Book of Westerns.* Eds. Ian Cameron and Douglas Pye. New York: Continuum, 1996: 294–301.

Hearn, Joanna. "'Ache for Home': Assimilation and Separatism in Anthony Mann's *Devil's Doorway.*" In *Hollywood's West: The American Frontier in Film, Television, and History.* Eds. Peter C. Rollins and John E. O'Connor. Lexington: University Press of Kentucky, 2005.

Howe, Winona. "Almost Angels, Almost Feminists: Women in *The Professionals.*" In *Hollywood's West: The American Frontier in Film, Television, and History.* Eds. Peter C. Rollins and John E. O'Connor. Lexington: University Press of Kentucky, 2005: 198–217.

Hutson, Richard. "Sermons in Stone: Monument Valley in *The Searchers.*" In *The Big Empty: Essays on Western Landscape as Narrative.* Ed. Leonard Engel. Albuquerque: University of New Mexico Press, 1994.

Kitses, Jim. "An Exemplary Post-modern Western: *The Ballad of Little Jo.*" In *The Western Reader.* 2nd ed. Eds. Jim Kitses and Greg Rickman. New York: Proscenium, 1999: 367–380.

———. "Peckinpah Re-visited: *Pat Garrett and Billy the Kid.*" In *The Western Reader.* 2nd ed. Eds. Jim Kitses and Greg Rickman. New York: Proscenium, 1999: 223–244.

Leinberger, Charles. *Ennio Morricone's* The Good, the Bad and the Ugly*: A Film Score Guide.* Scarecrow Film Score Guide, No. 3. Lanham, Md.: Scarecrow Press, 2004.

Liandrat-Guigues, Suzanne. *Red River.* London, British Film Institute, 2001.

Lyons, Robert, ed. My Darling Clementine*: John Ford, Director.* Rutgers Films in Print. New Brunswick, N.J.: Rutgers University Press, 1984.

McDonough, Kathleen A. "*Wee Willie Winkie* Goes West: The Influence of the British Empire Genre on Ford's Cavalry Trilogy." In *Hollywood's West: The American Frontier in Film, Television, and History.* Eds. Peter C. Rollins and John E. O'Connor. Lexington: University Press of Kentucky, 2005: 99–114.

Miller, Gabriel. "Shane Redux: *The Shootist* and the Western Dilemma." *Journal of Popular Film and Television* 11 (1983): 66–77.

Niver, Kemp R. *The Battle at Elderbrush Gulch.* Ed. Bebe Bergsten. Los Angeles: Locare Research Group, 1972.

Prats, Armando. "Outfitting the First American: 'History,' the American Adam, and the New Hollywood Indian in *Dances with Wolves, The Last of the Mohicans,* and *Geronimo: An American Legend.*" In *The Image of the American*

West. Eds. Will Wright and Steven Kaplan. Pueblo: University of Southern Colorado Press, 1997.

Pye, Douglas. *"Ulzana's Raid."* In *The Book of Westerns.* Eds. Ian Cameron and Douglas Pye. New York: Continuum, 1996: 262–268.

Rickman, Gregg. "The Western Under Erasure: *Dead Man.*" In *The Western Reader.* 2nd ed. Eds. Jim Kitses and Greg Rickman. New York: Proscenium, 1999: 381–404.

Rosenbaum, Jonathan. *Dead Man.* London: British Film Institute, 2001.

Sickels, Robert C. "A Politically Correct Ethan Edwards: Clint Eastwood's *The Outlaw and Josey Wales.*" *Journal of Popular Film and Television* 30 (2003): 220–227.

Simons, John L. "The Double Vision of Tragedy in *Ride the High Country.*" In *Sam Peckinpah's West: New Perspectives.* Ed. Leonard Engel. Salt Lake City: University of Utah Press, 2003.

Skerry, Phillip J. "Comic Elements in Peckinpah's *The Westerner.*" In *Sam Peckinpah's West: New Perspectives.* Ed. Leonard Engel. Salt Lake City: University of Utah Press, 2003.

Smetok, Jacqueline. "The American Eden: Regained and Lost Again in *Angel and the Badman* and *Witness.*" In *The Big Empty: Essays on Western Landscape as Narrative.* Ed. Leonard Engel. Albuquerque: University of New Mexico Press, 1994.

Springer, John Parris. "Beyond the River: Women and the Role of the Feminine in Howard Hawks's *Red River.*" In *Hollywood's West: The American Frontier in Film, Television, and History.* Eds. Peter C. Rollins and John E. O'Connor. Lexington: University Press of Kentucky, 2005: 115–125.

Staig, Lawrence, and Tony Williams. *Italian Westerns: The Opera of Violence.* London: Lorimer, 1975.

Stevens, Brad. *"Pat Garrett and Billy the Kid."* In *The Book of Westerns.* Eds. Ian Cameron and Douglas Pye. New York: Continuum, 1996: 269–276.

Sultze, Kimberly. "Challenging Legends, Complicating Border Lines: The Concept of 'Frontera' in John Sayles' *Lone Star.*" In *Hollywood's West: The American Frontier in Film, Television, and History.* Eds. Peter C. Rollins and John E. O'Connor. Lexington: University Press of Kentucky, 2005: 261–280.

Szaloky, Melinda. "A Tale Nobody Can Tell: The Return of a Repressed Western History in Jim Jarmusch's *Dead Man.*" In *Westerns: Film through History.* Ed. Melinda Szaloky. New York: Routledge, 2001.

Wanat, Matt. "'Fall in Behind the Major': Cultural Border Crossing and Hero Building in *Major Dundee.*" In *Sam Peckinpah's Westerns: New Perspectives.* Ed. Leonard Engel. Salt Lake City: University of Utah Press, 2003.

Weisser, Thomas. *Spaghetti Westerns—The Good, the Bad, and the Violent: A Comprehensive, Illustrated Filmography.* Jefferson, N.C.: McFarland, 1992.

Winkler, Martin M. "Tragic Features in John Ford's *The Searchers*." In *Classics and Cinema*. Ed. Martin M. Winkler. Lewisburg, Pa.: Bucknell University Press, 1991.

BIOGRAPHICAL WORKS

Autry, Gene, and Mickey Herskowitz. *Back in the Saddle Again*. Garden City, N.J.: Doubleday, 1978.

Balshofer, Fred J., and Arthur C. Miller. *One Reel a Week*. Berkeley: University of California Press, 1967.

Bond, Johnny. *The Tex Ritter Story*. New York: Chappell, 1976.

Brant, Marley. *Jesse James: The Man and the Myth*. New York: Berkley, 1998.

Canutt, Yakima, with Oliver Drake. *The Stunt Man: Autobiography of Yakima Canutt*. New York: Walker, 1979.

Carey, Harry, Jr. *Company of Heroes: My Life as an Actor in the John Ford Stock Company*. The Scarecrow Filmmakers Series, No. 42. Lanham, Md.: Scarecrow Press, 1994.

Cary, Diana Serra. *The Hollywood Posse: The Story of a Gallant Band of Horsemen Who Made Movie History*. 2nd ed. Norman: University of Oklahoma Press, 1996.

Davis, Ronald L. *Duke: The Life and Image of John Wayne*. Norman: University of Oklahoma Press, 1998.

Etulain, Richard. *The Hollywood West: Lives of Film Legends Who Shaped It*. Golden, Colo.: Fulcrum, 2001.

Evans, Max. *Sam Peckinpah, Master of Violence: Being the Account of the Making of a Movie and Other Sundry Things*. Vermillion, S.D.: Dakota Press, 1972.

Eyman, Scott. *Print the Legend: The Life and Times of John Ford*. New York: Schuster, 1999.

Fine, Marshal. *Bloody Sam: The Life and Films of Sam Peckinpah*. New York: D.I. Fine, 1991.

Ford, Dan. *The Unquiet Man: The Life of John Ford*. London: William Kimber, 1978. Reprint, 1982.

Fraser, Harry L., and Wheeler W. Dixon. *I Went That-a-Way: The Memoirs of a Western Film Director*. Scarecrow Filmmaker Series, No. 22. Lanham, Md.: Scarecrow Press, 1990.

Gallagher, Tag. *John Ford: The Man and His Films*. Berkeley: University of California Press, 1986.

Graham, Don. *No Name on the Bullet: A Biography of Audie Murphy*. New York: Viking, 1990.

Kerbel, Michael. *Henry Fonda*. New York: Pyramid, 1975.

Kiehn, David. *Broncho Billy and the Essanay Film Company*. Berkeley, Calif.: Farwell Books, 2003.

Lake, Stuart N. *The Life and Times of Wyatt Earp*. New York: Houghton Mifflin, 1956.

Levy, Emmanuel. *John Wayne: Prophet of the American Way of Life*. Metuchen, N.J.: Scarecrow Press, 1988.

McCarthy, Todd. *Howard Hawks: The Grey Fox of Hollywood*. New York: Grove, 2002.

McCoy, Tim, with Ronald McCoy. *Tim McCoy Remembers the West*. Garden City, N.J.: Doubleday, 1977.

McGhee, Richard D. *John Wayne: Actor, Artist, Hero*. Jefferson, N.C.: McFarland, 1990.

Mix, Paul. *The Life and Legend of Tom Mix*. New York: Barnes, 1972.

Nicholas, John H. *Tom Mix: Riding Up to Glory*. Oklahoma City: Persimmon Hill Books, 1980.

Pando, Leo. *An Illustrated History of Trigger: The Lives and Legend of Roy Rogers' Palomino*. Jefferson, N.C.: McFarland, 2007.

Rainey, Buck. *The Saga of Buck Jones*. Nashville, Tenn.: Western Film Collectors, 1975.

———. *The Fabulous Holts: A Tribute to a Favorite Movie Family*. Nashville, Tenn.: Western Film Collectors, 1976.

———. *The Life and Times of Buck Jones: The Sound Era*. Waynesville, N.C.: World of Yesterday, 1991.

Riley, Glenda. "Barbara Stanwyck: Feminizing the Western Film." In *The Hollywood West: Lives of Film Legends Who Shaped It*. Eds. Richard W. Etulain and Glenda Riley. Golden, Colo.: Fulcrum, 2001.

Robertson, Richard. "Steve McQueen and the Last Western." In *Back in the Saddle: Essays on Western Film and Television Actors*. Ed. Gary A. Yoggy. Jefferson, N.C.: McFarland, 1998.

Rogers, Roy, and Dale Evans, with Carlton Stowers. *Happy Trails: The Story of Roy Rogers and Dale Evans*. Waco, Tex.: Word, 1979.

Rogers, Roy, and Dale Evans, with Jane and Michael Stern. *Happy Trails: Our Life Story*. New York: Schuster, 1994.

Roth, Lane, and Tom W. Hoffer. "G. M. 'Broncho Billy' Anderson: The First Movie Cowboy Hero." In *Back in the Saddle: Essays on Western Film and Television Actors*. Ed. Gary A. Yoggy. Jefferson, N.C.: McFarland, 1998: 11–24.

Schackel, Sandra. "Barbara Stanwyck: Uncommon Heroine." In *Back in the Saddle: Essays on Western Film and Television Actors*. Ed. Gary A. Yoggy. Jefferson, N.C.: McFarland, 1998: 113–128.

Schickel, Richard. *Clint Eastwood: A Biography*. New York: Knopf, 1996.

Schoenecke, Michael K. "James M. Stewart: An American Original." In *Back in the Saddle: Essays on Western Film and Television Actors*. Ed. Gary A. Yoggy. Jefferson, N.C.: McFarland, 1998: 97–112.

Shepherd, Donald, and Robert Slatzer, with Dave Grayson. *Duke: The Life and Times of John Wayne*. London: Weidenfeldt, 1986.

Siegel, Don. *A Siegel Film: An Autobiography*. London: Faber, 1993.

Sinclair, Andrew. *John Ford*. London: Unwin, 1979.

Skerry, Phillip J. "Comic Elements in Peckinpah's *The Westerner*." In *Sam Peckinpah's West: New Perspectives*. Ed. Leonard Engel. Salt Lake City: University of Utah Press, 2003.

Slide, Anthony. *The New Historical Dictionary of the American Film Industry*. Lanham, Md.: Scarecrow Press, 1998.

Smith, Andrew Brodie. *Shooting Cowboys and Indians: Silent Western Films, American Culture, and the Birth of Hollywood*. Boulder: University of Colorado Press, 2003.

Smith, Ella. *Starring Miss Barbara Stanwyck*. New York: Crown, 1974.

Spittles, Brian. *John Ford*. London: Pearson, 2002.

Tydeman, William E., III. "Tom Mix: King of the Hollywood Cowboys." In *Back in the Saddle: Essays on Western Film and Television Actors*. Ed. Gary A. Yoggy. Jefferson, N.C.: McFarland, 1998: 25–42.

Walsh, Raoul. *Each Man in His Time: The Life Story of a Director*. New York: Farrar, Strauss and Giroux, 1974.

Weddle, David. *"If They Move . . . Kill 'Em!": The Life and Times of Sam Peckinpah*." New York: Grove, 1994.

White, Raymond E. "Roy Rogers: An American Icon." In *Back in the Saddle: Essays on Western Film and Television Actors*. Ed. Gary A. Yoggy. Jefferson, N.C.: McFarland, 1998: 77–96.

Wood, Robin. *Howard Hawks*. London: British Film Institute, 1983.

Yoggy, Gary A., ed. *Back in the Saddle: Essays on Western Film and Television Actors*. Jefferson, N.C.: McFarland, 1998.

———. "James Arness: Television's Quintessential Western Hero." In *Back in the Saddle: Essays on Western Film and Television Actors*. Ed. Gary A. Yoggy. Jefferson, N.C.: McFarland, 1998: 177–200.

Zinnemann, Fred. *A Life in the Movies: An Autobiography*. New York: Scribner's, 1992.

Zolotov, Maurice. *John Wayne: Shooting Star*. London: Allen, 1974.

WORKS DIRECTED AT A GENERAL AUDIENCE

Andreychuk, Ed. *The Golden Corral: A Roundup of Magnificent Western Films*. Jefferson, N.C.: McFarland, 1997.

Buscombe, Edward, ed. *The BFI Companion to the Western*. London: British Film Institute, 1988.

Cocchi, John. *Second Features: The Best of the "B" Films*. New York: Carol, 1991.

Everson, William K. *American Silent Film*. New York: Oxford University Press, 1978.

———. *Hollywood Westerns: Ninety Years of Cowboys and Indians, Train Robbers, Sheriffs and Gunslingers*. Secaucus, N.J.: Carol, 1991.

Eyles, Allen. *John Wayne and the Movies*. New York: Grossett and Dunlap, 1976.

———. *The Western*. New York: Barnes, 1975.

Fenin, George N., and William K. Everson. *The Western: From Silents to Cinerama*. New York: Orion, 1962.

———. *The Western: From Silents to the Seventies*. New York: Grossman, 1973.

Franklin, Joe. *Classics of the Silent Screen*. New York: Citadel, 1959.

Garfield, Brian. *Western Films: A Complete Guide*. New York: Rowson, 1982.

George-Warren, Holly. *Cowboy: How Hollywood Invented the Wild West*. Pleasantville, N.Y.: Reader's Digest, 2002.

Graham, Don. *Cowboys and Cadillacs: How Hollywood Looks at Texas*. Austin: Texas Monthly Press, 1983.

Hyams, Jay. *The Life and Times of the Western Movie*. New York: Gallery Books, 1983.

Lahue, Kelton C. *Winners of the West: The Sagebrush Heroes of the Silent Screen*. New York: Barnes, 1971.

Magers, Boyd. *Westerns Women: Interviews with 50 Leading Ladies of Movie and Television Westerns from the 1930s to the 1960s*. Jefferson, N.C.: McFarland, 2004.

———. *Best of the Badmen*. Albany, N.Y.: Empire, 2005.

Magers, Boyd, and Michael G. Fitzgerald. *Ladies of the Western: Interviews with Fifty-one More Actresses from the Silent Era to the Television Westerns of the 1950s and 1960s*. Jefferson, N.C.: McFarland, 2006.

Manchel, Frank. *Cameras West*. Englewood Cliffs, N.J.: Prentice, 1971.

Matthews, Leonard. *A History of Western Movies*. London: Royce, 1984.

Meyer, William R. *The Making of the Great Westerns*. New Rochelle, N.Y.: Arlington House, 1979.

Miller, Don. *The Hollywood Corral: A Comprehensive B Western Roundup*. New York: Popular, 1976.

Nevins, Francis M. *The Films of Hopalong Cassidy.* Waynesville, N.C.: World of Yesterday, 1988.

———. *The Films of the Cisco Kid.* Waynesville, N.C.: World of Yesterday, 1998.

Rothel, David. *The Singing Cowboys.* New York: A. S. Barnes, 1978.

———. *The Great Cowboy Sidekicks.* Waynesville, N.C.: World of Yesterday, 1984.

Sarf, Wayne Michael. *God Bless You, Buffalo Bill: A Layman's Guide to History and the Western Film.* Madison, N.J.: Farleigh Dickinson University Press, 1983.

Saunders, John. *The Western Genre: From Lordsburg to Big Whisky.* Short Cuts Series, No. 7. London: Wallflower, 2001.

Sennett, Ted. *Great Hollywood Westerns.* New York: Abrams, 1990.

Swann, Thomas Burnett. *The Heroine or the Horse: Leading Ladies in Republic Films.* New York: Barnes, 1977.

GENERAL WORKS

Brownlow, Kevin. *The War, the West, and the Wilderness.* New York: Knopf, 1979.

Katz, Ephrain. *The Film Encyclopedia.* New York: Perennial, 1979.

Limerick, Patricia. *The Legacy of Conquest: The Unbroken Past of the American West.* New York: Norton, 1987.

———. *Something in the Soil: Legacies and Reckonings in the New West.* New York: Norton, 2000.

Longman, Larry. *A Guide to Silent Westerns.* Westport, Conn.: Greenwood, 1992.

McGuire, James. *A Literary History of the American West.* Fort Worth: Texas Christian University Press, 1987.

Mellen, Joan. *Big Bad Wolves: Masculinity in the American Film.* London: Elm Tree, 1979.

Slide, Anthony. *The New Historical Dictionary of the American Film Industry.* Lanham, Md.: Scarecrow Press, 1998.

Smith, Henry Nash. *Virgin Land: The American West as Symbol and Myth.* Cambridge, Mass.: Harvard University Press, 1950.

Thomason, David. *A Biographical Dictionary of Film: Expanded and Updated.* New York: Knopf, 2004.

Tuska, Jon. *Close Up: The Contract Director.* Metuchen, N.J.: Scarecrow Press, 1976.

WEBSITES

Allmovie: www.allmovie.com
British Film Institute: www.bfi.org.uk
Cinema History: www.tc.umn.edu/~ryahnke/film/cinema.htm
Classic Film Guide: www.classicfilmguide.com/index.php?s=home
Classic Movies: www.thegoldenyears.org
Cowboy Pal: www.cowboypal.com
Film and Popular Culture Theory: www.gis.net/~tbirch/alitheory.html
Greatest Films: www.filmsite.org
In Focus Magazine: The Western: www.imagesjournal.com/issue06/infocus.htm
Internet Movie Data Base: www.imdb.com
The Old Corral: www.b-westerns.com/trio.htm
ReelClassics: www.reelclassics.com
Silent Era: www.silentera.com
Silent Film Stills Archive: www.silentfilmstillarchive.com
Vintage Reviews of Silent Movies: www.silentsaregolden.com/reviews.html

About the Author

Paul Varner was born in western Texas. After completing his undergraduate studies at Oklahoma Christian University in 1973, he attended the University of Tennessee in Knoxville from 1973 to 1981 where, along with his wife, Jeanine, he completed his MA and his PhD in English; he and Jeanine received their PhDs the same day. Since then Professor Varner has taught at Rochester College, Oklahoma State University–Oklahoma City, and Oklahoma Christian University, and at present he teaches in the English Department at Abilene Christian University in Abilene, Texas. He has two children—Bart, a musician, and Tess, a philosopher. Professor Varner has published widely on 18th-century English literature and current American poets. His published work on Westerns includes articles on Max Brand in the *Dictionary of Literary Biography* (Gale Research Press, 1978) and popular Westerns written since 2000 for *The Greenwood Encyclopedia of Contemporary Popular American Literature* (Greenwood Press). He is the editor of *Westerns: Paperback Novels and Movies from Hollywood* (Cambridge Scholars Press, 2008).